W9-ADD-702

Jacket reproduction courtesy of Alinari

John Navone SJ

Themes of St. Luke

Gregorian University Press - Rome

To the Jesuit Community
of Seattle University

THEMES OF ST. LUKE

PREFACE

Of many possible approaches to the study of the Third Gospel, this author has opted for a thematic approach, realizing that certain aspects of Lucan theology will thereby be highlighted at the expense of others. The examination of many distinct themes, despite their frequent overlapping, favors an appreciation of Lucan theology which is more analytic than synthetic. Notwithstanding the analytic emphasis of the thematic approach, the unity of Lucan theology will inevitably appear, inasmuch as all these themes are ultimately intelligible only as variations on the overriding Lucan theme of salvation in Christ.

An intelligent reading of the Gospel presupposes an awareness of the individual writer's themes. These themes intersect and illuminate each other. Several themes often occur in the same pericope.

The themes of one Gospel will often be found in the others; however, the perspective of the individual writer will inevitably color their treatment. None of the themes treated in this study has been selected on the assumption that it is exclusively Lucan.

This study does not aim at an exhaustive treatment of the themes selected. Such treatment might easily require a book for each theme. An attempt has been made to sketch a sufficiently large number of themes from the Third Gospel which as an ensemble might lead to an awareness of their subtle orchestration in the hands of the writer whose theological perspective unifies them into a meaningful work of art, intelligence and grace.

The themes of Luke's Gospel have been occasionally supplemented by a study of their counterpart in Acts, whenever this was thought especially helpful.

It is hoped that this book will be of assistance to those engaged in the ministry of the word.

Finally, to the editors of *The Bible Today* and *Scripture,* my gratitude for permission to use in this book articles which earlier appeared in their publications. The chapters, Fatherhood, Mercy, and Parallelism in the Glory and Humiliation of Christ appeared in *The Bible Today;* the chapters Joy, Prayer, Spirit, Temptation, and Way appeared in *Scripture.*

1.

THE LUCAN BANQUET THEME

Introduction.

The banquets of the Third Gospel are often historical events in the life of Jesus which Luke interprets as the fulfillment of the messianic prophecies (Isa 25. 6; 34. 6; 55. 1; 65. 11; Dt 12. 4; Zeph 1. 7). The prophetic tradition proclaimed that the Messiah would inaugurate eschatological happiness among the poor and the afflicted who would form his banquet community. [1] The banquet is an eschatological community-concept expressing Jesus' mission of restoring communion between God and man, and among men. [2]

The banquet is an eschatological concept. The consummation is compared to a banquet (14. 16-24). At the eschatological consummation the disciples will eat and drink with Jesus in the Kingdom of God (22. 30). Men will be gathered from all the corners of the earth to sit at table with the Old Testament saints (13. 29 = Mt 8. 11-12).

The days of the Baptist, which were the period of expectation, are superseded by the days of Jesus, which are the time of presence and fulfillment: "When John came, he would neither eat nor drink, and you say 'He is possessed.' When the Son of Man came, he ate and drank with you, and of him you say, 'Here is a glutton; he loves wine; he is a friend of publicans and sinners' " (7. 33-34).

---

[1] J. Schniewind, *Das Evangelium nach Lukas* (Göttingen, 1952, 62, remarks that Jesus is fulfilling his prophecied messianic mission when he gathers sinners into fellowship with himself.

[2] G. Ladd, *Jesus and the Kingdom* (London, 1966), 206.

[3] G. F. Moore, *Judaism in the First Centuries of the Christian Era,* II (Cambridge, 1927), 363.

Table fellowship with Jesus anticipates the eschatological consummation in the context of Jewish tradition, where the metaphor of the banquet is used to express messianic salvation.[3] It has been compared to an acted parable, which represents the fulfillment of Jesus' messianic mission of reconciling sinners with God by gathering them into his eschatological banquet community.[4]

I.

The dinner at the home of Simon the Pharisee (7.36-50), a uniquely Lucan story, is among the most important banquet scenes of the Third Gospel. It suggests that Jesus the Wisdom of God (11.49; 21.15) is an essential aspect of Lucan banquet theology; and that for those who receive Jesus in faith the Wisdom of God is simultaneously holding its banquet.

The Pharisees' criticism of Jesus for eating with sinners and the words about Wisdom, which precede the banquet account, also form a unit in Matthew's Gospel (Mt 11.19 = Lk 7.34-35). Luke, however, makes a different use of this unit by locating it before his banquet scene, where it now serves as a type of introduction in which the words about Wisdom give a cue to the interpretation of what follows.

Secondly, Luke has made a notable change in the text about Wisdom which harmonizes more with the communitarian aspect of the banquet theme which follows: "Yet Wisdom has been proved right *by all her children*" (7.35); whereas, Matthew's text has "... by her actions" (11.19).

These changes suggest that the significance of the banquet which follows should be interpreted as the fulfillment of Israel's Wisdom tradition, in which Wisdom invites her children to instruction, happiness, life, conversion and friendship with God at the banquet which she herself has prepared:[5]

---

[4] G. Bornkamm, *Jesus of Nazareth,* tr. I. and F. McLuskey (London, 1960), 8.

[5] W. Grundmann, *Das Evangelium nach Lukas,* 169, remarks that Jesus is the speaker and bearer of Wisdom (cf. Lk 2.40,52); Wisdom is like a mother who gives life and education to her children. Those who believe in Jesus are the children of Wisdom. They have been reborn through the Wisdom that is Jesus; and it governs their lives like a mother who rules her children. They resemble their mother.

'And now, my sons, listen to me;
listen to instruction and learn to be wise,
    do not ignore it.
Happy those who keep my ways!
Happy the man who listens to me,
    who day after day watches at my gates
    to guard the portals.
For the man who finds me finds life,
    he will win favor from Yahweh;
but he who gives offence to me does hurt to his own soul,
    all who hate me are in love with death.'
Wisdom has built herself a house,
    she has erected her seven pillars,
she has slaughtered her beasts, prepared her wine,
    she has laid her table.
She has despatched her maidservants
    and proclaimed from the city's heights:
'Who is ignorant? Let him step this way.'
    To the fool she says
'Come and eat my bread,
    Drink the wine I have prepared!
Leave your folly and you will live,
    walk in the ways of perception.' (Proverbs 8. 32-36; 9.1-6)

The introduction sets the story within the context of the banquet controversies in which he is criticized for eating with sinners (5. 29-32 = Mt 9. 9-13 = Mk 2. 13-17 and 15. 1-3). The controversy centers on the nature of Jesus' prophetic mission. His eating with sinners prevents Simon's belief in the authenticity of his prophetic mission: *"If this man were a prophet,* he would know who this woman is that is touching him ..." (7. 39).[6] Thus, the Pharisees cannot believe that Jesus is an authentic prophet; they cannot perceive the further significance of the banquets. They offend Wisdom as Simon offends Jesus (7. 44-46) Cf. Pvbs 8. 36).

However, for the penitent woman, Jesus' taking his place at Simon's table has a meaning which Simon cannot comprend. His presence is the sign for her entrance (7. 36). The universal

---

[6] W. Grundmann, *Das Evangelium nach Lukas,* 171, recognizes the irony of this situation. Simon's criterion of a prophet is the ability to see through a person. He has in mind the sinful woman; however, Jesus satisfies this criterion in a way which surprises Simon. Jesus sees through Simon.

reconciliation, prophecied in terms of the messianic banquet, is at hand. The sinner is invited to Wisdom's table that she may live and walk in the ways of the Lord. Luke implies that Jesus is the ultimate and perfect realization of Wisdom. Jesus achieves everything Wisdom promises: "Your sins are forgiven" (7. 48): and "Your faith has saved you; go in peace" (7. 50).[7] Thus, Luke implies that Wisdom has also held her banquet at the home of Simon the Pharisee, and that not all of those present were aware of it.

The association of Wisdom with a banquet is based on the principle that human life is impossible without food; analogously, life as a son of God is impossible without Wisdom. Thus, in the Lucan banquet scenes instruction is given. Those who accept the wisdom of Jesus are rewarded (14. 14; 22. 28-30). They are forgiven (7. 48). Jesus' prophetic mission includes the communication of wisdom, not merely in the limited sense of doctrine, but in the complete sense of the life itself which that doctrine expresses. The quality of that life which it is his mission to communicate is described in Jesus' inaugural address in the synagogue at Nazareth:[8]

> The spirit of the Lord has been given to me,
> for he has anointed me.
> He has sent me to bring the good news to the poor,
> to proclaim liberty to captives
> and to the blind new sight,
> to set the downtrodden free,
> to proclaim the Lord's year of favor. (4. 18-19 = Is 61. 1-2)

The wisdom of Jesus expresses the life he communicates. It is a life which enriches men with a new freedom, a new vision of reality, and the grace of God. Its goodness transcends the

---

[7] W. Grundmann, *Das Evangelium nach Lukas,* 173, maintains that the three last verses indicate how the story is to be interpreted. They contain the consolation of God's forgiveness which is achieved through Jesus as the messianic prophet, who also acts as high priest. The Wisdom-Word of God is her peace and forgiveness. The woman is moved by Jesus' word which she receives in faith. It evokes a loving gratitude. W. Manson, *Luke,* 85, believes that the woman's love is the proof of her forgiveness, and not its ground; Simon, on the other hand, has no idea of the need for forgiveness. This story is only in Luke.

[8] Cf. R. Schnackenburg, *The Moral Teaching of the New Testament,* tr. J. Holland-Smith and .W O'Hara (London, 1965), 17.

hatred of enemies and makes men resemble God: "You will have a great reward, and you will be sons of the Most High, for he himself is kind to the ungrateful and the wicked" (6. 35).[9] The Lord has anointed Jesus with his Spirit for the purpose of achieving his prophetic mission of communicating this new life to the poor. They alone are disposed to receive it.

In his discourse on the destruction of Jerusalem, Jesus is presented as the source of wisdom.[10] Jesus assures his disciples that this wisdom will not fail them: "Keep this carefully in mind: you are not to prepare your defence, because I myself shall give you an eloquence and a wisdom that none of your opponents will be able to resist or contradict" (21. 15).

II.

The banquet scene of *the eleventh chapter* (*11. 37-52*) enables Luke to show how the teaching of Jesus clashes with that of the Pharisees." Jesus excoriates them for their extortion and wickedness (v. 39), for their meticulous formalism and pretentiousness (vv. 42-43), for their resistence to the prophets and apostles which the Wisdom of God had sent them (vv. 47-49).[12] Jesus teaches that they should give alms (v. 41); that they should not overlook justice and the love of God (v. 42). Luke clearly implies that Jesus knows the divine intention of history, when Jesus remarks: "And that is why the Wisdom of God said, 'I will send them prophets and apostles; some they will slaughter and persecute, so that this generation will have to answer for every prophet's blood' ..." (vv. 49-50). Jesus knows and teaches the Wisdom of God, which the scribes and Pharisees reject in rejecting him: "When he (Jesus) left the house, the scribes and the Pharisees

---

[9] Cf. *Ibid.*, 102, 153, 161-1628.

[10] W. Grundmann, *Das Evangelium nach Lukas*, 249, comments that this is a reference to that Wisdom which almost assumes the character of an hypostasis in Proverbs 8, 22-31 and Wisdom 7. 24-27. Jesus is its realization.

[11] T. W. Manson, *Luke*, 148, comments on v. 52, saying that the Pharisees obscured the will of God. They make true knowledge of God impossible (8. 10); nor have they entered the kingdom of God (7. 29-30).

[12] W. Grundmann, *Das Evangelium nach Lukas*, 250, asserts that in the history of salvation and judgment, Jesus and the apostles belong to that long line of prophets persecuted and rejected by Israel. This interpretation, he believes, historicizes the eschatological threat to them in vv. 44-48.

began a furious attack on him ... setting traps to catch him out in something he might say" (11. 54).

The discrepancy between the ways of Jesus and those of his contemporaries characterizes every Lucan banquet scene.[13] This discrepancy occurs between Jesus and the religious leaders of Israel: with the Pharisees of the old Israel (5. 29-32; 7. 34-50; 11. 37-54; 14. 1-24; 15. 1-32); and with the disciples of the New Israel (22. 1-32; 24. 13-35). The banquet controversies are those of the religious community.[14] It is significant that the first five are in the context of Judaism and concern the essential nature of Jesus' prophetic mission and of his call to Israel; the last two concern the problems of the New Israel. The Last Supper is a picture of the disputes, denials and crises of the new eschatological banquet community. The disciples of Emmaus are reproved: "You foolish men! So slow to believe the full message of the prophets!" (24. 25).[15] Jesus reproves the religious leaders of both Israels for seeking preeminent positions within the community: "Alas for your Pharisees who like taking the seats of honor in the synagogues ..." (11. 43); and "A dispute arose also between them about which should be reckoned the greatest, but he said to them ..." (22. 24).

The banquet theologies of the messianic prophecies, Wisdom literature and Third Gospel are especially concerned with the community of the people of God as a community. The messianic banquet prophecies anticipate perfect community among men and between mankind and God; the Third Gospel proclaims the fulfillment of Israel's eschatological expectations to the extent that the servant's invitation has been accepted.[16] Jesus has inaugurated Israel's long expected messianic banquet community; however, Israel's religious leaders are generally unaware of this. They invite Jesus to banquets at their homes (7. 36-50; 11. 37-54; 14. 1-24); they criticize him for banqueting with sinners (5. 29-32; 7. 34-50;

---

[13] P. S. Minear, "A Note of Luke 22. 36," *Novum Testamentum* 7 (1964), 128-134, notes that controversy characterizes important table conversations (Lk 5. 29; 7. 36; 10. 38; 11. 37; 14. 1; 22. 1).

[14] W. Grundmann, *Das Evangelium nach Lukas*, 132.

[15] Cf. J. A. Grassi, "Emmaus Revisited (Lk 24. 13-35 and Acts 8. 26-40)," *Catholic Biblical Quarterly* 26 (1964), 463-467.

[16] Cf. W. F. Ryan, "The Church as the Servant of God in Acts," *Scripture* 15 (1963), 110-115. Also, P. Grelot, "La vocation ministerielle au service du peuple de Dieu," *Recherches Bibliques* 7 (1965).

15. 1-3); nevertheless, they fail to recognize the real banquet which is simultaneously in progress. It is only the sinners and the tax-collectors, "the poor, the crippled, the blind and the lame," and the disciples who enjoy the beatitude of those who eat and drink at Jesus' table in his kingdom (14. 15, 22; 22. 30).

Luke interprets the rejection of Jesus' prophetic mission as the culpable rejection of the Wisdom of God: "And that is why the Wisdom of God said, 'I will send them prophets and apostles; some they will slaughter and persecute, so that this generation will have to answer for every prophet's blood that has been shed since the foundation of the world, from the blood of Abel to the blood of Zechariah ...' " (12. 49-51).[17] In Matthew's parallel text (23. 34-36) "the Wisdom of God" is not mentioned. The witness of all Israel's prophets to Jesus is the intention of the Wisdom of God in history. Thus, Luke implicitly identifies Jesus with the Wisdom of God speaking through Israel's prophets.

The peculiarly Lucan association of Jesus with the Wisdom of God (21. 15), especially in banquet contexts (7. 35; 11. 49), suggests that Jesus is the realization of that Wisdom whose activity is described in Proverbs (8. 32-36; 9. 1-6); and that he is also ecountered in his instruction, in the house which he has built, and at the banquet table where he serves the community that he has called together.[18]

III.

The Lucan banquet theology of the *fourteenth chapter* may be divided into three parts.[19] In the first part (vv. 1-6) Jesus'

---

[17] W. Grundmann, *Das Evangelium nach Lukas,* 250.

[18] W. Grundmann, *Das Evangelium nach Lukas,* 133, comments on the ecclesial context of Lucan banquet situations.

[19] Together with the journey motif the hospitality accorded to Jesus is a characteristic of Luke. He treats these two motifs as parts of a single whole. In Jesus "God himself visits the people, hidden in the guise of the wanderer refreshing himself as a guest in their home," according to W. Grundmann, *Das Evangelium nach Lukas,* 27-28. H. Flender, *St. Luke Theologian of Redemptive History,* tr. R. and I. Fuller (London 1967), 81, comments on the Lucan guest motif: "In Jesus God visits his people, entering into fellowship with them (1. 78)." He notes the soteriological aspect of the guest motif: "Fellowship with Jesus means forgiveness of sins and newness of life."

miraculous cure on the Sabbath, which takes place at a banquet, is an adequate sign for men of faith that he speaks and acts with the authority of the Lord of the Sabbath.[20] The work of the Sabbath is precisely that of sanctifying (Gen 2. 3) and thereby making whole and bringing to perfection. Jesus is the eschatological sign par excellence of the messianic banquet community's inauguration. Jesus contains the fullness of its reality. This is his communion with God which it is his mission to communicate.

In the second part (vv. 7-14) Jesus teaches men how to live among themselves, if they wish to share the happiness of the eschatological banquet community. He teaches that eschatological happiness belongs to those who are free of self-seeking. It is a mistake to seek positions of honor and to exalt oneself (vv. 8-11). When inviting guests, preference should be shown for the poor precisely because they have no means of reciprocating nor of repayment.[21] Such selfless generosity is even now a sign of good fortune; for repayment will be made at the resurrection of the just (vv. 12-14). Gratuitous generosity is the spirit with which Jesus teaches them to give a banquet: "When you give a banquet ..." (v. 12).

In the third part, the parable of the Great Banquet (vv. 15-24), Jesus teaches that it is only the poor, the crippled, the blind and the lame (v. 21) who have the proper dispositions for accepting the servant's gracious invitation to the Great Banquet:[22] the others who had been invited make excuses for declining the invitation, because they are too preoccupied with their immediate personal concerns. No one is excluded from the Great Banquet except by his own choice. The servant's invitation is universal.

---

[20] It is only those who have faith in Jesus who are capable of perceiving a second level of meaning in Jesus' banquet situations. On the first level, Jesus is the one invited to the banquet; on the second level, there is a reversal of roles, and Jesus is understood by Luke to be the one who is inviting everyone to his banquet in which communion with God is a present reality.

[21] T. W. Manson, *The Gospel of Luke*, 172, describes "the poor, the crippled, the blind and the lame" as those from whom the proud and ambitious turn with social and physical repugnance (Lk 14. 14). Manson interprets the same category in 14. 21 as those who are not so rich and satisfied with this world as to despise Jesus' invitation.

[22] Isaiah had prophecied the coming salvation in terms of the blind and the lame: "Then the eyes of the blind shall be opened ... tnen the lame shall leap like a deer" (35. 5). Those who accept the servant's invitation to the banquet have found their salvation; and these are the blind and the lame.

The transition between the second and third parts indicates that the Great Banquet parable is concerned with the invitation to eschatological happiness in the Kingdom of God.[23] Jesus' advice to his host closes on a clearly eschatological note with the assurance of a repayment "at the resurrection of the just" (v. 14). The same motif is reiterated in the dinner guest's exclamation: "Happy the man who will be at the banquet in the Kingdom of God!" (v. 15).[24] The transition suggests a link between those who are rewarded at the resurrection of the just and those who attend the banquet in the Kingdom of God. It implies that those who accept Jesus' "banquet teaching" are simultaneously accepting the servant's invitation to the Great Banquet.[25] As participants of the messianic banquet community, their eschatological happiness is even now communicable to "the poor, the crippled, the lame, the blind" (v. 13). It is the happiness which derives from the spirit of Jesus and his teaching.

The verbal unity of repeated, interlocking words and phrases is a literary device which enables Luke to express the doctrinal unity of these complementary aspects of his banquet theology. The word "happy" (*makarios*) occurs with a clearly eschatological significance in both the assurance of Jesus (v. 14) and the exclamation of the dinner guest (v. 15). The key verb linking these correlative aspects of the Lucan banquet theology is "invite" (*kalein*), which occurs four times (vv. 13, 16, 17, 24). Thus, in the context of eschatological happiness, characterizing the banquet community, Jesus invites his hearers to invite others according to the spirit of his life and teaching (v. 13).

"The poor, the crippled, the lame, the blind" (v. 13) are they whom Jesus' hearers should invite.[26] It is Jesus who invites them through his hearers. In the parable of the Great Banquet the servant is told to go out quickly into the streets

---

[23] R.W. Funk, *Language, Hermeneutic, and Word of God* (New York, 1966), 172.

[24] R. Swaeles, "La parabole des invités qui se dérobent," *Assemblées du Seigneur* 55 (1962), 35; R. Bultmann, *Die geschichte der Synoptischen Tradition* (Göttingen, 1931), 113, notes a striking parallel with Apoc. 19. 9.

[25] R. Bultmann, *Die Geschichte,* 325, comments that all the materials from 14. 1-24 are linked together on the basis of their external relation to a banquet.

[26] J. Dupont, *Les Béatitudes* (Louvain, 1954), 193-209, stresses the importance of the poor in Lucan theology. See Lk 9. 58-60: the obligations of this world are no excuse for putting off the call of the kingdom.

and alleys of the town and to bring to the banquet "the poor, the crippled, the blind and the lame" (v. 21). The servant accomplishes his mission of bringing this category of men to the banquet: "Sir, said the servant, your orders have been carried out" (v. 22). The poor actually constitute the eschatological banquet community, even though they are not the only persons invited.

The spirit of Jesus and his teaching, with regard to inviting those who can make no repayment, implicitly corresponds to that of the Lord at the Great Banquet at whose table are found the poor. [27] In both cases the poor cannot make a repayment for what they receive, whether it be for the invitation which they receive from Jesus and his hearers or for that which they receive from the Lord of the Great Banquet and from his servant. Luke has explicitly defined the poor as those who cannot repay the good that is done for them (v. 14). [28]

This is the community of "the poor, the crippled, the blind and the lame" in which the prophecied salvation of God is realized:

> 'Courage.' Do not be afraid.
> 'Look, your God is coming,
> vengeance is coming,
> the retribution of God;
> he is coming to save you.'
> Then the eyes of the *blind* shall be opened,
> the ears of the deaf unsealed,
> then the *lame* shall leap like a deer
> the the tongues of the dumb sing for joy;
> for water gushes in the desert,
> streams in the wasteland,
> the scorched earth becomes a lake,
> the parched land springs of water.
> The lairs where the jackals used to live
> become thickets of reed and papyrus ...
> And through it will run a highway undefiled
> which shall be called the Sacred Way;
> the unclean may not travel by it,

---

[27] R. Swaeles, *art. cit.*, 45.

[28] In Isaiah's prophecy of the eschatological banquet all are invited, and especially the poor (55. 1-3; 65. 13). Psalms also contain this idea (22. 27; 23. 5; 78. 24-25, 27, 29).

nor fools stray along it.
No lion will be there
nor any fierce beast roam about it,
but the redeemed will walk there,
for those Yahweh has ransomed shall return.
They will come to *Zion* shouting for joy,
everlasting joy on their faces;
joy and gladness will go with them
and sorrow and lament be ended.

(Isaiah 35. 4-10)

This is the community which Jesus was sent to form, "He has sent me to bring the good news to the *poor,* to proclaim liberty to captives and to the *blind* new sight ..." (4. 18). Jesus identifies himself in terms of the community where his saving presence is felt: "Go back and tell John what you have seen and heard: the *blind* see again, the *lame* walk, lepers are cleansed, and the deaf hear, the dead are raised to life, the good news is proclaimed to the *poor* and happy is the man who does not lose faith in me" (7. 29). The poor, the blind and the lame participate in the Great Banquet.

Jesus' spirit of unselfish giving finds a parallel elsewhere in the Third Gospel, when a reward is assured those who lend to their enemies "without any hope of reward" (6. 35). A repayment is promised to those who invite the poor without seeking personal recompense (14. 14). The concept of not seeking a reward from the recipients of charitable actions is especially Lucan. The parallel Matthean text on loving one's enemies makes no mention of lending without hope of a reward (5. 44-45).

The ultimate motive for lending without seeking a reward from the beneficiary is that of communion with God: "... love your enemies, do good to them, lend to them without any hope of reward; then your reward will be a rich one, and you will be *sons of the Most High,* because he is generous to the thankless and the unjust. Be merciful *as your Father* is merciful" (6. 35-36).[29] Again: "Forgive us our sins; we *too* forgive all those who trespass against us" (11. 24). If God acts in a certain way, his sons will, by the fact of their sonship, act accordingly. Luke expresses communion with God in various ways. In the case

[29] A. R. C. Leaney, *The Gospel according to St. Luke,* (London, 1958), 138.

of the lender, he expresses it in terms of sonship; in the case of those who are attending a banquet, he explains it in terms of a banquet. The kind lenders will be "sons of the Most High"; the gracious hosts, Luke implies, will resemble the Lord of the Great Banquet. In each case, good is done without seeking to profit from the recipient, because the agent lives according to the spirit of Jesus' life and teaching. This is the spirit of *agapē* not *erōs,* love of an end that overflows rather than the desire of an end that uses means.

IV.

At the beginning of Jesus' public ministry, the Pharisees disapprove of his banqueting with sinners (5. 29-32).[30] Luke repeats this critical refrain at the beginning of his *fifteenth chapter* (*15. 1-2*), where it becomes the key to the interpretation of the entire chapter: "Now the tax collectors and sinners were all drawing near to hear him. And the Pharisees and the scribes murmured, saying, 'This man receives sinners and eats with them.'" The redactional unity of this chapter is formed by three parables which answer the criticism of the Pharisees expressed in the opening verses.[31]

In the parallel parables of the lost sheep (15. 4-7) and of the lost coin (15. 8-10) Jesus compares the joy of those who have recovered what they had lost with the joy of God over the conversion of sinners. In both parables friends and neighbors are invited to share in the joy of recovery (15. 6, 9). The final parable of the chapter, the Prodigal Son (vv. 11-32), is a classical illustration of the divine love for the repentant sinner. The second part of the parable teaches that it would be wrong for anyone

---

30 T. W. Manson, *The Gospel of Luke,* 55, comments on Lk 5. 29-32: "A physician of souls, Jesus will not like the Pharisees, wait for sinners to come to him, but will go to them. Over against the Pharisaic idea of salvation by segregation he acts upon the new principle of salvation by association (cf. 19. 9-10)."

31 E. Rasco, "Les Paraboles de Luc XV," *Ephemerides Theologicae Lovanienses* (1967), 165-183, provides an excellent analysis of this chapter, which he interprets as Jesus' answer to the Pharisees' criticism of his eating with sinners; H. B. Kossen, "Quelques remarques sur l'ordre des paraboles dans Luc. XV," *Novum Testamentum* (1956), I, 75-80, notes the remarkable parallel in the order of these three parables with Jeremiah 31. 10-20.

to object, like the eldest son, the Pharisees and the scribes, at the divine welcome for repentant sinners. It it also Jesus' appeal to the hearts of his critics that they should share his redemptive joy by changing their dispositions toward their brother and towards him whom they are to recognize as having a father's heart for all. [32]

The fifteenth chapter is an invitation to share the divine joy in the return of sinners. The Pharisees cannot accept it without a radical change of outlook. Jesus formulates the invitation in his parables and in his way of acting which reflects the joy of God welcoming sinners and inviting all to rejoice with him. [33] Without making any kind of christological statement, the parable is a veiled assertion of authority: Jesus claims that he is acting in place of God as his representative. Thus, Luke links these three parables with the public ministry of Jesus and the criticism of the Pharisees.

V.

The account of *the Last Supper* is a third major exposition of Lucan banquet theology (22.1-38 = Mt 26.20-35 = Mk 14.17-25). It offers several parallels with the banquet theology of the fourteenth chapter.

The participants in both banquet situations are concerned about their personal prestige and status. Jesus disapproves of this attitude: "... do not take your seat in the place of honor" (14.8). When the dispute arises at the Last Supper about which of the disciples should be considered the greatest, Jesus says: "Among the pagans it is the kings who lord it over them, and those who have authority over them are given the title Benefactor. *This must not happen with you*" (22.25). [34] At the first banquet, Jesus says: "... make your way to the lowest place and sit there (14.10). At the Last Supper, his teaching is similar: "... the greatest among you must behave as if he were the youngest, the leader as if he were the one who serves" (22. 26-27).

---

[32] C. H. Giblin, "Structural Considerations on Luke 15," *Catholic Biblical Quarterly* 24 (1962), 29.

[33] J. Jeremias, *The Parables of Jesus*, tr. S. H. Hooke (London, 1954), 154.

[34] Cf. A. B. Du Toit, *Der Aspekt der Freude im urchristlichen Abendmahl* (Winterthur, 1965), 89.

In both banquet situations Jesus speaks of a servant. In the parable of the Great Banquet Jesus relates: "When the time for the banquet came, he sent his *servant* to say to those who had been invited, 'Come along: everything is ready now'" (14. 17). At the Last Supper Jesus tells his disciples: "Yet here I am among you as a servant" (22. 27).

At both banquets Jesus promises an eschatological reward to those who faithfully follow him in his teaching and trials. Those who invite the poor to their banquets without seeking repayment will find happiness, because repayment will be made to them at the resurrection of the just (14. 14). At the Last Supper Jesus tells his disciples: "You are the men who have stood by me faithfully in my trials; and now I confer a kingdom on you, just as my Father conferred one on me: you will eat and drink at my table in my kingdom, and you will sit on thrones to judge the twelve tribes of Israel" (22. 28-30).[35]

At both banquets explicit mention is made of a kingdom. In the first banquet a guest exclaims: "Happy the man who will be at the banquet in the Kingdom of God" (14. 15). At the Last Supper, Jesus tells his disciples that he has longed to eat the passover with them before his passion, because he would not eat it again, "... until it is fulfilled in the kingdom of God" (22. 16). Again: "I shall not drink wine until the kingdom of God comes" (22. 18). Jesus confers the kingdom on his disciples which he has received from his Father (22. 29); and promises them that they shall eat and drink at his table in his kingdom (22. 30).[36]

The kingdom of God is the source of eschatological happiness (14. 15). It is the gift of Jesus and his Father (22. 29); and it is described as the eschatological banquet community of Jesus and his faithful disciples (22. 30).

An exclusively Lucan text in the eschatological pericope urging readiness for the Master's return offers a striking parallel with Jesus' role as servant and Master at the Last Supper: "Happy those servants whom the master finds awake when he comes. I tell you solemnly, he will put on an apron, sit them down at table and wait on them" (12. 37).[37] The eschatological banquet

---

35 Cf. H. Conzelmann, *The Theology of Saint Luke*, tr. G. Buswell (London, 1960), 201; cf. 155, n. 1.

36 Cf. A. B. Du Toit, *Der Aspekt der Freude*, 89, 91.

37 H. Flender, *St. Luke*, n. 98, notes the portrayal of the second coming

community and its master, whose service creates and maintains it in existence, is adumbrated in the pericope on the Master's return and precisely delineated in the account of the Last Supper. The master's service at the table of his followers is the reward for the servants who are found to be faithful when he returns.

The order, and to a considerable extent the material, of Luke's treatment of the Last Supper is unique among the gospels.[38] In contrast with Matthew, Luke places Jesus' promise to the apostles of governing the twelve tribes of Israel within the context of the Last Supper and of the eschatological banquet community. In Matthew we read: "I tell you solemnly, when all is made new and the Son of Man sits on his throne of glory, you will yourselves sit on twelve thrones to judge the twelve tribes of Israel" (19. 28). In Luke, the promise of governing the new Israel, the Church, is in a twofold banquet context: (1) Luke locates within the historical event of the Last Supper, an historical banquet; (2) Luke joins it with the specific promise of eating and drinking at Jesus' table in his kingdom. Luke writes: "... and now I confer a kingdom on you, just as my Father conferred one on me: you will eat and drink at my table in my kingdom, and you will sit on thrones to judge the twelve tribes of Israel" (22. 30).

In the Lucan account of the Last Supper the apostles are taught to imitate the nature of Jesus' kingship, which is explained in terms of service at the table fellowship of the eschatological banquet community (22. 27).[39] The apostles must rule the kingdom which Jesus has conferred on them with the same spirit with which Jesus rules in the kingdom of his Father. Through the conferring of the kingdom, the apostles are now ruling over the new Israel which is united in the table fellowship of its King's table.[40] The unity and existence of the eschatological banquet community are achieved through the service and sacrifice

---

as the return of Jesus from the heavenly feast in this text; however, Jesus in v. 37 comes to serve his own. By the use of Johannine terminology (Jn 13. 4) the text is applied to present encounter with Christ which Flender believes includes the Lord's Supper. The exalted Christ "comes" again and again to his own, until he comes at the end of the ages for the redemption of the body (Lk 21. 28).

[38] Cf. R. Tannehill, "A Study in the Theology of Luke-Acts," *Anglican Theological Review* 43 (1961), 198.

[39] *Ibid.*, 199.

[40] *Ibid.*, 201.

of Jesus. The verb which Luke uses for expressing the conferring of the kingdom on the apostles is *diatithemai* (22. 29). It means 'to dispose of property by a will'. Within the context of the Last Supper it clearly suggests the act of one who is about to die; and, therefore, that the death of Jesus is associated with the conferring of the kingdom and with the existence of the banquet community where he serves. [41]

Jesus' service at the table of his banquet community identifies it. [42] When Jesus sits at table and breaks bread, the disciples at Emmaus recognize their Lord (24. 30). The life and activity of Jesus' banquet community is expressed in the breaking of bread (Acts 2. 42, 46): "They remained faithful to the teaching of the apostles, to the brotherhood, to the breaking of bread and to the prayers" (v. 42); and, "They went as a body to the Temple every day and met in their houses for the breaking of bread" (v. 46).

In two texts of Acts, Luke stresses the fact that Jesus and his disciples eat *together* by the use of three verbs which are compounds with *syn-*: 1. 4 refers to Jesus' "eating with" the apostles; 10. 41 speaks of the apostles' "eating with" and "drinking with" Jesus. As the Emmaus story shows, the table fellowship of Jesus' banquet community consists both in the fellowship of Christians with each other and with their Lord.

From the actual banquets in which Jesus participates at the beginning of chapters 14, 15 and 22, Luke makes a transition to another banquet of which the actual banquets are symbols. [43] In chapters 14 and 22 the transition is made to the eschatological banquet which Jesus is inaugurating in fulfillment of Israel's prophecies: it is the Great Banquet to which the servant calls the invited guests who fail to respond, as well as "the poor, the crippled, the blind and the lame," who accept the invitation (14. 15-24); it is the banquet where the apostles will eat and drink

---

[41] *Ibid.*, 202.

[42] *Ibid.*, 200. Also, what Jesus is actually doing at table is seen as the fulfillment of the messianic banquet which would be served by the Messiah himself (Isa 25. 6): "The proof-from-prophecy is the central theological idea throughout the two volume work. Luke regards Jesus' own predictions of his suffering, death and resurrection, together with the Scriptural prophecies, as decisive proof that Jesus is the Christ, and that God has raised him from the dead. The theme of proof from prophecy is central to Luke's theology of history" (p. 199).

[43] P. M. Galopin, "Le Repas," *Assemblées du Seigneur* 55 (1962), 65.

at Jesus' table in the kingdom of God, which Jesus has conferred on them (2. 28-30). Thus there are two banquets simultaneously in progress. It is only for those who accept Jesus with faith that the first banquet suggests the second, the eschatological banquet to which the servant is inviting them, which he has conferred on them, and at whose table he serves (22. 27). In chapter 15 the transition is made from the Pharisees' criticism that Jesus is actually eating with sinners (v. 3) to the banquet celebrating the return of the prodigal son, who was dead and has come back to life (vv. 23-32). The eschatological dimension of the second banquet appears in its correspondence to the banquets of the messianic prophecies in which perfect reconciliation between God and man is expressed (Isa 55. 1-3; 65. 13).[44]

VI.

The *Emmaus account* (Lk 24. 14-35) exhibits close parallels with the events of chapter 20 in John's Gospel, which support an historical tradition for this entire Lucan resurrection material.[45] The scene emphasizes the messianic hopes of the disciples based on Jesus' mighty words and deeds (24. 19, 21); and it stresses a present glory.[46] Jesus' interpretation of scripture affirms the present fulfilment of Christ's glory (24. 27). The late afternoon setting for the meal is a Lucan characteristic closely connected with Jesus' healings and meals (Cf. Lk. 4. 38-40; 5. 29-38; 7. 36-50; 9. 10-17; 11. 37-41; 14. 1-24; 22. 14ff.; 24. 36ff.). The actions of Jesus at table are of special importance for Luke: "... he took the bread and said the blessing; then he broke it and handed it to them" (24. 30). Luke describes the same four elements in the feeding of the five thousand (9. 10-17), the Last Supper (22. 19), and partially in the account of Paul's shipwreck (Acts 27. 35).

---

[44] J. Daniélou, "Les repas de la Bible et leur signification," *Maison-Dieu* 38 (1950), 3.

[45] J. Jeremias, *The Eucharistic Words of Jesus* (New York, 1966), 150, note 2; also John A. Bailey, *The Traditions Common to the Gospels of Luke and John* (Leiden, 1963), 85-102.

[46] Cf. J. Dupont, "The Meal at Emmaus," *The Eucharist in the New Testament: A Symposium*, ed. J. Delorme (Baltimore, 1964), 114; N. Huffman, "Emmaus Among the Resurrection Narratives," *Journal of Biblical Literature* 64 (1945), 216-217.

Jesus' action has a revelatory character which opens the disciples' eyes and enables them to return to Jerusalem and spread the good news (24. 33-35).[47]

In the Emmaus account the true interpretation of scripture concerning the Messiah together with the actual recognition of the Messiah depend upon table fellowship with Christ.[48] The risen Christ effectively reveals himself in a banquet context. Twice in the Emmaus account is the recognition of Christ in the "breaking of bread" emphasized (24. 31, 35). The revelation has a twofold aspect: Jesus reveals the type of Messiah he is, as well as his present Lordship and fellowship with his own.

Luke associates the feeding of the five thousand and the Last Supper with the "breaking of bread" in the early Church by his linking of three aspects of these banquet occasions: the deeds of the Messiah; the hope and promise of the continuing fellowship; and the presence of the Messiah and his Age.[49]

Luke emphasized Jesus' identity as Messiah by the context of the Emmaus account in which the mighty words and deeds of Jesus and the disciples' hope that he was the Messiah are specified. The wisdom which Jesus displays here, as elsewhere (Lk 2. 41-52), is also a special trait of the Messiah.[50] The risen Lord is the Messiah; he makes his presence known and felt through table fellowship with his own.

After convincing the disciples that Jesus is the Messiah (vv. 25-27), He manifests himself to them and disappears. In the Emmaus pericope the scripture proof occurs before the manifestation of Jesus' resurrection. In the Jerusalem scene (24. 36-43), in which Jesus convinces his disciples of the identity between his crucified and his glorified body, the scripture proof (24. 44-48) comes after Jesus' self-revelation (vv. 36-43). The fact of Jesus' Messiahship is the presupposition for the encounter with the risen Lord (v. 61). The unbelief of the Emmaus disciples in

---

[47] Counterparts of the Emmaus account occur in the Old Testament narratives in which God or his representatives visit incognito, leaving after a meal and recognition (Genesis 18. 1-16; Judges 6. 11-22).

[48] E. C. Davis, *The Significance of the Shared Meal in Luke-Acts*, a doctoral dissertation accepted at the Southern Baptist Theological Seminary (A-xeroxed at Ann Arbor, 1967), 107-108.

[49] *Ibid.*, 108.

[50] Cf. H. Strack and P. Billerbeck, *Kommentär zum Neuen Testament aus Talmud und Midrasch* II (München, 1924), 152, 438; III, 636, 673.

Jesus' Messiahship (v. 21) must be overcome before the risen Lord can reveal himself to them.

VII.

The Lucan treatment of the banquet theme is characterized by several aspects which deserve special notice.

Healing is an aspect of the Messianic Age which Luke often associates with the banquet theme.[51] A healing account immediately precedes the Lucan banquet narration of Levi's call (5. 27-32), the feeding of the five thousand (9. 10-17), the dropsical man at the Pharisee's banquet (14. 1-11), the restoration of sight to the blind man (18. 35-43) immediately before Jesus' invitation to the home of Zaccheus (19. 1-10). The healed are invited and sought for the divine banquet table (Lk 5. 17; 6. 19; 9. 2, 42; Acts 9. 34).[52] Luke connects closely references to healing and the Kingdom of God (Lk 6. 19; 7. 7; 9. 2, 11). Healing is offered to those who will accept the invitation to the Kingdom (Acts 9. 34; 28. 27). The importance of healing as a sign of the Messianic Age is underscored in Luke's programmatic quotation from Isaiah's prophecy concerning the mission of the Messiah (4. 18). Luke links healing with his banquet narratives as an indication that the time of the Messianic Banquet is *now*, in the feeding of the five thousand, in banquets with sinners.[53] The healings are sufficient signs for men of faith that the Messiah himself is present at his table. The Lucan emphasis on the present does not diminish his concern for the eschatological character of the banquet (cf. 12. 37-40; 14. 15-24; 22. 16).

Lucan banquet scenes have a *revelatory character*.[54] This especially true in the case of repentant sinners (5. 29-32; 7. 36-50; 19. 1-10). They reveal the realization of Old Testament hopes for forgiveness and fellowship with God in the New Age: "Messias-

---

[51] For healing as an aspect of the Messianic time see II Baruch 29. ff.

[52] E. C. Davis, *The Significance of the Shared Meal*, 57.

[53] C. H. Dodd, "The Sacrament of the Lord's Supper in the NT," *Christian Worship*, 73. Dodd holds that Jesus invites the crowd to a feast in the sense of a parable — "Come, for all things are ready" In other words the Kingdom has come.

[54] E. C. Davis, *The Significance of the Shared Meal*, 72.

zeit ist Vergebungszeit."[55] The feeding of the five thousand (9. 10-17) is a scene of revelation, a foreshadowing of the Messianic Banquet, immediately followed by the Great Confession (9. 18-21), which emphasizes its revelatory character.[56] In the Emmaus account the banquet theme has the same revelatory character and is similarly followed by the immediate confession of faith in the risen Christ by the disciples (24. 33-35). Tax collectors are always associated with the banquet theme (3. 12; 5. 27; 7. 29; 15. 1; 10. 10). Luke implies that the significance of Christ is revealed to them in the banquet context.

A contrast between *the world's banquet and the heavenly banquet* is suggested by the Lucan treatment of the banquet theme.[57] Man does not live by bread alone (4. 4). The rich fool will enjoy the feast of this world (18. 16-21). The rich man enjoys this world's banquet while Lazarus suffers (16. 19-31); however, Lazarus will ultimately enjoy the banquet that really counts at the bosom of Abraham. Simon the Pharisee gives this world's banquet (7. 36-50) and is oblivious to the Messianic Banquet which the sinful woman recognizes and in which she participates. Blessed are those who hunger, because they will be filled (6. 21). Those who are now filled will go hungry (6. 25). Those whom this world's banquet fills, will not enjoy the eschatological banquet. That is the one which really counts: the joyous feast of the messianic community.

VIII.

In both Lucan volumes the banquet theme is strategically located. In the first it is associated with the call to discipleship (Lk 5. 27-31), with the Great Confession (9. 10-17); it appears in the center of the "Journey" section (ch. 14), before the Passion (22. 15-38) and after the Resurrection (ch. 24). The theme appears at the beginning of Acts (1. 4), in the central section (10. 41; 11-18; 15), and at the close of the volume (28. 23).[58]

---

[55] J. Schniewind, *Das Evangelium nach Markus* (Das Neue Testament Deutsch, Teilband 1. 9.), (Göttingen, 1960), 24; Cf. Jeremias, *Eucharistic Words*, 204-205.

[56] E. C. Davis, *The Significance of the Shared Meal*, 76.

[57] *Ibid.*, 79, 121.

[58] See E. C. Davis, *The Significance of the Shared Meal in Luke-Acts*, 174-175.

The banquet theme is associated with the extension of the messianic community. Beginning with Jesus' post-resurrection meals with the Eleven (1.4), the theme extends to the joyful fellowship of the Jerusalem community (2.42), to one of the Chosen who had formerly rejected the invitation to enter it (Paul, 9.9, 19), to outcasts among the Chosen (Aeneas, 9.34), to the "God-fearing" Gentile, Cornelius (10.1-11.18) and to the Gentile Philippian jailer (16.234). The divine invitation to the messianic banquet extends to all nations.

The vision of Peter (10.9-16), in the context of the Cornelius story, may also imply the Messianic Age and its Banquet. The food in this vision has been interpreted as a symbol of the New Age and its Banquet in which all mankind is invited to participate.[59] Peter is portrayed as extending the invitation to the Messianic Banquet. His words imply that his actual table-fellowship with the risen Lord empowers his invitation to others to participate in the same fellowship:

> "Now we are those witnesses — we have eaten and drunk with him after his resurrection from the dead — and he has ordered us to proclaim this to his people and to tell them that God has appointed him to judge everyone, alive and dead" (10.41-42).

In three of the four accounts of the post-resurrection meals (Lk 24.44-49; Acts 1.4; 19.41-42) Jesus charges his disciples to receive the Spirit and to announce the New Age. Their obedience to his command enables the ever widening circle of the Banquet community to reach the four corners of the Gentile world.

---

59 *Ibid.*, 165; Peter is reproached for having *eaten* with Gentiles (11.3); whereas, his closing rhetorical question (11.17) is intended to justify his having *baptized* them. This fusion of Peter's two actions implies the association of the two divine interventions which motivated them: the "cleansing" mentioned in the vision (10.5; 11.9) and the gift of the Holy Spirit (11.17).

SOME OLD TESTAMENT BANQUET TEXTS

Exodus 24. 9-11

Moses went up with Aaron, Nadab and Abihu, and seventy elders of Israel. They saw the God of Israel beneath whose feet there was, it seemed, a sapphire pavement pure as the heavens themselves. He laid no hand on these notables of the sons of Israel: they gazed on God. They ate and they drank.

Deuteronomy 12. 5-7

You must seek Yahweh your God only in the place he himself will choose from among all your tribes, to set his name there and give it a home. There you shall bring your holocausts and your sacrifices, your tithes, the offerings from your hands, your votive offerings and your voluntary offerings, the firstborn of your herd and flock; there you will ear in the presence of Yahweh your God and be thankful for all that your hands have presented, you and your households blessed by Yahweh your God.

Leviticus 7. 11, 15; 22, 29-30

This is the ritual for the communion sacrifice offered to Yahweh: ... The flesh of the victim must be eaten on the day when the offering is made (v. 15). If you offer Yahweh a sacrifice with praise, do it in the acceptable manner; it must be eaten the same day ..." (22. 29-30).

Isaiah 25. 6-10 (Messianic Banquet)

On this mountain,
Yahweh Sabaoth will prepare for all peoples
a banquet of rich food, a banquet of fine wines,
of food rich and juicy, of fine strained wines.
On this mountain he will remove
the mourning veil covering all peoples,
and the shroud enwrapping all nations,
he will destroy Death for ever.
The Lord Yahweh will wipe away
the tears from every cheek;
he will take away his people's shame
everywhere on earth,
for Yahweh has said so.
That day, it will be said: See, this is our God
in whom we hoped for salvation;
Yahweh is the one in whom we hoped.
We exult and we rejoice
that he has saved us;
for the hand of Yahweh
rests on this mountain.

Isaiah 55. 1-3 (The food of the poor)
Oh, come to the water all you who are thirsty;
though you have no money, come!
Buy corn without money, and eat,
and, at no cost, wine and milk.
Why spend money on what is not bread,
your wages on what fails to satisfy?
Listen, listen to me, and you will have good things to eat
and rich food to enjoy.
Pay attention, come to me;
listen, and you soul will live.

Isaiah 65. 13-14
Therefore, thus speaks
the Lord Yahweh:
You shall see my servants drink
while you go hungry.
You shall see my servants drink
while you go thirsty.
You shall see my servant rejoice
while you are put to shame.

Ecclesiasticus 24. 19-22 (From the Discourse of Wisdom)
Approach me, you who desire me,
  and take your fill of my fruits,
for memories of me are sweeter than honey,
  inheriting me is sweeter than the honeycomb.
They who eat me will hunger for more,
  they who drink me will thirst for more.
Whoever listens to me will never have to blush,
  whoever acts as I dictate will never sin.

Psalm 22. 26
The poor will receive as much as they want to eat.

Psalm 23. 5
Your prepare a table before me
  under the eyes of my enemies;
you anoint my head with oil,
  my cup brims over.

Psalm 78. 24, 25, 27, 29
he rained down manna to feed them,
he gave them the wheat of heaven;
men ate the bread of Immortals,
he sent them more food than they could eat.
he rained down meat on them like dust;
birds as thick as sands on the seashore.
They all had enough and to spare,
he having provided what they wanted.

Zephaniah 1.7
Silence before the Lord Yahweh!
For the day of Yahweh is near.
Yes, Yahweh has prepared a sacrifice,
he has consecrated his guests.

The Song of Songs 5.1
I come into my garden,
my sister, my promised bride.
I gather myrrh and balsam.
I eat my honey and my honeycomb,
I drink my wine and my milk.
Eat, friends, and drink,
drink deep. my dearest friends.

NOTES

B. Cooke, "Synoptic Presentation of the Eucharist as Covenant Sacrifice," *Theological Studies* 21 (1960), 1-44. The Last Supper inaugurates a new relationship between God and men, continually dynamic because it involves man's sacrificial submission to God's will, sacramental because it is expressed in the anamnesis of Christ's own eucharistic action. The idea of covenant, identical with that of kingdom, dominates the thought of the Synoptic Gospels, although the word *diatheke* itself is restricted to the text of the Last Supper.

J. Dupont, "Le repas d'Emmaüs," *Lumière et Vie* 31 (1957) 77-92. The pertinent texts from Luke and the context of the Greek mentality for whom Luke wrote would not lead to an interpretation of the "breaking of bread" as an ordinary gesture. This justifies a eucharistic interpretation of this text. The explanation of the Scriptures prepares for the recognition of the living and present Christ, while "the breaking of bread" gives to the believer the living and present risen body of Christ.

A. Feuillet, "Les grands étapes de la fondation de l'Église d'après les Evangiles Synoptiques," *Sciences Ecclesiastiques* 11 (1959), 5-21. The establishment of a new people of God is part of the messianic work of Jesus which is confirmed by three of the data of the Synoptics relative to the Church: [1] the choice of the Twelve, their number, their office and the names given them; [2] the promise to Peter after his confession at Caesarea; [3] the Last Supper as a gesture instituting a new religion and the foundation of the Church, the new banquet community.

J. Giblet, "La parabole de l'accueil messianique (Luc 15, 11-32)," *Bible et Vie Chrétienne* 47 (1962), 17-28. The parable of the Prodigal Son is addressed to the Scribes and Pharisees (Lk 15. 1-2) to explain

Jesus' eating with sinners. The feates has messianic overtones (Isa 25.6; Ps 23.5) and is clearly a type of salvation. Jesus is not condemning the Pharisees, but is inviting them to join the banquet community.

E. Galbiati, "Gli invitati al convito (Luca 14.16-24)," *Bibbia e Oriente* 7 (1965), 129-135. Luke seems to give the historical setting of this banquet because he mentions an actual banquet (v. 15). Following the parable of the Great Banquet Luke has a passage concerning detachment from all things (vv. 25-33) which implies Luke's moral interpretation of all that precedes. Luke's version of the banquet appears to be a parable with some possible allegorical traits in vv. 22-23 where the command to compel entry suggests the Church's missionary task. The early Church may have interpreted this as an exhortation to convert the Gentiles. The Talmud speaks of a publican of Ascalon who in the first century B. C. invited the counselors of the city to a banquet; when they did not come, he invited the poor to be his guests.

H. Kosmala, "'Das tut zu meinem Gedächtnis'," *Novum Testamentum* 4 (1960), 81-94. Jesus asks his disciples to do something in remembrance of him. J. Jeremias, *Die Abendmahlsworte Jesus* (3rd rev. ed., 1960), interprets the phrase as: "Do this, that God may remember me," "that my remembrance may come before God." However, Kosmola notes that there is no prayer in the early Church which asks God to remember the Messiah. The Christian prayer is directed to Christ. Therefore, in the invitation Jesus asks the disciples to break the bread (before the meal) and to drink the cup (after the meal) in remembrance of him. The content of the anamnesis of Jesus cannot be separated from the following and imitation of him. The liturgical action symbolizes full participation in the suffering and death of the Lord. This remembrance is verified in the following and imitation of Jesus; on the other hand, this following and imitation is only possible in the constant remembrance of Jesus.

E. Linnemann. "Überlegungen zur Parabel vom grossen Abendmahl, Lc 14: 1524/Mt 22.1-14." *Zeitschrift für die Neutestamentliche Wissenschaft* 51 (1960), 246-255, dismisses Lk 14.22f as an allegorical emplification, asserting that these verses are an integral part of the parable. Definite measures are taken to exclude the guests who refused the invitation to the banquet. The refusals were not absolute; there were excuses for coming at a later time. The invited wished to finish their work beforehand (14.18) and come later. Therefore, the sense of the parable, according to Linnemann, is that he who does not *now* subject himself to God's dominion will soon find that it is too late.

R. Morgenthaler, *Die lukanische Geschichtschreibung als Zeugnis*, Part I (Zurich, 1949), 156, suggests the following structure of balanced pairs in the Lucan account:

The Calling of the Tax Collector Levi (5.27-32)
  Pharisees and sinners (7.36-50)
    Merciful Samaritan and unmerciful Jews (10.29-37)
      Martha and Mary (10.38-42)
        First table parable (14.7-11)
        Second table parable (14.14-14)
        Third table parable (14.15-24)
        The Lost Sheep (15.3-7)
        The Lost Coin (15.8-10)
        The Lost Son (15.11-32)
      The Rich Man and Lazarus (16.19-31)
    The Grateful Samaritan and the Ungrateful Jews (17.11-19)
  Pharisees and sinners (18.9-10)
The Call of the Tax Collector Zacchaeus (19.1-10)

Morgenthaler remarks that the basic theme uniting these 14 diverses elements is indicated at the beginning: "The healthy do not need a physician, but those who are sick. I have not come to call the righteous, but sinners to repentance" (5.3132). Merciful and grateful Samaritans are contrasted with unmerciful and ungrateful Jews. Levi and Zacchaeus are paired as two sinners who accept Jesus and receive him im at their homes The banquet theme is explicit in the first case and implicit in the second. Simon the Pharisee and the Pharisee in the Temple are paired in their common contempt for sinners. Morgenthaler implies that the weakest parallel is that between Martha and Mary and the Rich Man and Lazarus. He suggests that John's Gospel may have made the Lazarus of the parable the historical brother of Martha and Mary, and that the death of Lazarus in the parable is behind the death of his counterpart in the Gospel of John. In two of the table-parables the poverty of men is explicitly mentioned (14.13, 21); it seems to parallel the "poverty" of God in stories of the lost. Thus the poverty of man and of God represents their mutual longing for each other; it is the poor who long for the kingdom and God who longs for what he has lost.

F. Mussner, "Das 'Gleichnis' vom Gestrengen Malherrn. Ein Beitrag zum Redaktionsverfahren und zur Theologie des Lukas (Lk 13.20-30)," *Trierer Theologische Zeitschrift* 65 (1956), 129-143. The model of this pericope is the parable of the great banquet in Lk 14.16-24. The "Master of the House" is Jesus and the banquet is already taking place in the Kingdom of Heaven (therefore not purely eschatological). All are invited but only those who have answered Christ's call to follow him enter through the narrow door leading to the banquet hall. Once the *kairos* has run out — Presumably when the banquet room is full — the Master will rise and shut the door. This is the final judgment. The discourse is prophetic in tone: it is both a warning to the unbelieving Jews and a promise of salvation to the Gentiles who answer the call of Jesus. In this passage the eschatology of Old Testament prophecy is radically denationalized.

The banquet hall is not Sion but heaven; and the people of God consists of both Jews and Gentiles. A study of these verses reveals that Luke has brough into a unified composition various sayings of Jesus regarding final salvation.

R. Orlett, "An Influence of the Early Liturgies upon the Emmaus Account," *Catholic Biblical Quarterly* 21 (1959), 212-219. For those Christians who had never seen Jesus alive, the experience of the two disciples epitomizes what they experienced at the early liturgical meetings from the readings and explanations of the Scriptures and from the *agape,* climaxed by the celebration of the Eucharist. Because the experience of the two disciples was considered as typical of the early Christian Eucharistic experience, in many retellings of the incident the Eucharistic terminology of "the breaking of the bread" came to be employed to describe the Emmaus meal.

F. Planas, "En el seno de Abraham," *Cultura Biblica* 15 (1958), 148-152. Lazarus reclines at Abraham's bosom as John reclined as Jesus' bosom at the Last Supper. Jn 1. 18 ("the only-begotten Son, who is in the bosom of the Father"), has been cited to support the banquet interpretation. Thus, Planas suggests the figure involved is that of the Messianic banquet in which Lazarus, as opposed to the Rich Man, participates.

J. Potin, "Les repas avec le Christ ressuscité et l'institution de l'Eucharistie," *Bible et Terre Sainte* 36 (1961), 12-13, observes that Luke describes the repasts of the risen Savior in terms similar to those for the Eucharist. The Last Supper inaugurated the Messianic Banquet and constituted the Church hierarchically. And after eating with his disciples the risen Christ gives them their mission (Lk 42. 28; Acts 1. 1-8). Luke implies that the repasts of Christ with his disciples represent all those who will believe in Jesus and be united with him and his apostolic community in the agape and table service of the Church, the Banquet community of the last days.

2.

CONVERSION

I — *Introduction*

The New Testament expresses the concept of conversion with words derived from the verbs *strephein* and *metanoein* with its corresponding substantive form *metanoia.*[1] The last two terms occur especially in the synoptic gospels. *Metanoein* occurs 16 times of which 9 are in Luke;[2] *metanoia* occurs 8 times of which 5 are in Luke.[3] Of the 14 times when Luke employs these two words, four alone belong to a common synoptic tradition.[4] The other ten occurrences are exclusively Lucan.[5] If the eleven occurrences of *metanoein*[6] (5 times) and *metanoia* (6 times)[7] in Acts are added, the Lucan predilection for this word becomes apparent. Luke manifests the same predilection for words deriving from *strephein,* both in their profane[8] and religious sense.[9] Mark and Matthew employ the word *epistrephein*[10] only once in the religious sense;[11] whereas, Luke employs it 3 times in his

---

1 *Metanoein* occurs 34 times, *metanoia* 22 times. This word study is based on R. Michiels, "La conception lucanienne de la conversion," *Ephemerides Theologicae Lovanienses* 41 (1965), 42-43.

2 Matthew 3. 2; 4, 17; 11. 20. 21; 12, 41; Mark 1. 15; 6. 12; Luke 10. 13; 11. 32; 13. 3, 5; 15. 7, 10; 16. 30; 17. 3, 4.

3 Matthew 3. 8, 11; Mark 1. 4; Luke 3. 3, 8; 5. 32; 15. 7; 24. 47.

4 Luke 3. 3 (Acts 13. 24; 19. 4) = Mark 1. 4 and Matthew 3. 2; Luke 3. 8 = Mt 3. 8; Lk 10. 13 = Mt 11. 21; Lk 11. 32 = Mt 12. 41.

5 Lk 5. 32 (Mt 9. 13 and Mk 2. 17); 13. 3, 5; 15. 7. 10 (Mt 18. 14); 16. 30; 17. 3 (Mt 18. 15), 4 (Mt 18. 21); 24. 47).

6 Rcts 2. 38; 3. 19; 8. 22; 27. 30; 26. 20.

7 Acts 5. 31; 9. 18; 13. 24; 19. 4; 20. 21; 26. 20.

8 *hupostrephein*

9 *epistrephein* (e. g. Acts 3. 26; Lk 23. 14; Acts 20. 30); *diastrephein* (Lk 9. 41; 23. 2; Acts 8. 10; 20. 30; *kestrephesthai* (Acts 7. 39).

10 This verb occurs 36 times in the New Testament of which 18 are in Lucan writings.

11 Mt 13. 15; Mk 1. 12; Acts 28. 27.

Gospel and 8 times in Acts,[12] which accounts for eleven of its nienteen occurrences with the religious sense in the New Testament.

II — *The Third Gospel*

In the peculiarly Lucan material of the Third Gospel the word *metanoia* first appears in a text explaining Jesus' mission. "I have not come to call the just, but sinners," is a text common to the synoptic tradition (Mt 9.13; Mk 2.17; Lk 5.32); however, Luke adds "to repentance" (*eis metanoian*).[13] Jesus expresses his prophetic mission with the phrase, "I have come to call". The Pharisees, who reject this call, are implicitly reprehended by this logion. Sinners are called to enter the kingdom because they alone have the necessary spirit of *metanoia,* humility and compunction; they are willing to admit their sinfulness.

The repentance of Nineveh is contrasted with the unrepentance of the Jews (11.29-32 = 12.39), and the towns of Galilee are less disposed to repentance than Tyre and Sidon, Sodom and Gomorrah (10.13-35; Mt 1.20-24). Jonah showed the Ninevites the way to God; now Jesus points the way, but his hearers, less responsive that the Ninevites, have refused to take it. Responsiveness is gauged in terms of repentance, which is the proper response to the person and preaching of Jonas and Jesus.

Conversion (*metanoein*) appears in the context of the massacre of the Galileans and of the collapse of the tower of Siloe (13.3, 5). Both events led Jesus' contemporaries to deduce that the victims had been punished for their sins. Jesus replies that the victims had sinned no more than other Galileans and the inhabitants of Jerusalem (13.2, 4). All are sinners and must re-

---

[12] Lk 1, 16-17; 22.32; Acts 3.19; 9.35; 11.21; 14.15; 15.16, 19; 26.18, 20; 28.27; 15.3.

[13] Cf A. Descamps, *Les Justes et la Justice dans les évangiles et le christianisme primitif* (Louvain-Gembloux, 1950), 155-156, does not interpret "the just" in an ironical sense, but as the truly just who have no need of being invited to *metanoia.* Only sinners, whom he interprets as Christians who have gone astray, must repent. They must return to the kingdom through a second conversion. He believes that in the first two Synoptics this text represents an appeal for a first conversion to Christianity and entrance into the kingdom. Because of the literary parallel with Luke 15.7, he concludes that in the Lucan account this text and the parables of mercy refer to a second conversion.

pent: "If you do not repent, you too shall perish" (13. 3, 5). Inasmuch as these two logia introduce the parable to the sterile fig tree (13. 6-9), their call for repentance would seem to be equally relevant to Luke's Jewish contemporaries.[14]

The introduction to the three parables of mercy (15. 1-2) reveals a contrast between the repentance of sinners and the self-righteousness of the Pharisees.[15] The same contrast occurs in the story of the Pharisee and the Publican in the Temple (18. 9-14). The parable of the Lost Sheep teaches that there is more rejoicing in heaven over one sinner who does penance than for ninety-nine who have no need of *metanoia* (15. 7). The parable of the Lost Coin mentions the joy of heaven for one sinner who repents (15. 10); and the parable of the Prodigal Son expresses the same joy at the return of the lost son (15. 13-24).

The three parables of mercy imply the active role and initiative of God for the recovery of what he has lost. As the parables of the Lost Sheep and Coin imply, conversion is achieved by the divine search for what has been lost. The Father of the Prodigal Son awaits and welcomes his son who had been dead (15. 32). Repentance is viewed not as a return to the law but to the person to whom the lost one belongs and who rejoices at the return.

The Lucan statement on fraternal correction interprets repentance within the context of the Christian community. The divine forgiveness which welcomes man's repentance must be reproduced in human relationships. The text is parenetic, a moral

---

[14] Cf. R. Michiels, *art. cit.*, 58.

[15] Cf. J. Jeremias, *Die Gleichnisse Jesu* (Zürich, 1952), 24-26 and 109-111, in contrast with A. Descamps, holds that the three parables of mercy in chapter 15 are clearly kerygmatic and that the Pharisees are the audience to whom they are directed. He gives an eschatological interpretation to joy (*chara*) and *metanoia*: God rejoices at the judgment (pp. 25, 110). R. Michiels, *art. cit.*, opts for neither the purely pastoral (Descamps) nor the purely eschatological (Jeremias) interpretation of these three parables. He maintains thet Luke has detached the concept of conversion from the eschatological, kerygmatic context which it possessed in the historical preaching of Jesus. He maintains that the historical *Sitz im Leben*, which is both eschatological and kerygmatic, is conserved by Luke in the criticism of the Pharisees' attitude: However, Luke suppresses any note of condemnation in his desire to emphasize the divine joy at the sinner's return. He holds that Luke is directing his attention to his Jewish contemporaries who still have time to repent in response to the preaching of the Church. Thus, Luke would be primarily concerned with the first conversion and not the second in these three parables.

instruction on relationships among Christians (17.4 = Mt 18.15, 21-22):

> If your brother does something wrong, reprove him and if he is sorry (*metanoese*) forgive him. And if he wrongs you seven times a day and seven times comes back to you and says, "I am sorry", you must forgive him (*metanoō*).

Luke is apparently considering a matter which concerns only two of the community: in Matthew the offence is more public. Luke does not mention appealing to the community. He is more concerned with the moral problem of the individual Christian who must follow the example of God and of Jesus in forgiving his repentant brother (11.4 = Mt 6.12).

In the story of Lazarus and the rich man, the latter requests that the former be sent to his five brothers to encourage them to repent (16.30). It is implied that if they do not repent, they shall also find themselves in Hades. Abraham responds that even the sign of the resurrection from the dead, a clear reference to Jesus, [16] would not convince them; furthermore, the five brothers have Moses and the prophets. Conversion is possible, if the brothers listen to them; there is still time for repentance.

The last instructions of the risen Christ concern the apostolic mission of preaching repentance (Lk 24.46):

> So you see how it is written that Christ would suffer and on the third day rise from the dead, and that, in his name, repentance for the forgiveness of sins would be preached to all the nations, beginning from Jerusalem.

The word *epistrephein,* in the religious sense, appears in the exclusively Lucan description of the Baptist as the New Elijah (1.16,17):

> ... he will *bring back* many of the sons of Israel to the Lord their God. With the spirit and power of Elijah, he will go before him *to turn* the hearts of fathers towards their children and the disobedient back to the wisdom that the virtuous have, preparing for the Lord a people fit for him.

Peter's denial and repentance are foreseen by Jesus (22.32): "I have prayed for you that your faith not fail, and that when *you have turned* again strengthen your brethren."

---

[16] R. Michiels, *art. cit.*, 59.

Although Luke does not expressly employ the word for conversion, he clearly communicates this understanding of Peter's first encounter with Jesus. The words of Peter at his own conversion were a confession of his sinfulness (5. 8): "Depart from me, Lord; I am a sinful man." The expression, "Depart from me" (*'exelthe 'ap' 'emou*) expresses reverent fear before a divine manifestation such as that experienced by the Hebrews who were afraid to encounter Yahweh (Ex 20. 19). Yahweh's revelation to Isaiah (6. 5) produced reverential awe. The expression also describes personal sinfulness. Peter departed and wept bitterly when he saw Jesus after his denial (22. 62). Luke would seem to employ this expression to signify conversion from a state of sinfulness. In Stephen's description of the call of Abraham and Moses (Acts 7. 3, 7), God tells both to "depart" (*exelthein*) from their native lands: "After they depart, they shall worship me in this place." Conversion from life under a false god, equivalent to a state of sinfulness, to the worship of the true God is described in geographical terms. Such a conversion is implied by Elijah's departure from Samaria (1 Kgs 17. 3). As Abraham, Moses and Elijah had been told to depart from an unclean land, Jesus is told by Peter to depart from himself, a sinner.

III — *Acts*

In the Book of Acts *metanoia* is opposed to ignorance, such as that which explains the distorted concept of the kingdom of God and led the Jews to the condemnation of Christ (3. 17; 13. 27); and which in pagans explains their failure to know the true God and their proper relationship to him (17. 30).[17] *Metanoia* requires the acquisition of knowledge and instruction (20. 20). Paul required the instruction of Ananias to come to the knowledge of Christ.

[17] Cf. J. Dupont, *Le Discours de Milet* (*Lectio Divina*, 32), (Paris, 1962), 82-83, notes in Paul's speech at Miletus the distinction in preaching to Jews and to pagans implied in the sentence: "I have preached to you ... urging both Jews and Greeks to turn to God and to believe in our Lord Jesus" (20. 21). The conversion of the Gentiles implies that they must repent of their idolatrous, polytheistic past and embrace a monotheistic faith in the one true God. The Jews already believe in Him; it is the second part of the sentence that primarily concerns them. They must recognize Jesus as Messiah and Savior.

Metanoia is a grace for both Jews (5. 31) and Gentiles (11. 18). It requires a turning away from sin (2. 26) and is a condition for forgiveness (2. 38; 3. 19). It presupposes a view of reality with which one's past conduct has been in conflict. The acceptance of Christ and his revelation achieves a liberation from sin impossible under the law of Moses (13. 29). The inward change of heart is authenticated by works (26. 20), and effectively symbolized by baptism (2. 38, 41). Repentance is the effect of the Spirit's operation in converts (11. 15-18).

Diverse elements which characterize conversion appear in the kerygmatic speeches of Acts 2-13.

The diverse stages of the conversion process are specified in Peter's first speech (2. 38-40):

> You must all *repent* and be baptized in the name of Jesus Christ for the forgiveness of your sins, and you will receive the gift of the Holy Spirit. The promise that was made is for you and your children, and for all those who are far away, for all those whom the Lord our God will call to himself ... Save yourselves from this perverse generation.

(1) *metanoia,* (2) baptism, (3) the remission of sins, (4) the gift of the Holy Spirit, (5) participation in the fulfillment of the salvation promises, (6) liberation and salvation constitute the phases of the conversion process. The Jews must repent for the crucifixion; *metanoia* and baptism are conditions for their forgiveness.

Peter's second speech specifies diverse elements that should lead to a radical reappraisal of one's life (3. 19-21):

> Now you must *repent* and *turn to* God, so that your sins may be wiped out, and so that the Lord may send the time of comfort. Then he will send you the Christ he has predestined, that is Jesus, whom heaven must keep until the universal restoration comes which God proclaimed, speaking through his holy prophets.

Repentance (*metanoein*), turning to God (*epistrephein*), the remission of sins, the expectation of the Second Coming, participation in the fulfillment of the salvation promises constitute the conversion process. The time for conversion is *now.* The kerygmatic call to conversion, to the condition for the divine blessing, is made in the christological context of the resurrection and exaltation of Jesus (3. 26):

> It was for you in the first place that God raised up his servant and sent him to bless you by *turning* every one of you from your wicked ways.

Repentance is associated with the ignorance of the Jewish people (3. 17-18):

> Now I know, brothers, that neither you nor your leaders had any idea what you were really doing; this was the way God carried out what he had foretold, when he said through all his prophets that his Christ would suffer.

The speeches of the fourth and fifth chapters repeat the call to conversion and the offer of salvation (4. 12; 5. 28-32). In the tenth chapter, Peter speaks of the guilt of the people of Jerusalem for the death of the Messiah (10. 39). Faith is demanded of Cornelius and his household as a condition for forgiveness (10. 42, 43).

Paul's speech to the Jews of the dispersion at Antioch of Pisidia blames the inhabitants of Jerusalem for the crucifixion (13. 47); consequently, there is no call to *metanoia*. Faith is necessary for forgiveness and justification (13. 38-49).

The kerygmatic speeches of Acts 2-13 appeal to the Jews of Jerusalem to repent for their role in the death of the Messiah; they emphasize the resurrection and exaltation of Jesus.[18] The risen Lord is the core of the apostolic preaching. God has established his kingdom through the risen Christ who realizes the kingdom of God. The delay of the Second Coming drew attention to the time between the resurrection and the Second Coming. Thus, Luke focuses on the present reign of the risen Christ and his action within the Church.[19]

The speeches of Peter in Acts contrast the divine action in the resurrection of Christ with the Jewish role in his death. The Third Gospel contrasts the culpability of those who conspired against Christ with the innocence of Christ. *Metanoia* is linked with the crime of the crucifixion.[20] The guilt of those responsible

---

18 R. Michiels, *art. cit.*, 47.
19 *Ibid.*, 48.
20 *Ibid.*

should induce them to a saving *metanoia* and a heartfelt reappraisal of what they have done. The apostolic preaching, calling for *metanoia,* affords the occasion for their conversion. After the ultimate rejection of the apostolic word of God, the apostolic preaching will be addressed to the Gentiles (10. 46), who will accept it (10. 48).

Conclusion

In the synoptic accounts *metanoia* is an eschatological concept in the tradition of the prophetic Old Testament speeches condemning the people of Israel and calling them to conversion. Thus, the Baptist calls Israel to conversion in preparation for the eschatological judgment and Jesus similarly demands repentance for admission into the eschatological kingdom. [21] In this context, conversion is conceived as the collective act of the entire people; it is unique in that it occurs once for everyone. [22] It involves a total change of heart and a return to God as a condition for entrance into the kingdom of God. The eschatological concept of *metanoia* in the Third Gospel characterizes the Baptist's preaching, Jesus' condemnation of the cities by the Sea of Galilee, the logion on the preaching of Jonas at Nineveh, the call to repentance (13. 3, 5) introducing the story of the sterile fig tree, and the story of Lazarus and the rich man. [23] It is found in Acts where conversion is mentioned as a necessary preparation for the Second Coming when Jesus shall judge mankind (3. 19-21; 10. 42; 17. 30-31). [24]

Occasionally Luke detaches texts on *metanoia* of the common synoptic tradition from their originally eschatological context, and inserts them into a new context which indicates a conversion that is individual and partial as opposed to collective and absolute. He does this because he considers the promises of salvation as realized within the Church. *Metanoia* is, in these passages, viewed within the context of the moral behavior of Chris-

---

[21] Cf. H. Conzelmann, *Die Mitte der Zeit* (Tübingen, 1954), 90-92 and 104-111, notes the Lucan tendency to deescatologize the concepts of the "kingdom ' and "metanoia". The three stages of salvation history are the time of Israel, of Christ and of the Church.

[22] R. Michiels, *art. cit.,* 75.

[23] *Ibid.,* 76.

[24] *Ibid.*

tians (5. 32; 15. 7, 10; 17. 3, 4; 24. 47).[25] In some texts Luke seems to view *metanoia* as a permanent moral disposition characterizing the new life of Christians (Lk 3. 8; 17.3-4; Acts 26. 20).[26]

Lucan soteriology is essentially ecclesial. The promised salvation is present in the Church and affords the opportunity of repentance for Jews and Gentiles.[27] The risen Christ reigns in his Church. The time of the Church is the time for conversion. The antithesis between Israel and the Gentiles, progressively elaborated in the Third Gospel and Acts, culminates at the end of Acts when it is clear that salvation has passed from the Jews to the Gentiles, from Jerusalem, the Holy City to Rome, the center of the pagan world. It passes to those who would be converted.

NOTES

H. B. Kossen, "Quelques remarques sur l'ordre des paraboles dans Luc XV et sur la structure de Matthieu xviii 8-14," *Novum Testamentum* 1 (1956), 75-80. Luke 15 presents three parables on repentance (the lost sheep, coin, and son). Matthew records only one of these. The early Christians studies the Old Testament and noted in the margin references to Christ. The teaching about Christ followed the references made by various "schools," and are thus connected to the order of Old Testament texts. Parallels to the Lucan ordering of these three parables can be found in Jer 31. 10-14, 15-17, and 18-20. Parallels to Matthew's ordering of material can be found in Jer 31. 7-9 and 10-14.

M.-F. Lacan, " Conversion et Royaume dans les Evangiles synoptiques," *Lumière et Vie* 9 (1960), 25-47. The Synoptics present Jesus as proclaiming the link between conversion and the kingdom of God. Mark describes conversion in terms of that faith which gives access to the kingdom and to life. Thus, Jesus calls men to faith, to fundamental conversion. Luke stresses the universality of salvation and the call to conversion (24. 47). Luke links joy and renunciation with conversion whose ultimate cause is the Father's mercy. Matthew emphasizes conversion in the context of the missionary community and its preaching to all nations (28. 19-20).

---

[25] *Ibid.*

[26] *Ibid.*, Cf. G. W. H. Lampe, "The Holy Spirit in the Writings of St. Luke," ed. D.E. Nineham, *Studies in the Gospels* (Oxford, 1955), 185-187.

[27] Cf. H. Schürmann, "Evangelienschrift und kirchliche Unterweisung. Die repräsentative Funktion der Schrift nach Lk 1, 1-4," *Miscellanea Erfordiana* (*Erfurter Theol. Stud.*, 12), (Leipzig, 1962), 48-73, esp. 68, maintains that Luke understands the realization of eschatological time in the time of Christ and in that of the Church. In both the possibility of conversion is offered to hearers of the Christian message. Luke understands salvation history in terms of promise and fulfillment.

3.

FAITH

In the Age of Jesus, faith has three distinct aspects: it is christological; it is charismatic; and it is associated with Jesus' miraculous power of healing. [1]

Only once in the Lucan account does faith (*pistis/pisteuō*) have an explicitly christological sense. In this case it is a question of unbelief rather than belief (22. 67): "If you are the Christ, tell us". "If I tell you," he replied "you will not believe me..." A christological understanding, according to S. Brown, offers the best interpretation for faith in the episode concerning the calming of the storm (8. 25) and in Christ's prayer that Peter's faith would not fail (22. 32). In each case the faith of the apostles is in question. [2]

"Charismatic faith", expressing confidence in one's own power of working miracles, is imparted by Jesus but does not focus on his person. This particular sense of faith appears in the apostles' words to the Lord, "Increase our faith" (17. 5). [3]

In the Age of Jesus faith in Jesus' miraculous power occurs in the miracle stories deriving from Mark or Q. [4] The centurion's faith in this power is so great that he believes Jesus can cure his servant even from a distance (Lk 7. 9/Mk 8. 10). The paralytic's friends exhibit the same faith in Jesus' miraculous power, when they lower the paralytic from the hole in the roof (Lk 5. 20/Mk 2. 5).

A secondary relationship between faith and forgiveness emerges in this same pericope, when Jesus responds to this

---

[1] S. Brown, *Apostasy and Perseverance in the Theology of Luke* (Rome, 1969), 39.

[2] *Ibid.*

[3] *Ibid.*; See B. Vawter, *The Four Gospels* (Dublin, 1967), 268.

[4] *Ibid.*, 37; See A. Richardson, *Miracle Stories of the Gospels* (London, 1941).

manifestation of faith by forgiving the paralytic's sins before performing the desired miracle. The relationship of faith and forgiveness has a special meaning for Luke, because it squares with the missionary situation in the Age of the Church, where faith, understood as the acceptance of the Christian kerygma (Acts 26. 18), obtains forgiveness.[5]

The situation of Jesus' miracle-working corresponds to that of the Christian mission. Luke perceives this in the words of Jesus related twice by Mark: "Your faith has healed you" (8. 48/ Mk 5. 34; 18. 42/Mk 10. 52). *Sōteria,* which means both "health" and "salvation", is generally associated in Acts with the forgiveness of sins; consequently, the notion of faith as the requisite for *sōteria* corresponds with the association of faith and forgiveness.[6] The parable of the sower (8. 12; cf. Acts 16. 31), in its Lucan version, reveals that the former formulation is also linked with the missionary situation.

The dialogue between Jesus and Jairus reveals Luke's interest in the relationship between faith and *sōteria.*[7]. The Marcan parallel is simply a call to faith (5. 36); whereas, Luke adds another element: "Only believe, *and you will be saved*" (8. 50). The relationship between faith and *sōteria* has a missionary background which appears twice where Luke employs the phrase "Your faith has healed you". In the first of these exclusively Lucan pericopes no miracle ocrurs; in the second it can hardly refer to the miracle reported.

The parable of the two debtors (7. 41-43) in the story of the sinful woman (7. 50) implies that the woman's sins have already been forgiven. Gratitude has impelled her great display of love. The reason for her forgiveness, Jesus explains, is not her faith, but her love (7. 47); consequently, the conclusion that her faith has saved her (7. 50) is unexpected.[8]

The same problem arises in the healing of the ten lepers

---

[5] *Ibid.*, 37; See G. Bouwman, *Das Dritten Evangelium* (Düsseldorf, 1968). 53, 162-165.

[6] *Ibid.*, 37-38.

[7] *Ibid.*, 38; Brown notes that the Lucan addition, "and she will be healed" (8. 50) sounds strange after v. 49, in which the death of Jairus' daughter has been reported; however, the very inappropriateness of the addition reveals Luke's interest in linking the concepts of faith and salvation (healing).

[8] *Ibid.*, 38.

(17.19).[9] Only one Samaritan is addressed with the words, "Your faith has healed you"; therefore, the healing involved cannot refer to the cure which all ten enjoyed. By the same token, faith cannot refer to the obedience of the lepers in showing themselves to the priests. The words appear unrelated to the situation, if understood of the Samaritan alone. Gratitude, rather than faith, distinguishes him from the other nine (17.16). Furthermore, there is no conferring of salvation as in the forgiveness of the sinful woman (7.48).

Brown finds that the simplest solution to the difficulties in these two pericopes is to assume that Luke, in using the words "Your faith has saved you" as the conclusion for these episodes, understood them in terms of the missionary situation of the Church, without reflecting that this understanding scarcely suited the context in the Age of Jesus.[10] The concept of faith in Jesus' miraculous power is sometimes found anachronistically joined with acceptance of the Christian kerygma, a sense proper to the Age of the Church.

In Lucan writings the notion of faith (*pistis/pisteuō*) is used theologically in four contexts, where it means: belief in the law and the prophets (24.25; Acts 24.14; 26.27); belief in the Baptist (20.5/Mk 11.31); belief in the fulfilment of a divine prophecy (1.20,45; Acts 27.25); and belief in "a thing" (Acts 13.41).[11] There usages of the expression *pistis/pisteuō* contribute little to the comprehension of the Lucan notion of "faith". The same is true for his non-theological use of the word (16.11; Acts 17.31; Acts 9.26), signifying respectively "entrust", "proof", "believe" in a profane sense.

In the Age of the Church, Brown's study of this concept reveals a threefold use of the concept of faith, similar to that he established for the Age of Jesus:[12]

---

[9] *Ibid.*; See G. Voss, *Die Christologie der Lukanischen Schriften in Grundzügen*, (Bruges, 1965), 36,46.

[10] *Ibid.*, 39.

[11] *Ibid.*, 37.

[12] *Ibid.*, 47-48; Brown observes that Peter uses the faith-wrought healing of the lame man as the starting point for his preaching to the people and his appeal to penance and conversion, with a view to the remission of sins (3.12-19). Thus, faith in the miracle-working power of Jesus' name serves as a model for the faith in the Christian kerygma which is required for the forgiveness of sins (Acts 10.43). In the speech before the Sanhedrin the double meaning of *sōteria* (i.e. salvation and healing), which provides the

Belief in the miracle-working power of Jesus' name and of the apostles. This belief in Jesus' name is the starting point for the appeal for faith in the Christian kerygma (Acts 3.16; 14.9).

Charismatic faith, enabling the leaders of the community to work miracles and encourage the disciples to perseverance (Acts 6.5; 11.24).

Belief in Jesus as the Christ. This "belief" is now restricted to the initial acceptance of the Christian kerygma and probably designates, concretely, the externa *confession of faith* preceding and accompanying baptism.[13]

Brown discovers a fourth usage of "faith" which does not occur in the Age of Jesus, because "the faith" in this sense did not yet exist (i.e. *fides quae praedicatur*). This is the Christian kerygma itself, the content of the missionary preaching, in which Christians are admonished to persevere.[14]

---

basis for joining miracle and missionary appeal, is deliberately exploited (4.9, 12). In the name of Jesus the apostles are able to heal *and* to save (*sòzo*). In Acts the faith in Jesus' healing power which characterized the Age of Jesus is replaced by faith in the healing power of Jesus' name (3.16) and of the apostles (14.9). Cf. Brown, 40.

[13] "Faith" in the atypical case of Simon Magus (Acts 8.13) is not accompanied by an inner change, but designates an exterior action, such as the confession of faith pronounced at baptism. This "faith" did not come from the heart (Lk 8, 12), but was merely an external profession of membership in the Christian religion. For Luke, "faith" is normally accompanied by an inner change.

[14] The efficacy of Christian preaching must be understood against the Old Testament background for the Christian idea of preaching the good news (Isa 52.7). This was not merely a question of announcing "peace" and "good things", but of effectively bringing them about. Thus, the Christian gospel not only announces but actually effects salvation (cf. W. Grundmann, *Das Evangelium nach Lukas* (Berlin, 1966), 1.

4.

THE FATHERHOOD OF GOD IN ST. LUKE

St. Luke reproduces two of the Marcan references to God as Father: the reference to the Son of Man coming "in the glory of his Father" (Mark 8:28 - Luke 9:36); and the address in prayer, "Abba, Father" (Mark 14:36 - Luke 22:42). Luke clearly reaffirms the Marcan doctrine of God as the messianic Father of Jesus, the messianic Son.

St. Luke's use of the material which he shared in common with *Matthew* underscores the conviction that Jesus calls God his Father because he is himself the messianic Son, and that he calls God the Father of his disciples because to them he, as messianic Son, has willed to reveal him.

The prayer of thanksgiving (Luke 10:21 - Matthew 11:25-27) contains five references to God as Father. After the return of the seventy, Jesus gives thanks to his Father:

> "I thank thee, Father, Lord of heaven and earth, for hiding these things from the learned and wise, and revealing them to the simple. Yes, Father, such was thy choice." Then turning to his disciples he said, "Everything is entrusted to me by my Father; and no one knows who the Son is but the Father, or who the Father is but the Son, and those to whom the Son may choose to reveal him."

Unique Relationship of Messianic Son

Jesus addresses God directly as "Father"; he then refers to him as "my Father." He proceeds to draw attention to the unique and intimate relationship which exists between the Father and himself. At the express desire and through the agency of the messianic Son himself, it is possible for this unique and intimate relationship to be extended so as to include certain selected human beings as well. Those whom the Son chooses as the recipients of his revelation are able to know the Father; they are able to share the Son's relationship to the Father.

Both St. Luke and St. Matthew record four other passages in which Jesus addresses his disciples, the chosen few to whom the mystery of the kingdom is revealed. Jesus enjoins the disciples to "be perfect" (or "merciful") as their Father is "perfect" (or "merciful") — (Matthew 5:48 - Luke 6:36). Jesus teaches his disciples to address God in prayer directly as "Father" (Matthew 6:9 - Luke 11:2). Jesus assures his disciples that he knows their needs (Matthew 6:32 - Luke 12:30). Jesus assures them that he will give them the best of all possible gifts (Matthew 7:11 - Luke 11:13).

In material which Luke *alone* uses we discover the aspect of the divine fatherhood which appealed to him especially. The boy Jesus in the Temple replies to his parents' question: "Did you not know that I was bound to be in my Father's house?" (Luke 2:49). This episode presents Jesus as the messianic Son of the Father; from his earliest years Jesus is aware of his unique and intimate relationship to the Father. Jesus recognizes his obligation to carry out his Father's will.

The Father's Community of Sons

Jesus tells his apostles at the Last Supper, "And now I vest in you the kingship which my Father vested in me" (Luke 22:29). The reference is messianic, as is clear from the messianic promise which immediately follows: "You shall eat and drink at my table in my kingdom and sit on thrones as judges of the twelve tribes of Israel" (Luke 22:30). Jesus and his disciples form one royal community to whom the Father assigns the power of judgment. Through the agency of the messianic Son, the disciples share in that kingship which derives from the Father.

On the cross, Jesus twice addresses God as "Father" (Luke 23:34, 46). After the resurrection, in the upper room in Jerusalem, Jesus commissions the Eleven as his witnesses, "I am sending upon you my Father's promised gift" (Luke 24:49).

The Lucan passage, "Have no fear, little flock; for your Father has chosen to give you the Kingdom" (12:32), sheds more light on the relationship of the disciples to the Father. That

Jesus so frequently uses the imagery of shepherd and sheep when speaking either of God's purpose or of the disciples reveals that he regards his followers as a messianic community in the making. To them is given the kingdom, communion with the Father through Jesus himself. As well as being the Father of the Messiah, Jesus, God is also Father of the "little flock" of the faithful who acknowledge his messiahship.

The Freedom of Sonship

The divine fatherhood of God should bring the disciples of Jesus freedom from anxiety:

> And so you are not to set your mind on food and drink; you are not to worry. For all these are things for the heathen to run after, but you have a Father who knows that you need them. So set your mind upon his kingdom; and all the rest will come to you as well (Luke 22:29-31).

Jesus' story of the prodigal son speaks in unequalled terms of God's fatherhood (Luke 15:11ff.). Regarding this parable, Günther Bornkamm remarks that "We must not allow our view to be dimmed with regard to the fact that the father is the principal figure in this parable, however much we are told about the fate of the two sons" (*Jesus of Nazareth,* p. 126).

Jesus, according to St. Luke, speaks of God as Father both of himself and of his disciples. And this dual aspect is equally clear in the other evangelists. God is the Father of the Messiah and of all those who are members of the messianic, or Christian, community. Men become the sons of God by grace, in Jesus the Messiah, and not by nature. All the references to God as the Father of men are made in passages where Jesus is speaking with his disciples, with those who have accepted the revelation which he has freely chosen to make to them.

"My Father" and "Your Father"

"Father" on the lips of Jesus is found in all the gospel traditions; it is clearly implied by some of the parables or analogies (Luke 15:11ff.). Only Jesus uses the phrase "my Father" in the New Testament. This phrase occurs frequently in *Matthew* and *John,* four times in *Luke,* and never in *Mark.* Nevertheless, all the evangelists concur that the mission of Jesus is that of revealing and imparting his sonship. Although his sonship is in a most important sense unique, Jesus can bring it about that others share in and enter into it (Luke 10:22).

Through sonship Jesus and his disciples are united in the common cry "Father": This prayer represents the fulfilment of the messianic prophecy of 2 *Samuel* 7:14, "I will be his Father, and he will be my son" (cf. Ps. 89:26f.). The prayer "Father" professes a vital communion with the Father through a loving and obedient adherence to his Son. The prayer "Father" expresses the existential reciprocity of the Father-Son relationship, of vital dependence.

Jesus teaches constantly about the kingdom, or kingship, of God, but he who exercises this dominion is referred to, not as King, but as Father. Jesus often speaks of the Father with relation to himself in a different tone from that with which he speaks of the Father in relation to his disciples. Most of the passages in which the distinction made between "my Father" and "your Father" is explicit or implicit are concerned with the mission and authority of Jesus. One such passage occurs in St. Luke's infancy narrative (2:49; cf. also 22:29). The union of Jesus with his Father's will is stressed in the Passion account (Luke 22:41f.; 23:34, 46). The difference is clearest in his revelation that the Father and the Son know each other in a way which is not revealed and, by implication, cannot be revealed to anyone (10:21).

Shared Sonship

J. Jeremias remarks that no Jew would have dared to address God as Father in the manner of Jesus (cf. *The Lord's Prayer,* pp. 19f.). Jesus did it always, in all his prayers which are handed down to us, with the single exception of his cry from the cross, where he is quoting *Psalm* 22:1. Jesus spoke with God as a son would with his father. In addressing God as Father, Jesus revealed the ultimate mystery of his mission and authority. His prayer, "Father," contains *in nuce* his message and his claim to have been sent from the Father. In the Lord's Prayer Jesus authorizes his disciples to repeat the word "Father" after him.

He gives them a share in his sonship and empowers them, as his disciples, to speak with their heavenly Father in the same way a child would speak with his father. Through the gift of sonship the disciple repeats the prayer "Father," which proclaims his acceptance of, and entrance into, the kingdom of Jesus the Messiah.

NOTES

E. Yarnold, "The Trinitarian Implications of Luke and Acts," *Heythrop Journal* 7 (1966), 18-32. The Third Gospel and Acts imply a Trinitarian economy in which the Son is begotten by the Father through the intermediacy of the Spirit. The temporal mission of the Son reveals the intra-Trinitarian economy of the eternal generation of the Son. Luke links Jesus' Sonship with the Spirit in his account of the Annunciation, the Baptism and the Transfiguration. The Son gives the Church the Spirit he has received (Acts 2. 33).

5.

GRACE IN ST. LUKE'S GOSPEL

The word grace (*charis*) occurs 25 times in Lucan writings: 17 times in Acts, and 8 times in the Gospel.[1] The derived term *charizomai* occurs 4 times in Acts and 3 times in the Gospel. *Charisma* occurs once in the Gospel. Luke alone of the Synoptics employs the noun *charis* (it appears in John 3 times) and the verb *charizomai*.

In Luke-Acts *charizomai* always expresses the giving of something which is not due, but which reveals the favor of the giver toward the recipient. Jesus gives sight to the blind (7. 21). He speaks of cancelling a debt (7. 42 f.). Pilate's releasing of Barabbas is a favor granted the Jews (Acts 3. 14). The concept of doing a favor appears in Acts 25. 11, 16. Paul receives a favor in Acts 27. 24.

Favor appears as an action in Acts 24. 27 and 25. 3, 9. *Charis* has the sense of a reward in Luke 6. 35, though the nuance of favor is not lost, man's relation to God is never on the plane of strict justice (cf. Lk 17. 9).

Favor appears as a passive quality in Mary's finding favor in the sight of God (1. 30). Jesus grows in *charis* before God and men (2. 52); he is favored by God. Early Christians find favor among the people (Acts 2. 47; 4. 33).

Traditionalism and Novelty

The Lucan use of the word grace reveals both traditional and new perspectives. The traditional perspective appears when

---

[1] Lucan references to grace (*charis*) in his Gospel: 1. 30, 2. 40, 52; 4. 22; 6. 32, 33, 34; 17. 9; in Acts 2. 47; 4.)33; 6. 8; 7. 10, 46; 11, 23; 13. 43; 14. 3, 26; 15. 11. 40; 8. 27; 20. 24; 32; 24. 27; 25. 3, 9. The derivative charidzomai appears in the Gospel: 7, 21, 42, 43; and in Acts 3. 14; 25. 11, 16; 27. 24. Cf. T. W. Manson, "Grace in the N.T.," in *The Doctrine of Grace*, ed., Whitley (London, 1932); J. Moffat, *Grace in N.T.* (London, 1931).

Stephen speaks of the patriarch Joseph, associating grace with wisdom: "God was with him, and rescued him out of all his afflictions, and gave him grace and wisdom before Pharaoh, king of Egypt" (Acts 7. 10). God's grace is that which enables Joseph to win favor; it also gives Pharaoh access to Joseph's wisdom (Gn 41. 38).

Three Lucan texts in Acts which employ the expression grace in relation to the word of God reveal a new perspective for this concept: (1) At Iconium, Paul and Barnabas are assured in their preaching by the Lord who bears witness "to the word of his grace," granting signs and wonders to be done by their hands" (14. 3); (2) At Ephesus, Paul again proclaims his mission of witnessing to "the gospel and of the grace of God" (20/24); (3) Paul commends his disciples to God and "to the word of his grace" (20. 32). In these three texts concerning Paul, Luke writes of the preaching of the Christian message, which consists in the proclamation of the grace that God is offering man. God communicates to believers a grace which is actively present in the preaching of his word. Through the preaching of the gospel, even the Gentiles now share in the grace of God (Acts 14. 23, 26; 15. 40).

The Lucan account of the Annunciation presents a melange of texts containing traditional Septuagint formulas for the conferring of grace.[2] Thus, Mary had "found grace with God" (1. 30), as Noah (Gn 6. 8), as Abraham (Gn 18. 3), and David (I Sam 27. 5).

Grace and Joy

The Lucan themes of grace and joy are closely related.[3] Grace (*charis*) and joy (*chara*) derive from the same root. Grace emphasizes the external aspects of charm and beauty which evoke joy; it can refer to manifestation of those personal qualities which causes the beneficiary to rejoice. Joy is associated with the elated awareness of the grateful recipient. The Greek words *charis* and *chara* reveal the interrelationship of the subjective and objective, of the internal and external aspect of the same gracious, joy-giving event.

These two aspects are found in Barnabas' arrival in Antioch: "When he saw the grace of God, he rejoiced" (Acts 11. 23). The

[2] R. Laurentin, *Structure et Théologie de Luc I-II* (Paris, 1957) 64-90.

[3] M. Cambe, "*La charis* chez Saint Luc. Remarques sur quelques textes, notamment le *Kexaritomene*," *Revue Biblique* 70 (1963), 193.

success with which the preaching of the word of God had met in Antioch was the evidence evoking Barnabas' joy in the Lord.

The expression, "Hail (*kaire*), full of grace," (1.28) suggests that Mary's joy is her total responsiveness to the grace she has received. S. Lyonnet translates the angel's salutation as an invitation to rejoice in the prospect of messianic times: "Cry out for joy, *kecharitomene*!"[4] The Lucan "*kaire*" introduces the fulfillment of the messianic prophecy adumbrated in Soph. 3.14, Joel 2.21 and Zach. 9.9, *freedom* from fear, joy, and the presence of the Lord within the daughter of Sion are the key themes of this eschatological message. Of these three texts the two short triumphant messianic psalms with which the oracles of Sophonias ended come nearest to the angel's message:

> Cry our for joy, daughter of Sion,
> Shout for gladness, O Israel.
> Rejoice ... O daughter of Jerusalem,
> Yahweh is king of Israel in your midst (lit. in your womb)
> On that day they shall say to Jerusalem:
> Fear not, O Sion ....
> Yahweh your God is in your midst (lit. in your womb),
> a mighty Savior (Heb. *Yoshia'*).

Gabriel's message parallels the Sophonias text:

> Rejoice, you who are full of grace (*kecharitōmene*)
> The Lord (Yahweh) is with you ....
> Fear not, O Mary ....
> You shall conceive in your womb
> and bear a son.
> And you shall give him the name:
> Yahweh the Savior (Heb. *Yeshua'*).

Grace and Wisdom

Luke associates grace and wisdom in his references to the young Jesus among the doctors in the Temple (2.40, 52): "And the child grew and became strong, filled with wisdom; and the grace of God was with him"; and "Jesus increased in wisdom and stature, and in grace before God and man." In the first text, Jesus appears more as the object of God's grace; in the

[4] S. Lyonnet, "*Xaire Kecharitomène*," *Biblica* 20 (1939), 131.

second text, he is rather the subject of grace. The gift of God within Jesus pleases God and exerts an attraction over men.[5]

The grace which is quietly active in the person of the young Messiah will break out on the first day of his public ministry with his reading of Isaiah in the synagogue at Nazareth (4.22). All marvel at his "words of grace." But their comprehension of Jesus is superficial.[6] Luke's use of the phrase "words of grace" elsewhere (Acts 14.3; 20.24, 32), indicates that this is a technical expression in the Lucan writings which means "message of grace." I. de la Potterie, after weighing the different interpretations of this phrase, concludes that Jesus speaks of the grace of God and of his salvific will.[7] Jesus' Nazarene neighbors are astonished that the fulfillment of such a prophecy could be announced by someone who appeared so ordinary.

The references to the growth of the young Jesus find parallels in the infancy narratives of Sampson and of Samuel (1.80 and 2.40 with Judges 13.24; Lk 2.52 with I Sam. 2.26 and with Prov. 3.4). The interpretation of these texts, of course, surpasses the significance of the older formulas. Even Luke's language takes on a pauline coloring (Lk 1.28 with Eph. 1.7).

Plenitude Formulas

The word "grace" appears in formulas of plenitude, where it becomes part of a complex of terms with which it assumes an affinity of meaning.[8] The "plenitude formulas" begin with the adjective "full" (*plērēs*), followed by two determinants.[9] The seven men, for example, who are to be chosen from among the brethren to serve at table, are to be "full of the Spirit *and* of wisdom" (Acts 6.3). Stephen appears as a man "filled with the Holy Spirit *and* with faith" (Acts 6.5). The confident attitude of the Church at Antioch is described in terms of the disciples being "filled with joy *and* the Holy Spirit" (Acts 13.52). Lucan style is characterized by these "plenitude formulas" in which is

[5] M. Cambe, *art. cit.*, 199.

[6] Cf. H. Flender, *St. Luke Theologian of Redemptive History*, tr. R. H. and I. Fuller (London, 1967), 153.

[7] I. de la Potterie, *Excerpta Exegetica ex Evangelio Sancti Lucae*, informally published class notes (Rome, 1963-64), 130; Cf. de la Potterie, "L'onction du Christ," *Nouvelle Revue Théologique* 80 (1958), 231-32.

[8] M. Cambe, *art. cit.*, 199ff.

[9] Cf. G. Delling, *art.*, "*pleres*" in *TWNT*, VI, 284-85.

described fulness of the Spirit, of power, of grace, or of joy. All suggest that the Spirit is the cause of this fulness. They recall the same formula in John's Prologue (1. 14), "full of grace and truth."

Grace and Spirit occasionally appear as interchangeable (Acts 6. 8 with 10. 38). Stephen accomplishes his miracles in virtue of his fulness of "grace and power" (6. 10). The miraculous healings of Jesus were explained in terms of God's having anointed Jesus "with the Holy Spirit and with power" (Acts 10. 37), received at his baptism. Grace and power (*dunamis*) are frequently related. Stephen is "filled with grace and power" (Acts 6. 18).

Jesus' "words of grace" spoken at his inaugural discourse in the synagogue at Nazareth (4. 22), seen in the light of the relationship between grace and Spirit, can be understood as clearly inspired: "the Spirit of the Lord is upon me" (4. 18 = Isa. 61. 1). The Holy Spirit had descended upon him at his Baptism theophany, and event marked by a profound eschatological significance (cf. Isa. 63. 14, 19), signifying that Jesus' entire existence was in communion with the Holy Spirit.[10] The Baptism signified that he had received the eschatological gift of the Spirit to inaugurate his mission as the prophet foretold by Isaiah (142. 1).[11] The prophetic mission for which Jesus had been designated at his Baptism begins with his inaugural discourse at Nazareth. He had been designated to speak his "words of grace" at his Baptism; and he is able to speak them in virtue of the Holy Spirit which has descended upon him for the solemn inauguration of his divine mission as the prophet and creator of the messianic community. Thus, the Baptism, the Holy Spirit and the "words of grace" have a communitarian, as well as personal, significance which adumbrates the descent of the Spirit and the subsequent apostolic preaching which create the Christ-community at Pentecost.[12] In this sense, the Baptism marks the beginning

[11] *Ibid.*, 87. The author notes the two anointings in Luke: the Baptism, which is prophetic in character, and the Ascension, which is royal. The event is described as personal, communitarian, eschatological and messianic.

[12] *Ibid.*, 90. The author convincingly argues that the dove which descends upon Jesus at his Baptism symbolizes the new eschatological community, the Church. The dove in the O. T. symbolized the people of God. The dove signifies what the mission of Jesus would achieve, just as the tongues of fire at Pentecost represent what the mission of the Church would effect. The descent of the Holy Spirit in the form of the dove represents the new messianic community which would begin to exist in its fulness with

of Jesus' mission and that of Christianity in the Spirit-inspired preaching of the "words of grace." [13]

Through the agency of the Holy Spirit the "words of grace", of God's gracious gift of salvation in Christ, are spoken by Christ at the outset of his mission. The apostles and evangelists are those who have heard and believed the "words of grace" and share in the mission of Christ by accepting his commission to proclaim them. Thus, the Church is the place where the Holy Spirit creates anew and the exalted Christ manifests his presence through his "words of grace." Grace means the whole Gospel, which is "the good news of the grace of God" (Acts 20.24), and "the word of his grace" (Acts 13. 43; 14. 3). Grace is also the personal impact of the exalted Christ who spreads abroad the gospel and enables it to bear fruit (1 Cor. 15. 10; 2 Tim. 2. 1); thus, the missionaries are commended by the Church to the grace of the Lord (Acts 14. 26; 15. 40; 20. 32).

"Full of Grace"

The Lucan application of the expression "full of grace" to Mary (1. 28) suggests a "plenitude formula". Mary has been endowed with grace and called to rejoice. The Holy Spirit, the Power of God, has overshadowed her. The word "overshadow" suggests that Mary is the *locus* of a great presence. [14] This unusual word (four times in the Greek Old Testament) appears to have its most technical meaning in Exodus 40. 34: [15]

> Then the cloud covered the Tent of Assembly and the glory of Yahweh filled the Dwelling, And Moses could not enter the Tent of Assembly, because of the cloud that *overshadowed* it and of the glory of Yahweh with which the Dwelling was filled.

Old Testament annunciations offer analogies which contribute to an understanding of Mary's role in redemptive history. [16] There

---

the miracle at Pentecost; the tongues of fire do not represent the Holy Spirit, but that which he would effect, the baptism of the Church; the gift of tongues, would represent the unity of all nations in the Church under the action of the Spirit.

[13] M. J. Lagrange, *Evangile selon saint Luc*, (4th ed., Paris, 1927), 21.

[14] R. Laurentin, *Structure*, 73-79.

[15] A. Jones, *God's Living Word* (London, 1963), 164.

[16] Cf. J. P. Audet, "L'Annonce à Marie," *Revue Biblique* 63 (1956) 346-74.

as the announcements of births, such as that of Isaac (Gn. 17-18), Sampson (Jg 13) and of the Emmanuel prophecies (Isa 7); there are announcements of missions, such as that of Moses (Ex 3-4) and of Gideon (Jg 6). The parallel for the message to Mary derives from the angel's salutation to Gideon in Jg 6. 11-24, which is abbreviated here:

> "Yahweh is with you, valiant hero!" "With all respect, my Lord," answered Gideon, "If Yahweh is with us, how is it that all this is happening to us?" .... And the angel of Yahweh said to him: "Go ... and save Israel from the hand of Midian." "How am I to save Israel ... I am the least in my father's house," said Gideon, "If I have found favor in your eyes, give me a sign that it is you who speak."

Gideon is not addressed by his own name; he is given the name, "Valiant Hero," which indicates his future mission for a messianic deliverance of the people of God. Gabriel does not use Mary's name at the outset; instead, he greets her with a name of portent: *Kecharitomene, "Full of Grace."* Her new name designates the mission which she has been chosen to perform on behalf of the new messianic community. The phrase, "the Lord is with you," is in both the case of Gideon and Mary a promise assuring them of the divine assistance for the achievement of their mission, on behalf of the people of God. [17] Thus, *kecharitomene* is a statement of Mary's function and a description of her action as God's chosen agent for the messianic deliverance of his people. [18] *Kecharitomene* reveals Mary's mission; "the Lord is with you" guarantees its success. Her name, "Full of Grace," anticipates her dynamic function as the object of God's incomparable grace (favor). She rejoices in the acceptance of her mission to become the mother of the Messiah who shall achieve the liberation of the people of God.

---

[17] Cf. L. Cerfaux, *Recueil Lucien Cerfaux* (Gembloux, 1954), I, 50. Commenting on Elizabeth's "Mother of my Lord," i. e. of my lord the king, Mary is interpreted as the queen-mother, the *gebirah,* or Great Lady, of Judah's court, however, the focus of the narrative is always on the royal son.

[18] A. Jones, *God's Living Word,* 166-167, warns against trying to interpret this text as if it were an analysis of Mary's dignity or a treatise on her personal sanctity, rather than a statement of her function. It is not the personality of the messianic instrument that occupies the center of the narrative, but the child who shall be called "Son of the Most High" (1. 32-33).

The conception and birth of Jesus, his Baptism, and his inaugural address in the synagogue at Nazareth are closely united in the Third Gospel by the two Lucan themes of grace and the Holy Spirit. The Holy Spirit is explicitly mentioned in all three pericopes. The theme of grace appears in the first and third pericope; however, we must look to the second pericope, with its descent of the dove at the Baptism, to grasp the import of Jesus' "words of grace" in the third pericope. The theme of the Holy Spirit illuminates our understanding of the *kecharitomene* and the "words of grace" in the eschatological context of the messianic community which comes into being through the activity of the Holy Spirit, the receptivity of *"Kecharitomene,"* and the "words of grace" of the prophet-Messiah himself.

NOTES

A. Jones, "Background of the Annunciation," *Scripture* 11 (1959), 65-81. The "Rejoice, Full of Grace" (*kecharitomene*).. recalls the "Cry out for joy, daughter of Sion" passage from Zephaniah 3.14-17 as has often been noted by scholars such as Laurentin and Lyonnet. The Lucan Annunciation narrative uses Old Testament material abundantly and carefully. The reappearance of Gabriel recalls Daniel with its accomplishment of vision and prophecy (9.24). Gabriel's word "overshadow" may refer to the indwelling Glory (Ex. 40.34). The study of the literary form of "annunciation" by Audet with its appeal to the angelic annunciation to Gideon (Jdg 6.11-24) leads to the conclusion that "Full of grace" is not a personal compliment but, like "valiant hero" in the address to Gideon, an announcement of function. This view squares with both the perspective of the Lucan account and with the Semitic mentality.

6.

JERUSALEM

The Gospel of Luke begins and ends in the Temple at Jerusalem (1. 5; 24. 63). Luke highlights Jerusalem and the Temple more than any other Synoptic.[1] Jerusalem is the place where redemptive history is fulfilled.[2] Jesus has to die in Jerusalem (13. 33). The disciples must stay in Jerusalem to receive the power of the Holy Spirit (24. 49; Acts 1. 4), and to become witnesses, "beginning from Jerusalem" (24. 47; Acts 1. 8). The exalted Lord appears either in Jerusalem or nearby (21. 13, 18, 33, 52). The community assembles in Jerusalem, "in the temple as the place which belongs to the people of God, the true Israel" (Acts 2. 46; 3. 1-3; 5. 20, 25, 42). The authority of the expanding Church is kept "in the hands of the authorities in Jerusalem" (8. 14-25; 11. 2, 22; 12. 25; 13. 13). Even Paul must go to Jerusalem to receive his authorization (9. 27; 15. 2, 22).

Luke distinguishes between the city and the Temple in the story of the triumphal entry and in Jesus' stay there before his death; between the people and their leaders.[3] The people listen to Jesus in the temple (20. 1), coming early in the morning to hear him (21. 38). They hang upon his words (19. 48) and are shocked at his death (23. 48). The high priests and leaders of the people who plot to murder Jesus are contrasted with them (19. 47).

---

[1] E. Lohse, *TWNT* VII, 330.

[2] The travel account actually has no locale, only the motif "on the way" — "to Jerusalem". In 13. 32 it appears that the journey is willed by God ("I must go"). Jesus' death will not only be in Jerusalem but also by means of Jerusalem (13. 34). For this purpose Jesus had "set his face to go to Jerusalem" (9. 51) for "the days drew near for him to be received up," and on the mountain Moses and Elias had spoken "of his departure" (*exodus*) which he was to accomplish at Jerusalem" (9. 31).

[3] H. Flender, *St Luke Theologian of Redemptive History,* tr. R. H. and I. Fuller (London, 1967), 107.

The preaching of the apostles in Jerusalem (Acts 3. 11) is linked with the motif of the people listening to Jesus in the temple.[4] There is still time for the people to repent and accept the Christ of Israel. They were not fully responsible for the crucifixion, because they did it "in ignorance" (Acts 3. 17). The same opportunity holds for the Pharisees. They disappear from the passion narrative with the implication that they are not culpable for the crucifixion.[5] As in the case of Gamaliel (Acts 5. 34), they represent that segment of the Jewish leadership which is receptive to the Christian message.

If Jerusalem is the place of salvation, it is also the place of judgment. Through her rejection of the Christ Jerusalem becomes the scene of judgment and brings destruction upon herself (13. 34). Jesus meets the traditional fate of the prophet in Jerusalem (13. 33). The acclamation from Ps 118 which Jesus receives at his triumphal entry (19. 38, cf. also 13.35) means fulfilment for the disciples, but judgment for Jerusalem because of its rejection of Jesus.[6] The passion is framed by two scenes which focus on the impending judgment. In one (19. 41-44) Jesus weeps over the city; in the other the people weep for Jesus (23. 27-31).[7] Jesus himself interprets the destruction of Jerusalem in his temple discourse (21. 5): it represents the wrath of God over his disobedient people, which had been foretold in the scriptures (21. 20-24). Thus, God wills that the center of the new Israel should shift from Jerusalem to Rome (Acts 23. 11). Jerusalem in God's chosen center from which will spread his salvation (9. 31, 51, 53; 13. 22, 33; 17. 11; 18. 31; 19. 11; 24. 47-49, 52; Acts 1. 8, etc.).

The Temple retains its importance at the beginning of the Christian period. Jesus makes his way to the Temple and delivers his final teaching on the Law and the Last Things.[8] At the Temple Jesus speaks of the future significance of Jerusalem

---

[4] Luke not only emphasizes Jesus daily teaching in the Temple (20. 1, 37 restate 19. 47), but he also breaks Mark's close tie with the episode of the Temple cleansing in order to stress Jesus' authority to teach (20. 2) rather than his authority to cleanse the Temple.

[5] H. Flender, *St. Luke,* 108.

[6] *Ibid.*

[7] H. Conzelmann, *The Theology of Saint Luke,* tr. G. Buswell (London, 1960), 133.

[8] *Ibid.,* 164.

(21. 22). The primitive Church remains loyal to the Temple (Acts 2. 46; 5. 42); however, in the story of Stephen it comes to terms with the problem of the Temple: "It was Solomon who built God's house for him. Even so the Most High does not live in a house that human hands have built" (Acts 7. 47-48). The argument is addressed to the Jews; in 27. 24, it is addressed to the Greeks.

Stephen argues his case about the Temple at a time when Christians prayed there.[9] When Luke wrote about Stephen's martyrdom, the problem of freedom from the Law and the Temple had already been solved. Thus, Conzelmann believes that Luke is the first evangelist who describes the past of the Christian community as past.[10]

"Jerusalem" is a key Lucan word. It occurs 30 times in the Third Gospel and 57 times in Acts; it is found only 10 times in Matthew and 14 times in Mark. Its connection with the Passion is especially underscored in the Lucan account of the Transfiguration, when Moses and Elias speak of Jesus' "Exodus to Jerusalem". Only Luke designates the Passion as an *exodus,* as a departure from this world (9. 31). This word occurs in only two other New Testament texts where it signifies the departure from Egypt (Hb 11. 22), and where Peter describes his own approaching departure (2 Pt 1. 15). R. Laurentin believes that the context of the Transfiguration suggests that Jesus' exodus will be a return to the Father whose voice is heard in the cloud of glory which envelops him (9. 35-36).[11] The return to the Father which is evoked as the positive aspect of the *exodus* is explicitized in John's Gospel (13. 1; 17. 1, 5).

Jesus' journey to Jerusalem is associated with his "assumption" (*analempsis*): "When the days drew near for his assumption, he resolutely took the road for Jerusalem" (9. 51). The "days" that Luke mentions would seem to imply that the assumption embraces Jesus' death, resurrection and ascension, the series of events which constitute his exaltation (cf. Acts 1. 2, 22).

Laurentin affirms that *analempsis* signifies the entire pascal mystery, designating it in terms of its last act.[12] It is the ascension in which Jesus joins his Father (Acts 1. 4, 7) in order to send

---

[9] *Ibid.*, 165.
[10] *Ibid.*
[11] R. Laurentin, *Jésus au Temple* (Paris, 1966), 96.
[12] *Ibid.*, 96, 98.

the Spirit. Thus, the *exodus* and the *analempsis* would seem to be analogous concepts closely associated with Jerusalem and Jesus' exaltation. The theme of the ascent towards the high place, the dwelling place of God, has a rich symbolic value associated with these two concepts. At the Transfiguration (9.28) Jesus ascends the mountain to pray; the road to Jerusalem must be traversed as a necessary phase in the course of Jesus' life leading to the ascension (9.51). The ascent to Jerusalem is a common biblical theme. The Psalm of Zion (46, 48, 76, 87), in markedly eschatological terms, hymn the glories of Jerusalem which is both the dwelling place of the Most High and the goal of pilgrimage (Ps. 87 and 122).[13]

Another typically Lucan word closely linked with Jesus' journey to Jerusalem is *poreuomai,* "to go", "to set out", "to be on one's way." The expression occurs 146 times in the New Testament. The Lucan writings account for 88 appearances of the word. The word is associated with Jesus' redemptive mission in Jerusalem: "it is necessary for me to go (*poreuesthai*) today and tomorrow and the day following, for it is impossible that a prophet should die outside Jerusalem" (13.33). The expression is associated with the mystery of Jesus' *exodus* and *analempsis* and the accomplishment of his redemptive mission in Jerusalem: "The Son of Man goes (*poreuetai*) as it has been decreed" (22.22). The transcendent reality of Jesus' departure, expressed by the concepts of the *exodus* and *analempsis,* is not explicit in 22.22; however, it becomes clearer in Acts where the verb *poreuomai* describes his ascension: " ... they were gazing into the sky as he went" (*poreuomenou*); and " 'Jesus will return in the same way which you have seen him depart' " (*poreuomenon*) (Acts 1.10, 11). Thus, R. Laurentin affirms that Jesus journey and ascent to Jerusalem symbolize the pascal mystery and his departure for a more mysterious place, until the time "when he comes in his own glory and that of the Father and of the holy angels" (9.26).[14]

Commenting on eschatology in the Gospel of Luke, W. Robinson shows that Luke presented Jesus' eschatological address (Lk 21) as only one topic among the others taken up in Jesus' public teaching.[15] The Lucan form of that address would indicate

---

13 *Ibid.,* 97.
14 *Ibid.,* 97-98.
15 W. C. Robinson, *The Way of the Lord* (Dissertation, University of Basel,

that Jerusalem's destruction fulfilled prophecy but was not connected with the final events. Luke was more concerned to show the reliability of prophecy rather than to push the arrival of the kingdom farther into the future.[16] In his treatment of Jerusalem Luke also wished to teach that in Jesus' approach to Jerusalem the way of the Lord came near. This was the redemptive-historical time of Jerusalem's visitation, and her destruction was retribution for rejecting the Messiah.[17] Although Luke disassociates Jerusalem's fate from the eschaton, he has not abandoned hope for the future coming of the kingdom.[18] He refers to it twice in connection with the coming of the Son of Man (17.22; 21.25). Assurance with regard to the coming of the end is derived from the example of Jesus' ministry and by knowing the nature of God's reign of grace which providentially embraces the future life and work of the Church.[19] According to Robinson, Luke interprets the delay of the parousia in terms of the ongoing way of the Lord, whereby the times of divine visitation would continue as they had in the time of Israel and especially during the ministry of Jesus.[20] Thus, Luke expresses redemptive history's movement from the Jews to the Gentiles geographically in Acts by the portrayal of the way of the Lord from Jerusalem to Rome.

NOTES

K. Baltzer, "The Meaning of the Temple in the Lukan Writings," *Harvard Theological Review* 58 (1965), 263-277, writes that the Temple in the Old Testament was the place of worship, the center for the administration of law and justice, a place of asylum, and in many respects the center of Israel's life. Various theological concepts concerning the Temple existed simultaneously and influenced on another. Such were especially ideas concerning the Temple as the place of the presence of God, of His name, of the glory of Yahweh (i.e. the "mighty presence" or *kabod Yahweh*). This

1962), 70-72. Luke 21 presents eschatology as one doctrine among others. It is not restricted to an inner circle of disciples as in Mk 13.3.

[16] *Ibid.*, 72-80. Luke 21.7 does not ask about the final events (21.25) but asks the date and sign of the things "of the temple." The question regarding the fall of Jerusalem (21.7) is not the same as that about the kingdom (17.20).

[17] *Ibid.*, 80-98. The author notes that in the Old Testament the expression "visitation" (*episkeptomai, episkope*) often indicated the dynamic presence of God in blessing or in retribution.

[18] *Ibid.*, 98-111.

[19] *Ibid.*, 70.

[20] *Ibid.*, 71.

last concept appears in the Old Testament, the intertestamental literature and in the Qumran writings. The Jewish Shekinah speculation expected the *kabod* to return at the end of time.

In the early Christian writings the variety of Jewish Temple traditions are still evident. As a matter of course the first Christians continue the Temple observances. However, the Christian community is regarded as the new Temple as is also Christ Himself (Jn 2. 21). The Temple figures prominently in the third Gospel especially in Lk 1 and 2. Moreover, Luke so arranges Jesus' temptations that the last one occurs at the Temple. Furthermore, when Jesus said: "your house is forsaken" (Lk 13. 35), His statement would mean (cf. Ez. 10. 18; 11. 23) that God will withdraw His presence from the Temple and from Jerusalem.

With the Palm Sunday account Luke's concept of the Temple becomes very clear. According to him the sole purpose of Jesus' entry into the city is to take possession of the Temple (Lk 19. 45). In Luke, "when Jesus enters the Temple or is in the Temple, the Temple is really the Temple. To state it more precisely, Jesus and the *kabod* are connected." The connection appears in Luke in his account of the transfiguration, in the ascension, and in Jesus' reference to the Second Coming (Lk 21. 27). The Temple, even after its destruction, presented a problem for Christians, a problem which Luke solved by his christology. "For him Christ is the presence of God, because Christ, *kabod/doxa,* and spirit are related."

W. Käser, "Exegetische und theologische Erwägungen zur Seligpreisung der Kinderlosen Lc 23. 29b," *Zeitschrift für die Neutestamentliche Wissenschaft* 54 (1963), 240-254. The incident about the women of Jerusalem originally consisted of 23. 27-28. Distinctively Lucan traits appear in the next two verses (29-30) only loosely connected with v. 28. Luke would seem to have added these verses because he likes to state important facts three times (Pilate thrice asserts that Jesus is guiltless), and Luke gives the third mention of the fall of Jerusalem (Lk 19. 39-44; 21. 5-36; 23. 29-31). The ruin of Jerusalem means the end of Israel as a people, as state, and as the community of God. The new and spiritual Israel replaces the Israel according to the flesh.

A. F. Klijn, "Joden en heidenen in Lukas-Handelingen" (Jews and Gentiles in Luke-Acts), *Kerk en Theologie* 13 (1962), 16-24. The literary analysis of Lk 13. 22-30; 13. 34-35; 19. 11-27; 1939-44 leads to the deduction that for Luke the rejection of Israel is final. Unlike Paul, Luke does not hold the view of Paul that only as a consequence of Jewish unbelief salvation has reached the Gentiles Rom 11. 12, 25) and that the gospel had to be preached first to the Jews and, as a favor, to the Gentiles.

Both groups were destined for the gospel from the beginning; therefore, in the Lucan perspective the promises to Israel have not been transferred to the Church. As opposed to Mt 8, 11 where the Gentiles will sit with the patriarchs in the kingdom, Luke 13. 28 affirms that the unfaithful Jews of his day will see the patriarchs sit in the kingdom *and* the Gentiles will come to sit in it. He does not assert that they will sit *with* the patriarchs. The Church is not the new Israel into which the Gentiles find admittance (contrast with Rom 11. 17-19). Because Israel has rejected its salvation, there is no more Israel; there are only individual Jews, of whom many have received the gospel. In Luke conception of God's saving plan, Jerusalem is the point of departure and *arche* of God's saving work and Rome, the capital of the Gentiles, represents "the ends of the earth" (Acts 1. 8).

G. Rau, "Das Volk in der lukanischen Passionsgeschichte, eine Konjektur zu Lk 23. 13," *Zeitschrift für die Neutestamentliche Wissenschaft* 56 (1965), 41-51, notes that with one major exception (Lk 23. 13), Luke's references to the Jewish people in his Passion story and its sequel show that they are universally friendly to Jesus but opposed to their own leaders (19. 49; 20. 1, 6, 9, 16, 19, 26, 45; 21. 38; 23. 27, 35, 48; 24. 19-20). The disparity is not explained by saying that Lk 23. 13 followed another source than Mark. Rather, as P. Winter holds, the text of 23. 13 should read *tou laou*, not *kai ton laon*: the people as such are not present to condemn Jesus, but only their rulers.

Two arguments support this reading. (1) The change from *tou laou* to *kai ton laon* was a scribal error. (2) The phrase *tou laou* is to be read in the light of Luke's whole *Tendenz*: the Jewish people approve of Jesus; their rulers do not. This antagonism between the people and their leaders is well expressed in Lk 20. 26 where because of it the rulers must refrain from condemning Jesus. Similarly the possibility of the rulers' deceiving Pilate by false accusation (Lk 23. 2) is guaranteed only by the people's absence. The *ochlos* of Lk 22. 47, the *hapan to plethos auton* of 23. 1, the *tous ochlous* of 23. 4 and the *pamplethei* of 23. 18 do not refer to the Jewish people as a whole, but only to those who follow their rulers. The people as a whole reappear only at Lk 23. 26-31, where characteristically they mourn for Jesus, whereas Jesus reproaches not them but their leaders. Thus 23. 13 does not contradict the Tendenz of Luke's conscious reinterpretation of Mark.

By way of contradict the Tendenz of Luke's conscious reinterpretation of Mark. Jewish nation by their accepting responsiblity of Jesus' death (27. 24-25) does not occur in Luke. In contrast with Mark, Luke even omits that Evangelist's reference to the custom of releasing a prisoner to the people on the feast day (Mk 15. 6-8) so that in one more instance Luke absolves the people as such from the guilt of choosing Barabbas over Jesus.

P. Simson, "The Drama of the City of God. Jerusalem in St. Luke's Gospel," *Scripture* 15 (1963), 65-80. Luke portrays the role of the Holy City from the beginning of the New Testament until the time when it is no longer the spiritual center of the world. Jesus' birth, temptation (4. 1-13), and "exodus" (9. 28-36) take place in Jerusalem. Jesus journeys to the hostile city which kills the prophets, rejects her king, and perseveres in her blindness: "behind Jesus' passion, the shadow of another passion stands out: the passion of Jerusalem." Luke alone presents the life of Jesus as a unique, resolute "going up" to Jerusalem. It remained for the Fourth Gospel to describe the New Jerusalem.

7.

LUCAN JOY

The Vocabulary. Many expressions in Luke-Acts indicate joy: *makarios* and *makarızo* (blessed and to bless),[1] *chara* and *chairein* (joy and to rejoice),[2] *doksa* and *doksazein* (glory and to glorify),[3] *agalliasis* and *agalliáō* (exuberant joy and to rejoice exuberantly),[4] *'aínein* (to praise),[5] *eulogein* (to bless),[6] *eirēnē* (peace),[7] *euphrainein* (to gladden or to feast),[8] *megalunō* (magnify),[9] and *skirtaō* (to leap for joy).[10]

---

1 *Makarios*: (exclusively Lucan texts) 1, 45; 11, 27; 14, 14, 15; Acts 20, 35; 26, 2; (in common texts) 6, 20, 21,22; 7, 23; 10, 23; 12, 43, 37, 38. *Makarizo*: 1, 48.

2 *Charein*: (exclusively Lucan), 1, 14, 28; 10, 20; 13, 17; 16, 32; 19, 6, 37; 23, 8; (common texts), 6, 23; 15, 5; 22, 5; Acts 5, 41; 8, 39; 11, 23; 13, 48; 15, 31.

Charizesthai: 7, 21, 42; Acts 3, 14; 25, 11; 27, 24.

Chara: (exclusively Lucan), 1, 14; 2, 10; 15, 7; 24, 41; Acts 8, 8; 12, 14; 13, 52; 15, 13; (common texts), 8, 13; 24, 52; 10, 17.

3 *Doksa*: (exclusively Lucan), 2, 9, 14, 32; 9, 31, 32; 14, 10; 17, 18; 19, 38; 24, 26; Acts 7, 2, 55; 12, 23; 22, 11; (common texts), 4, 6; 12, 27; 9, 26; 21, 27.

Doksazein: 2, 20; 4, 15; 7, 16; 13, 13; 17, 15; 18, 43; 23, 47; Acts 11, 18; 21, 20; 3, 13; 4, 21; 13, 48; (common texts), 5, 25, 26.

4 *Agalliasi*: 1, 14, 44; Acts 2, 46. This word is not found in the other Synoptics.

Agalliao: 1, 47; 10, 21; Acts 2, 26. This word occurs once in the Synoptics (Mt. 5, 12).

5 *Ainein*: 2, 13, 20; 19, 37; 24. 53; Acts 2, 47; 3, 8, 9. This word does not appear in the other Synoptics.
10, 36; 24, 2; (common texts), 10, 5; 12, 51; 8, 48; 7, 50; Acts 16, 33; (common) texts), 9, 16; 19, 38; 13, 35.

7 *Eirene*: 1, 79; 2, 14; 11, 21; 14, 32; 19, 38, 42; 24, 36; Acts 12, 20, 7, 26; 9, 31; 10, 36; 24, 2; (common texts), 10, 5; 12, 51; 8, 48; 7, 50; Acts 16, 33; (common) Lk. 2, 29.

8 *Euphrainein*: 12, 19; 15, 23, 24, 29, 32; 16, 19; Acts 2, 26; 7, 41. This word does not appear in the other Synoptics.

9 *Megaluno*: 1, 46, 58; Acts 5, 13; 10, 46; 19, 17. The word occurs once in the other Synoptics (Mt. 23, 5).

10 *Skirtao*: 1, 41, 44; 6, 23. The word occurs in Luke alone. A. Schmoller, *Handkonkordanz* (Stuttgart, 1963, 13th ed.) serves to indicate the occurrences of these words. W. F. Moulton and A. S. Geden, *A Concordance to the Greek Testament* (Edinburgh, 1926, 3rd ed.) also serves this purpose. A. Plummer,

'Aineo, doksazo, eulogeo and *megalunō* focus more on the religious activity evoking joy than on the subjective state of the person rejoicing. These four words express joy at the recognition of salvation in progress. [11]

'Eirēnē expresses that peace which encompasses the whole man, his body and soul, as well as the relationship between himself and his world. Luke does not restrict it to an inner peace of soul. [12]

'Euphraino occurs in the parable of the merciful father (15, 23; 32) where it expresses the joy of the father who has found his son. [13] The term expresses the communal joy of feasting, of being together at a banquet.

Makarios involves the external conditions that ground interior happiness. [14]

'Agalliao and *chairein* are more concerned with the interior dimension of personal happiness. [15] *Agalliaō,* with one exception, is found exclusively in the infancy narratives where it describes Zachary's reaction to the birth of John (1, 14), John's reaction in Elizabeth's womb to the arrival of Mary (1, 44), and Mary's responsiveness to the presence of God within her, "My spirit *rejoices* in God my Saviour" (1, 47). The repetition of the same verb helps Luke to stress how these events are innerlocked in the achievement of the same divine plan.

'Agalliao is an especially Lucan term. It occurs six times in Luke-Acts (four times in the Gospel) and only three times in the rest of the New Testament. This expression of jubilant and thankful exaltation is always involved with the theme of God's help. [16] It refers to the eschatological act of divine salvation which is supremely the theme of rejoicing.

The Gospel according to St. Luke, Intern. Crit. Comm. (Edinburgh, 1922, 5th ed.) is an aid for the peculiarly Lucan usage of these terms.

[11] See especially G. Kittel and G. Friedrich eds., *Theologisches Worterbuch zum Neuen Testament* (Stuttgart, 1933).

[12] Kittel, *op. cit.*, vol. II, 400ff. J. Comblin, "La paix dans la théologie de saint Luc", *Revue Biblique* 32, 1956, 439-460, finds more of a political sense in the term than can perhaps be justified.

[13] R. Bultmann in Kittel, *op. cit.*, vol. II, p. 772ff.

[14] Bertram and Hauck, Kittel, *op. cit.*, vol. IV, pp. 365ff.

[15] R. Bultmann, Kittel, *op. cit.*, I, 19-21; A. B. Du Toit, *Der Aspekt der Freude im urchristlichen Abendmahl* (Dissert. Univ. of Basel, 1965), pp. 24f.

[16] *Art. cit.*, Kittel, *op. cit.*, p. 20.

Chairein and *chara* occur in the four primary Lucan contexts for the theme of joy: in the infancy narratives (3 times), in the beatitudes (once), in the Travel Narrative (9, 51-19, 27), (8 times), and in the resurrection narratives (twice).[17] It expresses Zachary's joy in his son (1, 14); the joy of the people in John (1, 14); the angel's greeting to Mary (1, 28); the message of good news to Joseph (2, 10). In every case joy is related to the recognition of the present salvation process and experienced in the measure that one participates in it. Zachary, John in his mother's womb, Simeon, Anna, Joseph and Mary rejoice, because the call to salvation is also a call to joy.

Together with *skirtaō, chairein* and *chara* describe the inner dimension of Luke's last beatitude: "Blessed are you when men hate you... Rejoice in that day, and leap for joy" (6, 22f.). *Charein* expresses the joy of the seventy disciples in their mission (10, 17); the deeper cause of joy asserted by Jesus (10, 20); the people's reaction to Jesus' saving power (13, 17); the joy of discovery when the shepherd finds his lost sheep (15, 5); the joy in heaven over one repentant sinner (15, 10); the joy of the father whose son returns (15, 32); the joy with which Zaccheus receives Jesus (19, 6), the last occurrence of the term in the travel narrative. *Chairein* conveys the disciples' joy at the resurrection appearance (24, 41) and as they return to Jerusalem after the Lord's ascension (24, 52).

The Travel Narrative (9, 15-18, 54) contains most of the peculiarly Lucan material. The plan for Christian joy presented in the beatitudes (6, 20-23) is considerably clarified by the Travel Narrative.[18] There are twently references to joy and ten pericopes in which this theme is basic within the Travel Narrative.[19]

---

[17] M. Cambe, "La *charis* chez saint Luc", *Revue Biblique* 70, 1963, pp. 193-208.

[18] Cf. J. Dupont, *Les Béatitudes* (Bruges, 1954), 78; Cf. A. George, "Tradition et redaction chez Luc. La construction du troisième évangile," *Ephemerides Theologicae Lovanienses* 43 (1967), p. 109; cf. X. Leon-Dufour, "L'évangile selon saint Luc", *Introduction à la Bible* II (Tournai, 1959), p. 252; "Luc, évangeliste du dessein de Dieu, est en même temps l'homme qui précise jusqu'où va concretement l'exigence du message évangelique. Mieux que Mt et Mc il indique qu'il faut porter la croix 'chaque jour' (9, 23). Mais en même temps il manifeste mieux le Saint-Esprit à l'oeuvre et la joie déversée au coeur des croyants."

[19] *Agalliao*: 10, 21; *chairein* or *chara*: 10, 17, 20; 13, 17; 15, 5, 7, 9,10, 32; 19, 6; *euphraino*: 15,23, 24, 29, 32; *makarios*: 10, 23; 11, 27, 28; 12, 37, 38,)43; 14, '4, 15. The pericopes in which joy is a dominant motif: the apostles should

Some characteristics of joy may be catalogued as follows:

1. *Willingness to accept a mission* conditioned the joy of the seventy at the signs that the kingdom of God has wrought (10, 17). The disciples rejoice that even the demons are subject to them.

2. *Belonging to God,* Jesus tells his disciples, is a deeper motive for their rejoicing rather than their power over demons. The joy of participation in the divine mission ultimately derives from the fact that the disciples belong to God, "...rejoice that your names are written in heaven" (10, 20).

3. Mission is intimately connected with *eschatological joy.* The disciples rejoice over the signs of the coming consummation. Their joy is based on the conviction that salvation is a present reality and will be such even more in the future. Theirs is the joy of rising hopes and deepening faith in the fulfilment of the divine promises based on the growing evidence which is recognized by those who actively participate in their realization. Reicke writes that the Travel Narrative is sustained by a genuine ecstasy of eschatological joy which intensifies with the progressive realization of the divine plan of salvation.[22]

4. *The Father's effective salvation of the Anawim* brings joy to Jesus (10, 21). The Father's plan and action of salvation delight Jesus. He rejoices at the revelation of grace to the poor and humble faithful. (The second half of the Parable of the Prodigal Son relates Christian joy to that of Christ. The Christian is called to participate in Christ's joy in the Father's work of salvation in ourselves and others.)

5. *The Joy of Jesus is in the Holy Spirit.* It is only Luke who refers here to Jesus' joy in the Holy Spirit: "At that time,

---

rejoice that their names are written in heaven (10,)17-20); Jesus' joy over the Father's self-revelation to the poor (to the *anawim* [10, 21-22]); those who hear and keep the word of God are genuinely happy (11, 27-28); happy is the servant who is ready for his Lord's return (12, 35ff.); happy is the man who invites the poor to his table (14, 12-14); the parable of the messianic banquet and its eschatological joy (14-15-24); the three parables of joy in finding what had been lost (chapter 15); Zaccheus' joy in the salvation which came to his home (19, 1-10).

20 B. Reicke, *The Gospel of Luke,* tr. by R. Mackenzie (Richmond, 1964), p. 79.

21 W. Grundmann, *Das Evangelium nach Lukas* (Berlin, 1959), p. 213, suggests the Old Testament background (Ex. 32, 32ff., Is. 4, 3) of the expression, "names written in heaven".

22 B. Reicke, *op. cit.,* p. 79.

Jesus was filled with joy by the Holy Spirit and said, O Father, who art Lord of heaven and earth..." (10,21). Matthew gives the same prayer (11,25-27) but not the opening phrase, which is Luke's own, and characteristic in bringing together three of his favourite themes: joy, prayer and the Holy Spirit. In prayer Jesus is closest to the Holy Spirit and to his Father in a union of ecstatic joy.

6. *Hearing and keeping the word of God* is a source of blessedness: "Blessed are they who hear the word of God and keep it!" (10,38-41). Christian joy is based on sharing the same spirit that was in Christ and not on physical ties.

7. *Joy is enduring* because the word of God from which it originates is enduring. Mary sat at the feet of Christ, listening to his words. The joy of those who hear the word of God and keep it is hers. She is wiser than Martha, because what she has "shall not be taken from her" (10,38-41); his words "will never pass away" (21,33).

8. *The work of Jesus* in healing the crippled woman is a sign of the presence of the kingdom of God and of the joy of God's benevolent reign. "All the people rejoiced" because a daughter of Abraham had been saved from the bond of Satan (13,16). Thus, the kingdom of God in the words and saving work of Jesus brings joy to the multitudes.

9. *Preparedness for the Lord's visitation* is a prerequisite for joy: "Blessed are those servants whom the master finds awake when he comes; truly, I say that he will gird himself and have them sit at table, and he will come and serve them" (12,37). The Father has given Christians a kingdom (12,32) in which they may rejoice, provided that they are ready for it. Preparedness is maintained through participation in Christian life and worship (12,35; 17,26; 21,34).

10. *Poverty and renunciation* are preconditions for Christian joy, which indicate its trans-temporal origins. Christian joy does

---

[23] G.D. Delling, *Worship in the New Testament* (London, 1962) p. 24, states that primitive Christian worship is the work of the Spirit, and that this is abundantly clear from Acts. In this context he believes that *agalliasis* (exuberant joy) or *agalliasthai* (to rejoice greatly) are technical terms with signify an action of the Spirit, even where this connotation is not explicity give.. Du Toit, *op. cit.*, 29, comments: "Vielleicht hat Lukas Wert darauf gelegt, darzulegen, dass die jubelnde Begeisterung, die er von der Urgemeinde berichtet (Apg. 2,45; vgl. 2,26; 16,34) sich schonbei Jesus offenbart."

not derive from the wealth, pleasures and esteem of this world; in fact, it is actually precluded by them. The Lucan teaching on poverty and renunciation is an invitation to free one's spirit from these bonds for a joyous participation in the benevolent reign of God within his kingdom. Jesus advises the rich ruler to sell all that he possesses and give it to the poor that he might have treasure in heaven (18, 22); he adds that it is hard for the rich to enter the kingdom of God (18, 24). Luke's first beatitude (6, 20) promises the kingdom of heaven, and implicitly its joy, to the poor.

Inaugurating his public ministry in the synagogue of Nazareth, Jesus declares that "The Spirit of the Lord is upon me; he has anointed me, and sent me out to preach the gospel to the poor..." (4, 18). He is quoting Isaiah's prophecy of messianic joy for the *Anawim,* the faithful poor of Israel (Is. 61, 1-2). The poor are the privileged of the kingdom of heaven.

The Parable of the Sower (8, 5-15) teaches that the word of God cannot bear fruit if it is impeded by worldly cares, riches and the pleasures of life. Poverty and renunciation aim at freeing the Christian from these obstacles. Only then can the word of God produce Christian joy. This parable occurs in the other Synoptics; however, once or more of the same three obstacles to the word of God are found in exclusively Lucan material: Martha and Mary (10, 38-42); the Rich Fool (12, 16-21); the Rich Man and Lazarus (16, 19-31); the Prodigal Son (15, 1-31); Zaccheus (19, 1-10).

The Parable of the Great Banquet (14, 16-24) is followed by statements on the renunciation which a disciple must make (14, 25-33). The implication would seem to be that the messianic joy of the banquet demands a corresponding preparation on the part of its participants.[25] If this joy transcends every purely human joy, it is worth the sacrifice of the closest human bonds (14, 26).

---

[24] A. Schlatter, *Das Evangelium des Lukas,* S. 272, as quoted by Grundmann, *op. cit.*, p. 206, affirms that the following of Jesus gives his disciples a share in his work and a duty and service to fulfill. Thus, the Word of God requires a full and unconditioned dedication to its proclamation.

[25] J. M. Creed, *The Gospel according to St. Luke* (London, 1930), p. 193; J. Jeremias, *The Parables of Jesus* (London, 1963, English trans.), p. 196, makes much the same point as Creed: "Jesus drives home the exhortation: Do not act without mature consideration, for a thing half-done is worse than a thing never begun."

Lucan renunciation is basically a positive concept concerned with productivity. Its purpose is symbolized in the story of the tree which must be fertilized in the hope that it will bear fruit (13, 6-9). In another context it is the quality of the fruit that is uppermost (6, 43). In this case Luke implies that the quality of the fruit, of a man's way of life, is gauged by its worth and relevance to others. Good fruit gives nourishment and delight to others; it is not something which the tree keeps for itself. In this social context of renunciation, it is clear why Luke calls the rich man who "lays up treasure for himself" a "fool" (12, 16-21).[26]

Chapter 14: *the Messianic Banquet and the Joy of Perfect Community.* The eschatological and communitarian dimensions of Christian joy emerge especially in the fourteenth chapter where Luke presents the Parable of the Great Banquet (vv. 17-24). No evangelist has insisted so much on the banquet theme as Luke.[27] This entire chapter is situated in the context of a banquet.

The significance of this chapter derives from the prophetic and wisdom literature of the Old Testament, which had developed the banquet theme as an expression of the perfect happiness which God has in store for his faithful at the end of time.[28]

The eschatological banquet is served by God himself and its festive joy stems from the perfect intimacy between God and his creatures: "On this mountain the Lord of hosts will make for all peoples a feast..." (Is. 25, 6).

---

[26] Du Toit, *op. cit.*, p. 31, implicitly comments on the problem of security: "Der neue Inhalt des Lebens in der Umkehr ist die Freude. Sorge ist der Freude Feind. Darum durfen Jesu Nachfolger keinem Sorgen Raum geben, weder in bezug auf Essen oder auf Kleidung (Mt. 6, 25-34 par Lk. 12, 22-31; vgl. Lk. 21, 34) noch im Hinblick auf ihre Verteidigung, wenn sie vor Gericht stehen (Mt. 10, 19 par Lk. 12, 11). Die neue Lebens haltung offnet wieder den Weg zur Freude in Gottes Schopfung. Jetzt ist da kein Platz mehr für eine apokalyptische Verzweiflung an dieser Welt und an der Natur. In positiver Bejahung des alttestamentlichen Gedankens, dass alles, was Gott gemacht hat, gut ist (Gen. 1, 4. 10,)12, 18, 25, 31), entdekt der Glaubige in den Lilien des Feldes eine Schonheit, die die Pracht Salomons weit uberragt."

[27] P. M. Galopin, "Le Repas", *Assemblées du Seigneur* 55 (1962), p. 65; also H. Flender, on the table scenes, pp. 80-84.

[28] Galopin, *art. cit.*, pp. 59ff., comments on the abundance without end which characterized the Old Testament banquet tradition. Wisdom also offers a banquet (Prv. 9, 1-6) which is another aspect of the background for the teaching of Jesus at table.

The eschatological banquet realizes man's highest aspirations of perfect friendship with God and his fellow men. The messianic meal, prefigured by the gift of manna in the desert, represents the incomparable joy of perfect community with the Messiah and his followers. The messianic joy of the banquet is the gift of God, because the banquet itself is the gift of God; it is a joy which God has prepared for all mankind, "... the Lord of hosts will make for *all peoples* a feast".

Although the eschatological banquet is for all mankind, Isaiah teaches that it is especially for the poor (Is. 55, 1-3). The poor are the *Anawim,* those who remain faithful to Yahweh, as opposed to those who participate in the idolatrous and orgiastic banquets which celebrate false gods (Is. 65, 3-7). There shall be a reversal of roles at the end of time; the *Anawim* shall feast and the unfaithful shall be hungry (Is. 65, 13; Pr. 9, 1-6).

The prophets considered the covenant between Yahweh and his people under the symbol of a marriage. The psalmists and Deutero-Isaiah inserted the theology o fthe covenant into the context of the banquet. The convergence of these two lines of thought gave rise to the metaphor of the wedding banquet for designating entry into the future kingdom of the Messiah and the joy of communion with God.

The eschatological banquet symbolized the accomplishment of God's plan of salvation. It is doubtful that any of Jesus' Jewish hearers would have been unaware of the banquet theme and its significance. Jesus himself employed the wedding banquet as a symbol of ultimate happiness (Mt. 22, 1-24 = Lk. 14, 16-24; Mt. 25, 1-13 = Lk. 12, 35-38).

Jesus' banquets were a realization of the messianic and eschatological prophecies; and at the same time they are only the beginning of the ultimate realization of these prophecies. They promise more; they are signs of the beginning of the eschatological banquet.[29]

The banquets of Jesus are characterized by a joy which contrasts with the austerity and fasting of his precursor: "John the Baptist has come eating no bread and drinking no wine; and you say, 'He has a demon'. The Son of man has come

---

[29] Galopin, *art. cit.,* pp. 65ff.

eating and drinking; and you say, 'Behold, a glutton and a drunkard, a friend of tax collectors and sinners'." (7, 33-34).

Other characteristics of the eschatological banquet are found in the banquets of Jesus. He dines with the poor and the humble, with publicans and sinners. This displeases the Pharisees (7, 36; 11, 37; 14, 1-11). He dines with his friends at Bethany (10, 38-42), and with Zaccheus, the chief publican of Jericho (19, 1-10).

Jesus' banquets are in a salvation context. His critics complain, "He receives sinners and eats with them" (15, 2). Jesus answers that only the sick need a doctor; that he has not come to call the just, rather sinners (5, 31-32 - Mt. 9, 12). While dining with Zaccheus, Jesus declares that, "Today salvation has come to this house because he is also a son of Abraham" (19, 9). He has come to seek and save those who were lost. The banquet image serves to indicate salvation for even the Gentiles: "And men will come from east and west, and from north and south, and sit at table in the kingdom of God" (13, 29 — Mt. 8, 11).

The traditional concept of Yahweh's serving his people from his own abundance at the eschatological banuet is evoked in Jesus' feeding of the crowds who hungered for his word (9, 17) and at the Last Supper. The merciful father in the Parable of the Prodigal Son prepares a banquet as a sign of joyous exaltation over his son's return (15, 22-23).

The eschatological banquet is offered to all who hunger and thirst:

> "So, every one who thirsts, come to the waters; and he who has no money, come buy wine and milk without money and without price. Why do you spend your money for that which is not bread, and your labour for that which does not satisfy? Listen attentively to me, and eat what is good, and *delight yourselves* in fatness" (Is. 55, 1-2).

The blessedness of those who hear the word of Jesus and keep it (11, 28) is a fulfilment of the Isaian vision. The time for the banquet is now. Luke conceives of the kingdom of God as a banquet now arranged: it began with the preaching of Jesus and continues in the preaching mission of the Church: "... at the time for the banquet he sent his servant to say ..." (14, 17).

The story of the Great Banquet (14, 16-24) implies that messianic joy derives from responsiveness to the words of invitation and from participation in the banquet itself. In a spirit of eucharistic joy Christians are united with their Lord in the breaking of bread: "They continued to meet daily in the temple, breaking bread from home to home, they ate with joy and simplicity" (Acts 2, 46). This is the continuing *koinōnia* activity of the banquet community with its Lord until the time when, "you eat and drink at my table in my kingdom" (22, 30).[30]

The eschatological banquet tradition in the Lucan account reveals that Christian joy is essentially communal. Messianic, eschatological joy derives from the person of Jesus through whose redemptive work communion is re-established between God and man and among all men. After the Fall, man was unable to re-establish communion with God and neighbor on purely human resources. He suffered, because it was not good for him to be alone (Gn. 2, 18). The Lucan portrait of Christ, in the eschatological banquet context, is one of exuberant joy at the reversal of the human condition through the establishment of the agape-community.

Luke's banquet theology is suffused with a eucharistic joy in recognition of the gratuitous character of the invitation to enter into the eschatological agape-community. It is characterized by the joy of the *Anawim* who, recognizing their own poverty and misery before God and man, gratefully accept the salvation invitation that is offered them.[31] It is characterized by a universal joy in recognition of the fact that no one is excluded from the divine call to salvation within the eschatological banquet community. It is characterized by an eschatological joy, which is even now experienced in a process of salvation which is leading it to its full perfection at the end of time.[32]

---

[30] Cf. R. Tannehill, "A Study in the Theology of Luke-Acts", *Anglican Theological Review,* 43 (1961), pp. 195-203.

[31] Cf. P. B. Simson, Lk. 14, 1-11: Le code de bienséance de l'assemblée chrétienne," *Assemblées du Seigneur* 70 (1965), p. 38. Jeremias, *op. cit.,* pp. 192f., comments on the pericope of places at table and the following pericope of the messianc banquet: "Is Luke 14, 11 similarly intended to be a piece of practical wisdom, a rule of social etiquette? Surely not! The comparison with Luke 14, 14b, with 18, 14, and with Matt. 23, 12 shows that Luke 14, 11 is speaking of God's eschatological activity, the humbling of the proud and the exaltation of the humble on the Last Day." Jeremias sees 14, 11 as an "eschatological warning", which looks forward to the messianic banquet, and is a call to remounce self-righteous pretentions and to self-abasement before God.

[32] Grundmann, *op. cit.,* p. 298.

Chapter 15: *the Invitation to the joy of God in Jesus.* If the travel narrative contains the core of peculiarly Lucan thought, its fourteenth and fifteenth chapters present the nucleus of Luke's theology of joy. The eschatological banquet tradition, which dominates the fourteenth chapter and carries over into the Parable of the Prodigal Son in the fifteenth chapter, is a key to the Lucan theology of joy. The fifteenth chapter teaches that Christian joy consists in a willing, personal participation in God's own joy in effecting the salvation of mankind in Jesus.

The redactional unity of this chapter is more striking than that of the previous chapter. It is composed of three complementary parables which formulate an answer to the criticism of the Pharisees, which is expressed in the opening verses of the chapter: "Now the tax collectors and sinners were all drawing near to hear him. And the Pharisees and the scribes murmured saying, 'This man receives sinners and eats with them'." (15, 1-2).

In the opening parable of the lost sheep (15, 4-7), Jesus compares the behavior of the shepherd and his joy in finding his lost sheep, with that of God. The promise of Ezekiel is fulfilled: "As a shepherd seeks out his flock when some of his sheep have been scattered abroad, so will I seek out my sheep ... And I will set up over them one shepherd, my servant David, and he shall feed them: he shall feed them and be their shepherd" (34, 12; 23).

Jesus seems to imply that if his critics fail to rejoice with God at the conversion of sinners, they shall have no share in God's joy. There is still time for his critics to undergo a change of heart. This may be the import of the words introduced by "I tell you" in the statement, "Just so, I tell you, there will be more joy in heaven over one sinner who repents than over ninety-nine righteous who have no need of repentance" (15, 7).[34] Jesus warns the Pharisees of the danger in their attitude towards sinners and publicans. They show no mercy to those at whose salvation

[33] Luke obviously wishes the parable of the Great Banquet to be interpreted in a messianic sense by reason of his having inserted it as Christ's response to the beatitude in 14, 15. Cf. Jeremias, *op. cit.*, p. 42; R. F. Swaeles, "L'évangile (Lc. 14, 16-24): la parabole des invités qui se dérobent," *Assemblées du Seigneur* 55 (1962), pp. 36-37: "The parable in Lk. 14, 14, 1624 will share at one and the same time in these two aspects: the messianic proclamation and the parenetic warning. It marks the summit of the discourse at table by explicitly describing the beatitude of the Kingdom of God and the requisite condition for entering it."

[34] Cf. Grundmann, *op. cit.*, p. 307; cf. also Jeremias, *op. cit.*, pp. 132ff.

God rejoices. In contrast with the rabbinical saying which tells of God's joy in the destruction of the godless, Jesus affirms God's exuberant joy over the conversion of sinners.[35]

The second parable (15, 8-10) presents a woman in place of the shepherd. The identity of structure with the previous parable provides Jesus' revelation of the Father's mercy with a dual witness.[36] Luke recognizes the force of repetition for inculcating the importance of a key doctrine. As in the previous parable, the recovery of what had been lost is characterized by an outburst of joy which friends and neighbours are invited to share. Again, Jesus compares this to the joy of God at the return of a sinner. This time he employs the image of "the angels of God", ofr the heavenly court rejoices in God's own joy. Joy in God's saving mercy is the unique source of happiness. The third parable in this trilogy will make clear that those who do not share God's merciful attitude toward sinners cannot share his joy.[37]

If the significance of these two parables is almost identical in revealing the joy of God at the return of a sinner, they are likewise most similar in asserting God's persevering efforts made for his return. The image of the lost drachma gives perhaps a greater stress to the search, so much so that it suggests that God is attached to every man as if each were the only one."[38]

The point of the Lucan parables becomes more salient when compared with the parallel text on the lost sheep in Matthew (18, 12-14).[39] Luke stresses the joy of finding, whereas Matthew stresses the search. Luke underscores the joy of God in pardon-

---

[35] Cf. Grundmann, *op. cit.*, p. 308.

[36] E. Rasco, "Les Paraboles de Luc XV", *Ephemerides Theologicae Lovanienses* (1968), p. 168, presents the structures of the first two parables in a striking pattern which reveals their parallelism. The article is an excellent study of the theme of joy throughout the entire chapter. Grundmann, *op. cit.*, 306. Cf. Flender's study of what he calls, citing Morgenthaler (Die lukanische Geschichtsschreibung als Zeugnis, 2 vols., 1948-49) the "two-membered architectonic art of Luke," *op. cit.*, pp. 8ff. He notes in Luke stories about a man are often paralleled by stories about a woman: these parallels mostly occur in the special Lucan material. Even if they were already arranged in this way in his source, the passages from Acts show that Luke has deliberately and extended this type of parallelism.

[37] Cf. E. Galbiati, "La parabola della pecora e della drachmma ritrovata (Luca 15, 1-10)", *Bibbia e Oriente* 6 (1964), pp. 129-133.

[38] J. Cantinat, "L'évangile: Luc 15, 1-10", *Assemblées du Seigneur* 57 (1965), p. 38.

[39] Cf. J. Dupont, "La brébis perdue et la drachme perdue (Lk. 15, 1-10)", *Lumière et Vie* 34 (1951), Paroisse et Liturgie Suppl., pp. 15-23.

ing, whereas Matthew emphasizes Jesus' commissioning the strong, or the shepherds, to care for the weak. Luke reveals the heart of God, whereas Matthew teaches the duties of men. Luke defends the mercy of Jesus towards sinners; Matthew gives a rule for the apostles. According to Dupont, with Luke the parable retains its links with the concrete situation in the public ministry of Jesus when the Pharisees criticized his association with sinners; with Matthew the parable more directly reflects the situation of the primitive Church and of the pastoral responsibilities of its leaders.

The Parable of the Prodigal Son, the third of the trilogy, is the classical example of divine mercy.[40] This parable accentuates God's love for sinners in so far as God is compared to a father. Unlike the shepherd and housewife in the preceding parables, the father has the closest possible human relationship with what he has lost.[41] It is as if he had lost a part of himself: "While he was at a distance the father saw him and had compassion, and ran and embraced him and kissed him" (15, 20).

In the context of the general introduction at the beginning of the chapter (15, 1-2), the meaning of the second part of the parable is apparent: God's universal saving love is the source of all joy for those who are willing to accept it for themselves and for others. He who does not rejoice with God at the conversion of sinners will never know the meaning of Christian joy. No one can object, as the eldest son (15, 25-32), the pharisees and scribes, if Jesus associates with sinners in his effort to bring them back to their father.

The vocabulary of these three parables underscores the centrality of joy.[42] Some form of *charein* or *chara* depicts the joy of the shepherd (v. 5) and the father (v. 32), as well as the rejoicing in heaven over one who repents (vv. 7, 10). *Sunchairein* depicts the friends and neighbours rejoicing together with the shepherd and the housewife over their discover (vv. 6, 9).

Repeated images of joy occur in the third parable: *euphrainai* (feasting) in vv. 23, 32; the sound of music and singing (*sumphōnias*

---

[40] L. Cerfaux-J. Cambier, "Luc", *Dict. de la Bible Suppl.*, vol. 5, c. 587.

[41] No doctrinal explicitation follows the parable of the Prodigal as in the other two. The message is clear from the preceding parables and the introduction to the chapter. Cf. J. Cantinat, "Les paraboles de la misericorde Lc. 15, 1-32", *Nouvelle Revue Théologique* 77 (1955), p. 264.

[42] Rasco, *op. cit.*, p. 181.

kai chorōn) in v. 25. The very discovery of something that had been lost, the underlying experience of all the three parables, is itself an extended image of joy, most movingly expressed in the case of the father whose son has returned.

The frequent repetition of the notion of invitation and participation in vv. 6 and 9 (*sugkalei* and *sugcharete*) and "before the angels of God" (*chara enōpion tōn aggelōn tou Theou*) in v. 10 for example, emphasize the communitarian dimension of the Lucan theology of Christian joy. The same emphasis occurs in the father's request of the servants (v. 22) and in his repeated urging of the elder son to join in the rejoicing at his brother's return. It is a joy which one must share with others: the shepherd and the woman with their friends (cf. the prefixed verbs: *sugkalein, sugchairein*); God with his angels; the father with his servants and especially with the older son. [43]

The necessity of conversion is another underlying motif of the three parables. Conversion and the new way of life which corresponds to it are the indispensable basis of Christian joy. [44] In the first two parables two explicit references are made to the sinner who repents (*metanoia* in v. 7; *metanoiō* in vv. 7 and 10). The third parable relates the entire process of rupture and reconciliation. Paradoxically, in the second part of the parable it is the elder son who must undergo a change of heart before he can share in the joy of salvation: "he was angry and refused to go in" (v. 28). An irony emerges from the parable's dramatic shift: the elder son is the one who runs the risk of being really lost. [45]

Joy in the good news of universal salvation constitutes the theme of the entire chapter. Conversion of heart (*metanoia*) is the human prerequisite for sharing this joy. In the form of a parable Jesus mildly rebukes the Pharisees for their criticism voiced in vv. 1 and 2; he invites them to share in his joy by changing their dispositions toward their brother and toward Him whom they are to recognize as having a father's heart to all. [46]

This chapter expresses Jesus' invitation to all men, and particularly to the Pharisees who are called to be the religious leaders

---

[43] *Ibid.* Also, C. H. Giblin, "Structural Considerations on Luke 15, *Catholic Biblical Quarterly* 24 (1962), pp. 15-31.

[45] Cf. W. Michaelis, *Die Gleichnisse Jesu* (Hamburg 1956), p. 143.

[46] Giblin, *op. cit.*, p. 29.

of the people, to share God's own joy in the person and activity of Christ. This will demand a conversion from their own proud unconcern and contempt for sinners. It is an invitation which cannot be accepted without a radical change of outlook. Jesus formulates this invitation both by his words and way of acting which reveal the spirit and joy of God in greeting the sinner.[47] He who sees Jesus sees God and hears the invitation to rejoice with him. Whoever shares the spirit of God will not condemn Jesus' approach to sinners, His person is the gospel message. He is the stronger man who overpowers Satan (11, 22).[48] In his actions the merciful love of God for sinners becomes effectual. This is the claim of Jesus. Thus, without making any christological statement, the parable reveals itself as a veiled assertion of authority: Jesus makes the claim for himself that he is acting in God's stead, that he is God's representative.[49] The call to participate in God's saving love and joy is issued through Jesus, the image of the Father who performs the works of the Father.

E. Rasco notes that the parable remains mysteriously open: we do not know whether the elder son accepted the invitation.[50] The real question concerns ourselves: do we rejoice with God and with his Christ at the entry into the kingdom of our sinful brother? The total commitment in this response, Rasco concludes, allows us to enter the heart of Christ and, through him, unites us with the Father who offers his love to all.

The joy of Zaccheus (19, 1-10) is the final instance of rejoicing in the Lucan travel narrative. This story combines several of Luke's favourite themes, revealing the Lucan tendency to hold a large number of threads in his hand at once. The process of conversion (*metanoia*) begins when Zaccheus hears the words of Jesus with grateful joy; and, in typical Lucan fashion, Zaccheus evidences the sincerity of his conversion by the renunciation of his wealth in favor of the poor (19, 8). The banquet motif of conversion-agape provokes the characteristic complaint of the Pharisees that Jesus dines with sinners (9, 7; also 5, 29-30, where the same rebuke is registered when Jesus dines with Levi).[51]

---

47 Rasco, *op. cit.*, p. 182.
48 *Ibid.*
49 Jeremias, *op. cit.*, p. 182.
50 Rasco, *op. cit.*, p. 183.
51 P. Minear, "Luke's Use of the Birth Stories", from *Studies in Luke-Acts,* ed. by L. Keck-J. L. Martyn (New York, 1966), p. 116, described the

The joy of Zaccheus' response to the call to salvation contrasts with the sadness of the rich ruler who cannot bring himself to giving all his goods to the poor (18, 18-25). It contrasts with the plight of the rich fool (12, 16-21) who has completely missed the trans-temporal significance of life and has consequently closed himself off from genuine fulfilment. Only those who perceive the transitoriness of this world's wealth and use it for the good of the human community, like Zaccheus, find the authentic security of salvation joy. Thirdly, Zaccheus' joyful response contrasts with the attitude of the Pharisees who close themselves off from the kingdom and its messianic joy by the fact that they would exclude their fellowmen from it. They fail to recognize their own poverty and misery before God; consequently, they lack compassion for others in need of mercy (11, 41, 46, 52).

Resurrectional joy is manifest when Christ appears to the stunned disciples who "disbelieved for joy" (24, 41). Joy, not sorrow, was the apostles' reaction to Jesus' departure at the Ascension, and it remained a constant characteristic of the Christion life (24, 52; Acts 2, 46). [52] Its presence was especially noticeable in times of persecution (Acts 5, 41) and this appears natural when we see that it was closely connected with the Spirit's presence both in Jesus and in his disciples (10, 21; Acts 13, 52), and remember as well that the Spirit was to be present among the disciples above all in time of persecution (12, 11-12). Joy in persecution underscores the trans-temporal quality of Christian joy. Persecution was to be the lot of the Christian community (21, 12-18) and a source of blessedness (6, 3, 26); it is an assurance that the Kingdom of God is present and that its future consummation is at hand. The joy of the eschatological banquet has begun, and all mankind is invited to participate.

---

process of conversion in Luke: "There is a typical Lucan syndrome descriptive of the true response to God's redemption. It includes hearing, turning, repenting, praying, being forgiven, rejoicing, deeds appropriate to repentance, the gift of the Spirit, a people prepared and witnessing." See also W. C. van Unnik, "L'usage de *sodsein,* 'sauver', et des ses dérives dans les évangiles synoptiques", from *La Formation des Evangiles* (Bruges, 1957), Colloquium Biblicum Lovaniense, 192.

[52] B. Reicke, *op. cit.*, pp. 87-88; also, A. Hastings, *Prophet and Witness in Jerusalem* (New York, 1958), 166.

NOTES

J. Dupont, "La Brebis Perdue et la Drachme Perdue," *Lumière et Vie Supplément biblique,* 34 (1957), 15-23. Jesus often uses two closely related parables, symmetrically constructed, to illustrate some particular lesson. Luke 15. 1-10 is an example of the "double" or "coupled" parable. Others are found in Lk 14, 28-32; Lk 12. 2428. Luke tells these parables (i. e. lost sheep and coin) with an emphasis on the joy of God in finding what he had lost (i. e. the sinner). It justifies Jesus' solicitude for sinners. It illustrates God's solicitude and invites Jesus' critics to share the same joy.

D. W. C. Ford, *A Reading of St. Luke's Gospel* (London, 1957). Ford, in his commentary on the beatitudes (pp. 102-103), notes that after Jesus raised his eyes on his disciples, "Happy" is his first word. The keynote of Christ's way is set by this word. Ford comments that it is a way of joy before duty, inner satisfaction before striving, a gift before a command. (See the series of articles, "Complacency and Concern" by Frederick E. Crowe in *Theological Studies,* vol. 20 (1959) on the primacy of joy to striving.) In the beatitudes Christ teaches that joy is the first hall-mark of his authentic followers. Ford affirms that this joy has nothing to do with outward prosperity which may not in fact exist but it has everything to do with accepting in the faith of God life as it comes.

A. F. Walls, "In the Presence of the Angels' (Luke xv 10)," *Novum Testamentum* 3 (1959), 314-316, notes that *Chara enopion ton aggelon tou theou* has frequently been taken to refer to angelic joy, though no adequate parallels have been adduced to support this. Others hold that "the angels" is a periphrasis for "God"; however, Wall interprets the meaning as "God will rejoice before the angels." This then is analogous to the joy of the father in the company of his earthly household when the prodigal son returns.

8.

KINGSHIP

The Third Gospel has been called "a kingly gospel".[1] The reign of Christ appears in the Lucan account under the aspect of the royal person and that series of events by which he claimed his throne. Luke introduces the Kingdom of God as the object of Jesus' mission in Marcan contexts where it is absent (e. g 4. 43/Mk 1. 38; 9. 2/Mk 6. 7).[2] Luke narrates the birth of one who is to inherit the throne of David (1. 32). He alone of the Synoptics explicitly describes Jesus' entry into Jerusalem as that of a king (19. 38). It is only the Lucan account of the Last Supper in which Jesus bestows a kingdom upon his apostles (22. 18), and in which the good thief appears as the sole witness to the kingship of Jesus on Calvary (23. 42). The suffering of Jesus is the divine means whereby he enters into his glory (24. 26). The ascension marks the enthronement of the divinely chosen messiah-king who fulfills Israel's ultimate hopes (24. 51; Acts 1. 9.[3]

The kingship of Christ is a theme common to all the Gospels. It is affirmed in the synoptic accounts of Jesus' baptism (3. 22) and transfiguration (9, 35) when his Father proclaims his messiahship in terms of the oracles of the royal coronation (Ps 2. 7). The genealogy which links Jesus with David (3. 23-31), the confession of Peter (9. 20), and the prediction of Jesus' messianic entry into Jerusalem (13. 35) are other common synoptic texts.

Peculiarly Lucan aspects of Jesus' kingship appear in six pericopes of which the first is *the annunciation* of a son to Mary (1. 32-33): "He will be great and will be called Son of the Most

---

1 A. Hastings, *Prophet and Witness in Jerusalem* (London, 1958), 152.

2 A. R. C. Leaney, *The Gospel according to St. Luke,* Black's N. T. Commentaries, (2nd ed., London, 1966), 34.

3 R. Koch, "Ascensione di Cristo," J. Bauer, tr. L. Ballarini in *Dizionario di Teologia Biblica* (Brescia, 1965), 145.

High.[4] The Lord God will give him *the throne of his ancestor David;* he will rule over the house of Jacob for ever and his reign will have no end." The angel's words recall Old Testament passages about David's throne (2 Sam 7.16; Isa 9.6); about the Son of the Most High (2 Sam 7.14); about the endless reign (1 Kgs 1.31; Ps 45.7; 72.17; Dan 2.4). Mary's son will be a king.

The parable of the royal claimant (19.12-27/Mt 25.14-30) occurs just after Jesus has predicted his death for the third time (18.31-33), and has been addressed by the blind man of Jericho with the messianic title of son of David (18.38, 39). This parable, in which Jesus describes himself as the royal claimant (vv. 12, 14-15, 27), significantly precedes Jesus' entry into Jerusalem:

> A man of noble birth went to a distant country to be appointed *king* and afterwards return ... But his compatriots detested him and sent a delegation to follow him with this message, "We do not want this man to be our *king*"... "But as for my enemies who did not want me for their king, bring them here and execute them in my presence."

The long journey which the royal claimant must make to be appointed king suggests the journey which Jesus must make to Jerusalem where he will be rejected by his compatriots precisely for claiming to be the Son of Man (22.69).[5] His claim implies that he was divinely appointed to rule the People of God. The parable reveals that the messianic king assumes his sovereignty in stages. His kingship will be fully manifest when he returns to reward his faithful servants and to punish those who reject him.

Luke is the only synoptic who explicitly designates Jesus as a king when he describes *the messianic entry into Jerusalem* (19.28-44). By a series of literary parallels, Luke recalls the coro-

---

[4] A. George, "La royauté de Jésus selon l'évangile du Luc," *Sciences Ecclésiastiques* 14 (1962), 57-70, calls attention to these six pericopes.

[5] A. R. C. Leaney, *St. Luke,* 276, comments on Luke (22.69): "But from now the Son of Man will be seated at the right hand of the power of God." For Luke the event is cosmic and hidden from unbelieving eyes. As in the the other synoptics, the Lord is challenged as to his messiahship and answers about the Son of Man, whose destiny he has associated with suffering (9.22; 44; 18.31); but after the resurrection the suffering, now triumphantly past, is attached to the messiahship (24.26, 46). The expression "at the right hand" is messianic (cf. Ps 110.1). The conception of the Son Man is therefore joined with that of the Messiah, and suffering is associated with exaltation.

nation of Solomon: the words *epebibasan* (19. 35 = 1 Kgs 1. 33), *katabasis* (19. 37 = Kgs 1. 40), the jubilation of the people (19.37 = 1 Kgs 1. 40), the two references to peace (19. 38, 42).[6] The parallel with Solomon the king of peace seems to have been intended in a gospel where Jesus is also interpreted as the new Elias,[7] the new Moses[8] and the new Joseph.[9]

Jesus' prediction of the destruction of Jerusalem at the end of this episode (19. 41-44) parallels the conclusion of the preceding parable (19. 27). He cannot be rejected without disastrous consequences.

In the Lucan account of *the Last Supper* occurs the most explicit text on the kingship of Christ (22. 28-30):

> And now I confer a kingdom on you, just as my Father conferred one on me: you will eat and drink at my table in my kingdom, and you will sit on thrones to judge the twelve tribes of Israel.

The verb which Luke uses for expressing the conferring of the kingdom is *diatithemai,* which means "to dispose of property by a will." Within the context of the Last Supper it suggests the act of one who is about to die, and it clearly implies that the death of Jesus is associated with the conferring of the kingdom.[10] Jesus must suffer before his assumption of sovereignty as the messianic king; his entrance into his glory constitutes the pascal mystery.

The implied reunion of the twelve dispersed tribes which the apostles shall govern suggests the ideal, eschatological Israel.[11] Jesus' kingship is the supreme gift of his Father. He explains

---

[6] J. Comblin, "La paix dans la théologie de saint Luc," *Ephemerides Theologicae Lovanienses* 32 (1956), 454-456.

[7] See P. Dabeck, "Siehe, es erscheinen Moses und Elias," *Biblica* (1942), 180-189.

[8] This theme occurs in Acts (3. 15. 22; 5. 31; 7. 17-39). Cf. J. Jeremias, "Moses," TWNT, IV, 1942, 871-878, and A. Descamps, *Moïse, L'homme de l'Alliance* (Tournai, 1955), 171-187.

[9] See E. Sauffer, *Die Theologie des Neues Testament* (Stuttgart-Berlin, 1941), 222, 309, 323-325; and J. Dupont, *Les problèmes du Livre des Acts* (Louvain, 1950), 105-106; see Acts 7. 9-16.

[10] R. Tannehill, "A Study of the Theology of Luke-Acts," *Anglican Theological Review* 43 (1961), 202.

[11] P. Volz, *Die Eschatologie der jüdischen Gemeinde* (Tübingen, 1934), 344-348, 378.

that he has received the kingdom from his Father; he is king because he is the Son (1. 33; 22. 29-30). The establishment of the eschatological kingdom of the Father is achieved through the reign of the Father and the Son. His sovereignty or kingship can never be in opposition to that of his Father. Lucan parallelism underscores the solidarity of Christ's kingship with that of his Father (19. 11, 12-27; 22. 16-18, 29-30). Luke's originality consists in linking Christ's kingship with his passion and divine sonship.

Jesus' *messianic declaration before the Sanhedrin* (22. 67-70) reveals two distinctively Lucan aspects. The judges distinguish the titles of "the Christ" and of the "Son of God", enabling Luke to stress the new significance of the messianic titles. Secondly, Jesus *now* assumes his sovereignty; whereas in the Matthean and Marcan accounts of the trial, he speaks of his glorious return at the eschatological judgment. Jesus affirms that "from now on" (*apo tou nun*) the kingship is his (v. 69).

At the crucifixion *the good thief* is the sole witness to the kingship of Jesus (23. 40-43): "Jesus, remember me when you come into your kingdom". The account is exclusively Lucan. This confession significantly occurs in a context where the kingship of Jesus is conceived in purely political terms by the leaders of the people (v. 35), the soldiers (v. 36-37), and by the bad thief (v. 39). Jesus consistently rejects this concept (9. 21; 13. 35; 19. 42-45; 20. 41-44; 22. 67-70; 23. 2-3, 35-38). He enters into his glory through poverty, humble service and suffering.

Christ's entrance into the glory of his kingship has been described as "the keystone of Luke's theological arch, in preference to the future coming in glory apparently envisaged by Mark and Matthew. [13] Luke's interpretation of the cloud (21. 27) *in* which the Son of Man shall come in great glory is clear. [14] It is the cloud which marked the constant presence of Yahweh (Ex 14. 19, 24), which was present in the tent of meeting (Ex 33. 9-10) and which conceals the glory shining through it from within (Ex 24. 16-17), the glory which accompanies the Messiah throughout the entire Lucan Gospel. [15]

---

[12] A. George, *art. cit.*, 62.

[13] A. R. C. Leaney, *St. Luke*, 36.

[14] *Ibid.*

[15] Lucan texts on the kingship of Jesus correspond to the three phases

Through suffering Jesus enters into his glory and the reign thus inaugurated is delegated by the Spirit to the apostles. Both the Spirit and glory accompany the birth of the Messiah. The Baptist, his herald, is filled with the Spirit from his mother's womb (1. 15). The Messiah will reign forever (1. 33). The *glory* of the Lord shines around the shepherds at the Nativity and they are told that their *savior* is born (2. 9, 11). Simeon rejoices that his eyes have seen "thy *salvation*" which is a light for revealing to the Gentiles and the *glory* of Israel (2. 30-32). Luke alone prolongs the Baptist's proclamation from Isaiah 40. 3 to add two verses, which conclude with the words, "... and all flesh shall see the salvation of God." Jesus himself says that salvation has come to a son of Abraham (19. 9). The theme continues in Acts 2. 33, in Peter's sermon at Pentecost: "Exalted therefore to the right hand of God and having received the promise of the Holy Spirit from the Father, he has poured out this which you see and hear." Divine glory and salvation enter the world through Jesus, who after his suffering is exalted in the pascal mystery to the right hand of God whence he bestows the same Spirit he possessed from his birth, death and entrance into his glory.

In the Lucan perspective, Jesus' glory is that of a reigning king who is also a servant.[16] Jesus delegates his kingdom, enters his glory through his sufferings, death and resurrection, and rises to his throne at the right hand of his Father. The concept of the Son of Man is assimilated into that of the king.[17] Because Jesus now reigns, he will manifest the glory which he already possesses, which he has shown at the transfiguration, resurrection, and ascension, and in the appearances to Stephen and Paul.

---

of his royal progress. At the beginning of his account they announce the mystery of Jesus (1. 32-33, 43; 2. 11; 3. 22, 23-31). They occur at the time of his departure for Jerusalem, when Jesus sets out to realize the pascal mystery (9. 21, 35); and at the Last Supper (18. 38. 41; 19. 12-27, 35-38; 22. 29-30, 67-71; 23. 42-43; 24. 3, 26, 36, 46).

16 Luke contrasts assertions about Jesus' kingship with the mention of earthly rulers. The birth of the messianic king occurs in the days of Herod, king of Judea (1. 5). It occurs in Bethlehem because of Caesar Augustus' edict (2. 1). In the fifteenth year of Tiberius Caesar's reign (3. 1) Jesus receives his messianic anointing (3. 21-22) and rejects the devil's offer of worldly kingdoms (4. 5-6). Herod is mentioned before the confession at Caesarea (9. 7-9, 18-21); his threats are followed by the announcement of the messianic event which shall occur in Jerusalem (13. 31, 35). Pagan rulers are contrasted with the way Jesus exercises his kingship (22. 25-27).

17 A. R. C. Leaney, *St. Luke*, 37.

Luke envisages the restoration of all things (Acts 3.21) as the final and perfect manifestation of the divine kingship of Christ. In the interval before the glorious return of the Son of Man the Church must preach the good news of the kingdom to the ends of the earth.

NOTES

S. Aalen, "'Reign' and 'House' in the Kingdom of God in the Gospels," *New Testament Studies* 8 (1962), 215-240. Starting with the prophecy of Nathan (1 Chr 17.7-14), there is a tradition in Judaism in which "house" no longer means the royal family but the people of God. The kingdom of God corresponds to the Jewish expressions: the New Jerusalem, the Great Feast, the world to come and the house of God (Mt 12.25 = Mk 2.23). The kingdom means God's community or house (Mt 12.28 = Lk 11.20) whose presence is a fact. It is a house wwhere the gifts of salvation are available (Mt 11.12 = Lk 16.16).

G. F. Hawthorne, "The essential Nature of the Kingdom of God," *Westminster Theological Journal* 25 (1963), 35-47. Because the Pharisees' question revealed the wrong concept of the kingdom of God and overly stressed its space-time qualities, Jesus did not reply to their "When?" but tried to correct their view. The kingdom is not temporal and spatial; it is spiritual, consisting in the rule of God over the hearts of those who have gratefully accepted his loving and saving will.

A. Rüstow, "Entos hymon estin. Zur Deutung von Lukas 17: 20-21," *Zeitscrift für die Neutestamentliche Wissenschaft* 51 (1960), 197-224, states that when used with the genitive, *entos* can have the meaning "at your disposition," "within your power," "in the sphere of your influence and action," By adopting this meaning, the sense of Lk 1.7 20 ("The Kingdom of God is among you") would be: "It is foolish to wait eagerly for the parousia, to reckon the exact time of its coming or so seek a knowledge of its place, since the kingdom of God is within your reach. It rests with you to prove yourselves well disposed for its reception."

R. Sneed, "The Kingdom of God is Within You (Lk 17.21)," *Catholic Biblical Quarterly* 24 (1962), 363-382. Brown notes that behind the pronouncement story of Lk 17.20 lies one of the historical encounters between Jesus and the Pharisees who had heard him speak of the reign of God. Jesus dismisses reference to a date and turns the question to essentials by reminding his auditors that emphasis on externals does not effect the reign.

Sneed remarks that the disputed phrase of Lk 17.21b has philological support for the renderings "within you," "within your power" and "in your midst." However, precision in the interpretation of this phrase derives from a comprehension of the pericope's literary form. The unit is a pronouncement story, which in the oral period probably circulated as an independent unity, embodying a tradition on the internal aspect of the reign of God that is equated with the coming of the Holy Spirit. This view of the reign of God is especially pronounced in Luke-Acts in which the eschatological character of the coming of the Spirit is emphasized. The parallel between Lk 17. 10b. and Rom 14. 17 suggests that during the oral period there circulated a saying or story whose point was that Jesus had said that the reign of God was not realized by Mosaic observance, but by the reception of the Holy Spirit.

Thus, for missionary and catechetical purposes the tradition offered a welcome exposition of the relationship between Mosaic observance and the gift of the Spirit. Sneed concludes that Luke employs the pericope as a neutralizer for apocalyptic stimuli generated by the discourse in 17. 22-37. In sharp contrast to the latter, vv. 20f. affirm a present aspect of the reign of God.

9.

DIVINE MERCY AND HUMAN MERCY

In the Lucan account Jesus invites his disciples to be merciful as their heavenly Father is merciful. The Christian is committed to living according to the spirit of his heavenly Father, as expressed in and by Christ. In the Gospels of both Matthew and Luke, Jesus' injunction to conform to the spirit of his heavenly Father occurs at the beginning of his public ministry: "Be merciful as your heavenly Father is merciful" (Luke 6:36), and "Be perfect, therefore, as your heavenly Father is perfect" (Matthew 5:48).

Luke implies that being merciful is a life-long process, inasmuch as the literal translation of "be merciful" is "become merciful." The heavenly Father is always merciful, but the Christian *becomes* merciful.

The merciful goodness of the Father in the Lucan account is espeially evident in his attitude towards the lost. Luke alone recounts the story of the prodigal son, which speaks in unequalled terms of God's merciful fatherhood (15:11 ff.). It is the father's goodness that awakened the prodigal's confession and petition, which in turn are cut short by the same goodness (15:19, 21).

Non-Lucan Passages

The Lukan message presupposes an Old and New Testament frame of reference. The way of holiness which the Bible frequently underscores is embodied in the formula, "You shall be holy, because I, Yahweh, your God, am holy" (Lev. 19:2; cf. 11:44-45; 20:7, 26; 21:18). If holiness is the way of being which is proper to the God of Israel, then his people, bound to him in covenant fidelity, must be holy. In making Israel his people, Yahweh has made them a holy people, whose holiness derives from their community with him. Yahweh is with his people; as a consequence, they are a holy people.

Though the Old Testament does not contain the exact formulation of Luke, it does express the same idea. In *Deuteronomy,* for example: "(Yahweh) does justice for the fatherless and the widow, he loves the foreigner, giving him food and clothing. Love the foreigner, therefore, for you were foreigners in Egypt" (10: 18-19). The message is clear: Yahweh loves the foreigners, therefore his people must love them. Israel must live according to the same spirit, and act as Yahweh acts.

In the New Testament (1 Peter 1:15-16) the following recommendation occurs: "As he who called you is holy, be yourselves holy in all your conduct; since it is written, 'you shall be holy, for I am holy.'" Thus, the New Testament maintains a continuity with the Old in its doctrine on the law of holiness and its relation to resemblance and imitation.

Paul comments (Col. 3:12-13): "Put on then, as God's chosen ones, holy and beloved, the sentiments of compassion, kindness, lowliness, meekness and patience, forebearance; as the Lord has forgiven you, so your must also forgive." In his Epistle to the *Ephesians* (4:32-5:1), Paul writes: "Be good and full of compassion for one another, forgiving one another as God has forgiven you in Christ. Be imitators of God, as beloved children (i.e. of God)." Thus, Christians show that they are true children of their heavenly Father, for they have been generated by and live by his spirit.

Jacques Dupont (*Rivista Biblica,* 14, 146-149) observes that in speaking of the mercy of God, the Bible frequently joins "merciful" (*eleeson*) with "compassionate" (*oiktirmon*): "God is compassionate and merciful." The adjective for "merciful" occurs twenty-five times when speaking of God and five times for men; it is generally translated by the Hebrew word *ḥannûn.* "Compassionate," Dupont continues, is regularly rendered by *raḥûm*; it expresses the loving-kindness and deep affection parents feel for their children (e.g. Ps. 103:13). This word occurs thirteen times in the Bible. It qualifies God twelve times. Dupont concludes that mercy and compassion (loving-kindness) are preeminently divine attributes. Even though these are profoundly human sentiments, it is striking to observe that Israel generally reserves these words for the expression of Yahweh's solicitude for his children, especially when they are in trouble. In his revelation to Moses, Yahweh defines himself as the "God of loving-kindness and mercy" (Exod. 34:6).

The Lucan Emphasis

Luke 6:36 must be understood in a context where "compassion and mercy" are divine attributes which the disciples of Jesus are expected to manifest in their personal conduct. Luke concentrates on the character of our heavenly Father, rather than on duties imposed on the disciples. Because our heavenly Father is what he is, his true children will, as a matter of course, be like him.

The meaning of the divine mercy finds expression throughout Luke's Gospel. The parable of the lost sheep (15:4-7) is addressed to the scribes and pharisees who disapprove of Jesus' friendship with publicans and sinners. The parable emphasizes the joy of the shepherd in rediscovering his lost sheep; it represents the loving affection God has for sinners, his desire to pardon and reestablish them among his children. The parable reveals the sentiments of God and explains the conduct of Jesus, in whom the divine loving-kindness and compassion for sinners manifests itself. Luke pursues the same theme in the following parables of the lost drachma (15:8-10) and the prodigal son (15:11-32). In each case, Luke focuses on the sentiments and conduct of the heavenly Father, rather than on that of men, on the loving mercy and compassion that God has for sinners, rather than on the duty of the disciples to conform to this conduct. This is primarily a question of emphasis and focus; certainly, Luke implies that the true son of God will be like his Father.

In the parable of the importunate neighbor (11:5-8), Luke underscores the attitude of God, who is unable to be indifferent to our prayers. If a man, disturbed by an importunate neighbor, will not refuse what is requested of him, *a fortiori* God will not refuse to give what it necessary for those who ask it of him. The parable follows the Our Father; it draws attention to the fourth petition for our daily bread. The parable teaches what will be God's attitude toward our prayers; consequently, we may pray with confidence.

Matthew's commentary on the Our Father (6:14-15) has a different stress: "If you forgive men their trespasses, your heavenly Father will also forgive you; but if you do not forgive men their trespasses, neither will your Father forgive your trespasses." Matthew is primarily concerned with the Christian's duty to pardon offences. In a certain way, Matthew makes God's action depend on ours, whereas Luke emphasizes that our conduct should be based, or follow upon God's. Because God will not reject our prayers, we are able to pray with confidence.

Although Judaism had recognized the providence of God for his creation, it had the tendency to recognize the divine mercy only with regard to Yahweh's interventions on behalf of his chosen people. It is Jesus who reveals the goodness and mercy of God in its fulness; for God causes the sun to rise for the benefit of both the just and unjust, and the rain to fall on the good and the wicked (Matthew 5:45). Jesus reveals his heavenly Father. His parables are primarily concerned with enabling men to understand and love him. He explains his Father's actions in terms of parables: he is like the sower who throws grain on different parts of his field, like the man who sows the mustard seed, like the woman who puts a piece of leaven in the bread. In every case, Jesus refers to God's way of acting. This is the primary fact from which all else draws its significance, whether the phenomenon of nature or the conduct of men, and is the context of the teaching, "Be merciful as your heavenly Father is merciful" (Luke 6:36).

NOTES

H. Binder, "Das Gleichnis vom barmherzigen Samariter," *Theologische Zeitschrift* 15 (1959), 176-194. The parable of the Good Samaritan is not a lesson on love of neighbor. The wounded man is Jesus, who was rejected by the Jewish priesthood as unclean because He set Himself against the Temple and its worship. He alone is able to do for those who approach Him what the Jewish cultus could never do: give them access to grace. The conduct of those who pass by the wounded Jesus determines which one of the three (priest, Levite, Samaritan) has become a neighbor and has access to grace and the kingdom in Christ. Priests and been forbidden by Law to approach the dead (Lev 21.1); such contact made them unclean for cultic functions. Consequently, Luke's description of wounded man as "half dead" is most significant and the key to interpretating the parable. The Samaritan is separated from Jews in questions of cult.

B. Schwank, "'Wer ist mein Nächster?' (Lk 10.29), Eine Erklärung des Evangeliums de 12. Sonntags nach Pfingsten," *Benediktinische Monatschrift* 33 (1957), 292-295. The context of the Third Gospel and the entire Patristic tradition attest to the interpretation that we are to love our neighbor as Jesus the Good Samaritan, who saved mortally wounded mankind. And out of love for him we are to imitate him and help wounded mankind. Thus in Jesus the love of God and of neighbor coincide. The *formgeschichtliche* method is used to substantiate this interpretation of the Fathers who considered the Evangelists more as theologians than as reporters. This interpretation follows the advice of K. H. Schelkle "Über alte und neue Auslegung," *Biblische Zeitschrift* 1 (1957), 161-177, on the way upon which modern exegesis must enter.

10.

THE LUCAN "MUST"

"Must" (*dei*) occurs 44 times in Lucan writings of out the 102 times it is found in the New Testament.[1] The Lucan "must" expresses God's governing providence in the life of Jesus, as well as the necessity of accomplishing his Father's salvific will. It is particularly linked with the Passion which Jesus must undergo. The first text in which it is found in all the Synoptics alludes to the prophecies of Isa 53; Ps 118, 22; Os 6. 2: "The Son of Man must suffer much" (9. 22 = Mt 16. 21; Mk 8. 31).

The first occurrence in the Lucan Gospel is in the pericope which describes the finding of the child Jesus in the Temple: "I must be about my Father's business" (2. 49).[2] The six other times in which Luke makes use of this expression are proper to his Gospel. They concern the Passion, foretold in Scripture, which he must undergo:

> *13. 33*: I must go on my way today and tomorrow and the day following; for it cannot be that a prophet should perish away from Jerusalem. (Cf. Isa 53; Ps 118. 22; Os 6. 2).
> *17. 25*: First he must suffer many things and be rejected by this generation. (Cf. Isa 53; Ps 118. 22).
> *22. 37*: I tell you this scripture must be fulfilled in me, And he was reckoned among transgressors. (Isa 53. 13).
> *24. 7*: The Son of Man must be delivered into the hands of sinful men, and be crucified (Isa 53. 6, 12).
> *24. 26*: Was it not necessary that the Christ should suffer these things and enter into his glory? (Isa 53).

---

[1] The significance of the divine "must" in Lucan writings had been appreciated by H. Alford, Greek Testament, I (7th ed., London, 1874), 466: "... that *dei* so often used by Our Lord of his appointed and undertaken course..."

[2] J. Dupont, "Jésus à 12 ans," *Assemblées du Seigneur* 14 (1961), 38-40, comments on the Lucan "must" in general and especially anent this text. His views are restated by R. Laurentin, *Jésus au Temple* (Paris, 1966), 102-103.

24. 44: Everything written about me in the law of Moses and the prophets and the psalms must be fulfilled.

The Father's will and the Scriptures expressing it ground and designate the way which Jesus must follow. All the messianic prophecies must be accomplished. If the disciples at Emmaus had grasped the meaning of Scripture, they would not have been disillusioned by the Passion and death of Jesus. Luke repeats the same theme in his description of Paul's journey to Thessalonica's Jewish synagogue where "he discussed the Scriptures with them, explaining and proving that it was necessary for the Christ to suffer and to rise from the dead" (Acts 17. 3). "It was necessary" because the will of God, expressed in Scripture, would inevitably be accomplished. The Lucan "must" is associated with the will of God which "personally summons men and which fashions history according to its plan." [3] Jesus himself submits to that will (Lk 4. 43; 13. 33; 22. 37; 24. 44, and, in the context of the Passion, 9. 22; 17. 25; 24. 7, 26). So too do his witnesses (Acts 5. 29; 9. 6, 16; 14. 22, etc.).

Luke employs *dei* to bring out the necessity of the Passion. In 24. 7 Luke uses it as a subsequent proof that the Passion was part of the divine plan, by means of a reference back to one of Jesus' own statements. Comparison with 22. 37 reveals the harmony between Scripture and Jesus' own affirmation. Luke makes the demonstration of the necessity of the Passion in 24. 26 the climax of the Resurrection account. Jesus quotes the scriptural proof and refers to his earlier statements and thus completes the circle in 24. 27 and 44. H. Conzelmann notes that, when taken together with Acts 17. 3, these passages point to a usage that is already stereotyped, and to a fixed pattern of argument: it is from Scripture that the correct idea of the Messiah as a suffering Messiah is derived. The fulfillment is then confirmed by the historical Jesus. [4]

The idea of the progress of the Gospel according to plan underlies the necessity of a visit to the Temple (2. 49) and the fact that Jesus "must" proclaim the Good News (4. 43). Although the same concept occurs in Mark, Luke gives it greater precision and emphasis by showing that the plan can be seen throughout

[3] W. Grundmann, *art.*, "*dei*" in *TWNT* II (Eng. Trans.), 22.

[4] *The Theology of Saint Luke*, tr. G. Buswell (London, 1960), 153 n. 3, 154.

the course of Jesus' life. He reveals this progressive plan in the structuring of his Gospel. He describes a parallel progress in the history of the early Church. According to Conzelmann, Luke shows the three necessary stages in Jesus' ministry in 13. 33: "I must go on my way today and tomorrow and the day following..."[5] The Spirit teaches what one must say when called to declare one's faith (12. 12). The Christian way of life has its requisites (18. 1); among them is a fixed intention (19. 5). In Acts parallels occur in 3. 21, 4. 12. There is a link with Scripture (1. 16), and with the appointment of a witness (1. 22), with the Christian life (9. 16) and with the lot of Christians (14. 22).

The divine "must" cannot be resisted.[6] Luke often speaks of the futility of trying to withstand God. Gamaliel warns the members of the Sanhedrin not to oppose God (Acts 5. 39). Peter appears before the apostles in Jerusalem and defends his behavior in the case of Cornelius: "Who was I that I could withstand God?" (11. 17). Finally, the risen Christ tells Paul: "It hurts you to kick against the goad" (26. 14). Paul proves to King Agrippa that he could not be disobedient to the heavenly vision (26. 19). The divine "must" stands in contrast to the contingencies of history.[7] If it leads to the Passion, it also designates all the other events in the course of redemptive history. Not only does the divine "must" bring out the necessity of the Passion, but also of the entire ministry of Jesus implicit in the kerygmatic preaching. The Resurrection illuminates not only the Passion, but also Jesus' deeds and whole being (12. 49; 24. 26).

Paul's missionary activity is according to plan; in particular, he "must" see Rome (Acts 19. 21; 23. 11). The Lucan perspective of the divine purpose is conditioned by the divine "must" with regard to Jesus' life prior to his ministry (2. 49); within his ministry (9. 22; 17. 25; 24. 7, 26; Acts 17. 3); and subsequent to his earthly ministry until the restoration of all things (24. 26; Acts 3. 21).[8]

---

[5] *Ibid.*, 154 n. 1.

[6] H. Flender, *St. Luke Theologian of Redemptive History*, tr. R. H. and I. Fuller, (London, 1967), 143-44.

[7] The Lucan *"dei"* is noted by E. Stauffer, *New Testament Theology*, tr. J. Marsh (London, 1963), 26.

[8] W. C. Robinson, *The Way of the Lord* (Dissertation, University of Basle, 1960), 65.

11.

POVERTY

Poverty is a fundamental mark of blessedness in the thought of Luke (6. 20). The joy of the kingdom of God belongs to the poor. Mary exclaims: "My soul proclaims the greatness of the Lord and my spirit *rejoices* in God my savior; because he has regarded the *poverty* (*tapeinosin*) of his servant ..." (1. 46-47). Mary expresses the joy and eschatological hope of Israel's faithful poor (*anawim*) with words that recall theirs: "Yahweh heard our voice and saw our poverty and brought us out of Egypt" (Dt 26. 7).[1] The title of servant which Mary enjoys corresponds to that of the chosen people: "God has heard his servant, he has regarded my poverty ... and has given me a son" (4 Esd 9. 45). In this case the woman, the servant who speaks, is Sion. All generations shall call Mary blessed (1. 48) because through her the prophecies made about Israel are fulfilled: "All nations shall call you blessed, for you will be a land of delights." (Mal 3. 11). The Most High has done great things for Mary and the people of God whom she represents (1. 49): "God has done great things for you (i. e. Israel)" (Dt 10. 21). Thus, the Old Testament texts on poverty refer more often to the collectivity of Israelites rather than to individuals.[2]

The rest of the Magnificat confirms this interpretation. Luke makes a subtle transition from the graces conferred upon Mary

[1] R. Laurentin, *Structure et Théologie de Luc I-II* (Paris, 1957), 83.

[2] H. Sahlin, *Der Messias und das Gottesvolk, Studien zur Protolukanischen Theologie,* (Uppsala, 1945), 393-404; Israel is called God's servant (v. 54), recalling the suffering servant of Deutero-Isaiah. Mary declares, "Behold the handmaid of the Lord' " (1. 38). David is the servant of the Lord in the Psalms (e. g. 78. 70; 79. 3, 20); and the Israelites are servants of the Lord in Ps 79. 10. Israel is the servant of the Lord in Isaiah (40. 1; 48. 20). Again, the "poor man", the humble people who are oppressed, but who await God's vindication, are an important theme of the psalms (e. g. 9. 12, 17-20; 10; 12. 5).

to those conferred upon Israel. Because of her poverty, all generations shall call Mary blessed (1. 48). She is exalted because she is poor (*tapeinos*). This same exaltation shall be extended to all the poor (*tapeinoi*), to all who constitute the Israel of the spirit (1. 52): "He has pulled down princes from their thrones and exalted the poor" (*tapeinous*).[3] This transition from the individual to the collectivity within the theme of poverty enables Luke to affirm the identification of Mary and Israel.[4] Mary is the personification of the poor, of that privileged people chosen for salvation. She is the perfection of their poverty.

Mary describes herself as the servant of the Lord (1. 38, 48) at the moment when the glory of God comes to dwell within her (1. 35, 48-49). The poverty of the servant of the Lord is the reason why she has become the object of divine favor (*charis*) and messianic joy (1. 28).[5]

Jesus, the servant of the Lord (Acts 3. 13, 26; 4. 27, 30; cf. Lk 22. 27), is born in poverty and laid in a manger (2. 7, 12, 16); nevertheless, he is Christ the Lord (2. 11), and the angels sing at his birth (2. 13-14) and the glory of God appears on earth (2. 9). His birth is announced to the poor, to the shepherds in the fields. When Jesus is presented in the Temple, his parents make the offering of the poor (2. 24, cf. Lev 12. 8); none the less he is addressed as "the light for all the nations" and as "the glory of Israel" (2. 31-32). Here again the glory of God is manifested to Simeon and Anna, to the humble poor awaiting the salvation of Jerusalem (2. 38).

At the age of twelve, as a prelude to his mission, Jesus goes up to Jerusalem where he declares that he is the Son of God (2. 42); then he goes down to Nazareth, to obscurity. Thus, the glory of Christ is sporadically manifested to the obscure and humble poor of Israel who alone are capable of perceiving it. The poverty of Bethlehem, the submission of Jesus' parents to the

---

[3] A. Gelin, *Les Pauvres de Yahweh* (Paris, 1953), 156-159.

[4] R. Laurentin, *Luc I-II*, 84. Cf. E. Flood, "The Magnificat and Benedictus," *Clergy Review* 51 (1966), 205-210. Cf. R. Schnackenburg, "Das Magnificat, seine Spiritualität und Theologie," *Geist und Leben* 38 (1965), 342-357, comments that the thoughts of Mary are contained in the Magnificat which has been edited and placed within its framework by the author of the Infancy Gospel who thus conveys her personal thanks to God. In favor of her authorship is the fact that she spoke of herself as the servant of the Lord. No woman of the Old Testament was to be called blessed by all generations.

[5] *Ibid.*, 106.

law and the obscurity of Nazareth do not hide the glory of Israel from their eyes.[6]

When Jesus reads the lesson in the synagogue at Nazareth, he chooses the passage which describes his mission: "The spirit of the Lord has been given to me, for he has anointed me. He has sent me to bring the good news to the poor (*ptōchois*)" (4. 18). Later Jesus identifies himself for John's disciples in terms of those upon whom he is capable of exerting his own peculiar influence: "the *blind* see again, the *lame* walk, *lepers* are cleansed, and the *deaf* hear, the *dead* are raised to life, the good news is proclaimed to the *poor* (*ptōchoi*), and happy is the man who does not lose faith in me" (7. 23). Jesus identifies himself by the community which he has formed and where his impact is felt. It is only to the blind that he can give sight, and similarly with the others. It is only to the poor that the good news can be effectively proclaimed. His significance is grasped in terms of human needs which he alone can satisfy; and in terms of the community whose needs he satisfies.

Jesus begins his "sermon on the plain" as he began his sermon in the synagogue (4. 18), with a reference to the poor: "Blessed are you who are poor: the kingdom of God is yours" (6. 20). The lot of the rich is contrasted with that of the poor: "Alas for you who are rich: you have had your time of happiness" (6. 24). Thus, Luke maintains the contrast between rich and poor which he had introduced in his infancy narrative. Jesus is born poor. He is recognized by the poor, and his mission is to the poor. The rich, Luke would seem to imply, are those whose desires have already been satisfied by wealth, enjoyment, honor and esteem.[7] Of the wealthy Jesus has said: "How hard it is for the wealthy to enter the kingdom of God: It is easier for a camel

---

[6] *Ibid.*, 107.

[7] J. Dupont, *Les Béatitudes* (Louvain, 1954), 238: cf. P. Biard, "Biblical teaching on poverty," *Theology Digest* 14 (2, 1966), 153-154; cf. E. Wulf, "Vom Geist der Armut," *Geist und Leben* 38 (2, 1965), 135-146. For Wulf the possession of goods (riches) is an indispensable means for a man to develop his personality and thus to encounter the person of God. However, riches contain within themselves a mortal danger for man because sin has made him weak and avaricious. Therefore, the only proper relation to riches is that spirit of poverty which is gratuitously given by God and is exemplified in the life and teaching of Jesus and the apostles. The spirit of poverty is the spirit of the cross, of brotherly love and of being completely submissive and obedient to God's will.

to go through the eye of a needle than for a rich man to enter the kingdom of God" (18. 24). Wealth almost precludes genuine discipleship. Zacchaeus (19. 1-10) was "very rich"; it is only after he has given half his possessions to the poor that he is told salvation has come to his house.

Material poverty is one aspect of the beatitude; however, it is just as often accompanied by greed and unhappiness. The blessed poor are those whose material poverty permits the freedom of spirit which is necessary for following Christ. [8] The rich young aristocrat declined Christ's invitation because of his great wealth (18. 23): "At these words he was saddened; for he was a very rich man." The words of Christ saddened him, because his heart was not free to accept them. Christ's poor are blessed, because they are free. Concern for the retention or acquisition of wealth is not uppermost in their lives as it is for the rich fool (12. 15-21).

Material poverty does not guarantee Christian poverty. Further dimensions of the first beatitude are grasped in terms of the social conditions of Palestine at the time of Christ, when religion was of greater importance than economics or politics. [9] The social elite were those who carefully observed innumerable ritualistic perscriptions and who knew the Law. The social elite

---

[8] Cf. P. Bigo, "La richesse comme intendance, dans l'Evangile. A propos de Luc 16, 1-9," *Nouvelle Revue Théologique* 87 (3, 1965) 265-271. Bigo interprets the Parable of the Unjust Steward as an evil man who can show the Christian how to use riches to help the poor and to gain God's favor. Bigo justifies this interpretation with the context of Luke's whole treatment of riches in c. 16. Three sections control the passage's interpretation. (1) The parable's v. 9 which is closely parallel to v. 4 and so must not be separated from vv. 1-2. (2) The Parable of the Rich Man and Lazarus, later in the chapter, reaffirms the teaching of the Unjust Steward, that rich men are saved only by communicating their wealth to the needy. (3) Verses 9-13 stress a double attitude toward riches. (a) The riches of this life are alien to us. We have stewardship over them until we gain our own, real, spiritual riches later. (b) Riches are evil and unjust (vv. 9, 10, 11). Parable and chapter teach that riches becomes unjust and evil only if they are not communicated to the needy: cf. R. E. Brown, "Le 'Beatitudini' secondo San Luca," *Bibbia e Oriente* 7 (1965) (3-8). Brown holds that more than those in Matthew's, the Lucan Beatitudes insist upon actual poverty, hunger, suffering and persecution. Thus Luke reflects vividly the situation of the early Christians, most of whom were slaves. It is sometimes maintained that Luke condemns only excessive attachment to riches. This is incorrect; he condemns riches in themselves and glorifies that poverty which is accepted out of love of God.

[9] J. Dupont, *Les Béatitudes*, 220.

often condemned the masses who did not know the Law and considered them accursed (Jn 7. 49). The masses consisted of workers, peasants, merchants, tax-collectors and sinners. They were not all materially poor. Although many were richer than the Pharisees, they lacked the knowledge and minute practice of the Law which determined the social elite. The poor include the spiritually disinherited of Israel, the sinners who welcomed Jesus (e.g. 5. 27; 15. 1; 19. 1-10), and whom the Pharisees considered of no account. The Pharisees, on the other hand, were satisfied by the comfortable assurance that they alone were pleasing to God (18. 9).

Nevertheless, belonging to a class which the Pharisees despised would not suffice to explain the first beatitude. Only those poor are blessed who accept the Pharisees' estimation of themselves and judge themselves as the publican in the parable, who did not dare to raise his eyes to heaven, and beating his breast exclaimed, "My God, have mercy on me, a sinner" (18. 13). The blessed poor of Christ are they who have no claims on God. They are conscious of their spiritual misery and poverty before God; they alone are disposed to turn gratefully to Christ for salvation from their destitution.

The blessedness of the poor derives from the kingdom of God and not from the resources of this world. They very lack of these resources is a blessing when it leaves Christ's hearers free and disposed to accept the good news of salvation. Thus, the curse of poverty, in all its various aspects, is removed with a blessing; and *even* the poor, contemned by the Pharisees, enter the kingdom of God.

Luke stresses the predilection of Jesus for the spiritually disinherited: sinners, publicans, Samaritans. All these pariahs, often more despised than the materially poor, become the privileged in the merciful plans of God. The spiritually poor as well as the materially poor move Luke to profound compassion; they are the privileged of the messianic era. Because they suffer, they merit greater love.[10] The rich, on the other hand, are defined as those who have their consolation now (6. 24).

The word which Luke uses for poor (*ptōchos*) in the beatitude and elsewhere e.g. 4. 18; 7. 23) derives from the verb which means

---

[10] *Ibid.*

to cower or crouch; and it describes the abject poverty of one who is destitute. The two Hebrew words *ebion* and *ani* lie behind *ptōchos.*[11] The significant development of their meaning has three stages. Originally, they describe those who lack this world's resources (Dt 15.4, 11). Secondly, because of poverty, they go on to mean "downtrodden and oppressed" (Amos 2.6; 8.4). Thirdly, if a man is downtrodden, he has no influence, power or prestige, he cannot look to other men for help; consequently, he can only look to God for help (Amos 5.12; Ps 10.2). In the context of the beatitude, the poor are those who cannot trust to their own resources; they must turn to Christ for salvation.

The Lucan dialectic between wealth and poverty is heightened by the parable of the rich fool (12.16-21). The fool regards his wealth as a means of acquiring perfect happiness and security in this life: "My soul, you have plenty of good things laid by for many years to come; take things easy, eat, drink, have a good time." But God said to him, "Fool! This very night the demand will be made for your soul; and this hoard of yours, whose will it be then?" (12.19-20). The tragedy of the fool is explained in the last verse: "So it is when a man stores up treasure *for himself* in place of making himself *rich in the sight of God*" (12.21). The parable recounts the disastrous consequences of the self-centered existence, in which neither God nor neighbor play any vital role.

Jesus attacks the insatiable appetite for enjoyment and pleasure which absolutizes the value of this world's resources in the quest for happiness. The parable of the rich fool implicitly reveals the wisdom of the poor who are not engrossed in storing up treasure for themselves and who are none the less becoming rich in the sight of God.

Luke's view of poverty is not merely that of any absolute option for the future life; it also expresses his conviction that love for the disinherited and oppressed is a basically Christian attitude.[12] Generous giving to the poor is characteristic of authentic Christian love which does not seek to profit from its activities. Thus, Luke teaches that we should lend even to our enemies "without any hope of reward" (6.35), and that we should

---

[11] W. Barclay, *New Testament Words,* (London, 1964), 248.
[12] J. Dupont, *Les Béatitudes,* 210.

invite the poor to be our guests without hope of recompense (14. 14), because then we shall be "sons of the Most High" who is not self-seeking in his love for us (6. 36). All men are poor before God and cannot repay Him. We resemble Him as true sons when we give gratuitously. Luke's insistence on almsgiving would seem to be based on the principle that authentic Christians should spontaneously be moved to a loving compassion for those who need help (3. 11; 6. 30; 7. 5; 11. 41; 12. 33-34; 14. 14; 18. 22; 19. 8; Acts 9. 36; 10. 2, 4. 41).

Jesus warns those who hunger for riches that where their treasure is, there will their hearts be also. A man becomes what he loves; if he loves what perishes, he too shall perish. His life shall be meaningless (12. 15; 12. 23; 12. 33-34):

> "Watch and be on guard against avarice of every kind, for a man's life is not made secure by what he owns, even when he has more than he needs."
>
> "Life is more than food ..."
>
> "Sell your possessions and give alms. Get yourselves purses that do not wear out, treasure that will not fail you, in heaven where no thief can reach it and no moth destroy it. For where you treasure it, there will your heart be also."

The disciples must trust in the providence of their Father. If they set their hearts on his kingdom, their other needs shall be satisfied (12. 31-32). Only with the spirit of poverty will Christians be free to transcend the bondage of the human heart to the temporal order. [13] The imminence of death should motivate their unwordliness of spirit which does not seek ultimate security and satisfaction in the present order of things (12. 16-21). The poor of Christ do not expect more of the world than it can offer, consequently their blessedness is even now experienced.

Jesus challenges his followers to decision: "Whoever does not renounce all that he has cannot be my disciple" (14. 33). Poverty is viewed in terms of the kingdom which must be sought and of the Lord who must be followed at all costs, if that life which really counts is to be attained.

---

[13] J. M. Creed, *The Gospel according to St. Luke* (London, 1930), 175.

Jesus tells his host at a banquet that he should invite the poor who cannot repay him rather than those from whom recompense may be expected (14. 12-14). In this way he shall be rewarded at the resurrection of the just. Jesus then tells his host and his guests the parable of the Great Banquet to which the poor are invited and which they attend (14. 21-22). Those originally invited to the banquet decline the invitation because they are too preoccupied with their own special interests (14. 18-20). The poor are invited on the correct assumption that they are clearly disposed to accept whatever gracious hospitality is offered to them because of their basic destitution.

Jesus warns that one cannot be the servant both of God and of money (16. 13 = Mt 6. 24). His warning provokes the laughter of the Pharisees: "The Pharisees, *who loved money*, heard all this and laughed at him" (16. 14). Their love of money does not imply that they were wealthy; it means that they were servants of money rather than of God. Jesus unveils their hypocrisy: "You are the very ones who pass yourselves off as virtuous in people's sight, but God knows your hearts. For what is thought highly of by men is loathsome in the sight of God" (16. 15). Jesus knows of their loathesome love of money and warns them of its danger.

The story of the rich man and Lazarus is found in Luke alone (16. 19-31). Lazarus is called "the poor man" (vv. 20, 22); he is carried away after his death to the bosom of Abraham. The Jewish figure of speech evokes a picture of the messianic banquet where Lazarus reclines next to Abraham in the place of honor in Paradise for the just of Israel.[14] (Cf. Jn 13. 23; Mt 8. 11).

The rich man of the story has achieved all that the rich fool had hoped for (12. 10). The destitution of Lazarus does not preoccupy him. Ultimately both the happiness of the rich man and the misery of Lazarus come to an end. By the very fact that Luke does not expressly specify the culpability of the rich man, he underscores the danger of riches in general. The merits of Lazarus are likewise ignored: his ultimate destiny suggests the eschatological character of happiness.

---

[14] W. Grundmann, *Das Evangelium nach Lukas* (Berlin, 1956), 328; cf. 324-330.

The rich man dressed in purple (16. 19). The rabbis believed that God himself wore purple.[15] The position of the poor man who lay at his gate recalls that of the victim who the Good Samaritan found on the road (17. 31), and who had been similarly ignored.[16] Lazarus, his name, means "God helps"; he is patient and resigned. He is helpless, sick and famished. He would be most grateful for the scraps from the rich man's table (16. 21); however, the rich man does nothing to help him. Lazarus symbolizes the poor whom Jesus blesses (6. 10), and whose only hope is God.[17]

When the rich man dies he is buried in Hades (16. 23). Abraham tells him that when he had lived good things came his way (16. 25), recalling Luke's threat to the wealthy who enjoy their consolation in this life (6. 10). Just as Lazarus had longed for crumbs from the rich man's table, the rich man now longs for a drop of water from the finger tip of Lazarus (16. 21, 24). There is no question of revenge. Lazarus cannot help the rich man because of the great gulf which prevents any crossing from one side to the other. Even though Abraham is his "Father" (16. 24), he cannot help him. Had the rich man invited Lazarus to his table, he might have participated with Lazarus at his side now.[18] The situation recalls Jesus' advice: "When you give a banquet invite the poor ... that they cannot repay you means that you

---

15 *Ibid.*, 327.

16 *Ibid.*

17 *Ibid.*

18 *Ibid.*, 329. Cf. D.A. Carraro, "La Enseñanza Biblica sobre la Pobreza," R*evista Biblica* 28 (2, 1966) 73-78. Poverty is a fundamental theme of the NT for the spirit of poverty is the source of all riches. Moses (Num 12. 3) and Christ (2 Cor 8. 9) are ideals of poverty. The truly poor in spirit seek justice; they seek to relieve misery (Deut 15. 11; Zeph 3. 12; 2. 3). They know their weakness and are aware that God is their heritage (Jer 15. 20). In every poor man exists a sacrament of Christ's presence, for he forsook his divine privileges and became obedient unto death (Phil 2. 6 ff.) and became poor that we might becomes rich (2 Cor 8. 9). Poverty is a foundation of Christian existence, enabling that love without which nothing has value: cf. F. Stein, "A Pobreza na Biblia," *Revista Eclesiastica Brasileira* 24 (2, 1964), 309-328. The author shows that the biblical concept of "poverty" signifies a complex of virtues which needs to be carefully understood; *Vie Spirituelle* 111 (511, 1964) has the following articles under the general title "L'Eglise des pauvres." The fourth interpretation is well presented by them.

R.-L. Dechslin, "La communauté des pauvres de Jésus-Christ," 667-681.
B. Gardey, "Scandale et folie de la pauvreté," 696-706, 682-605.
C. Ranwez, "Bienheureux les pauvres," 696-706.
J.-M.-R. Tillard, "Le salut, mystère de pauvreté," 707-728.

are fortunate, because repayment will be made to you at the resurrection of the just" (14. 14).

The rich man wishes Lazarus to be sent to warn the rich man's five brothers so that they might avoid Hades (16. 27). Abraham responds that they already have Moses and the prophets to whom they should listen (16. 29). Luke implies that Moses and the prophets still avail to lead men to Abraham's bosom.

The Lucan Gospel is a message of hope for the poor. Luke's compassion for the poor and sinners is balanced by his stern warnings to the self-righteous, self-centered and pleasure-seeking (18. 28-30). Luke expresses a compassion which profoundly respects the unfortunate poor despite their physical, economic, social, moral and religious inferiority.[19] Besides the question of Luke's personal love for the poor, there is the fact that the majority of Christian communities consisted of the poor, suffering and despised. The Church remained the community of the "poor of Yahweh". Poverty is an historical sign of the people of God, the privileged recipients of his compassion. Luke understands that the poor are repulsed by this world and are therefore better disposed to turn their hopes toward heaven. This is a blessing; whereas the rich are cursed by their total immersion in and satisfaction with this world's resources. Luke's compassion for the poor is genuine because it is concerned with their temporal as well as spiritual welfare, with the temporal exigencies of the spiritually privileged.

Between the Age of Jesus and the Age of the Church a difference in the practice of renunciation occurs as a result of the change in the actual conditions of discipleship. Participation in the resourceless, itinerant existence of the master during the Age of Jesus (Lk 9. 58) necessarily excluded the disciple's retention of private property.[20] In a single act the disciple irrevocably surrendered all his possessions to the poor because their retention, even in part, would have implied his desire to retain the option of returning to his former state of life. Such a compromise belies the disciple's absolute committment to the Way

---

[19] J. Dupont, *Les Béatitudes*, 338-342.

[20] S. Brown, *Apostasy and Perseverance in the Theology of Luke* (Rome, 1969), 102.

of Jesus (Lk 9.62).[21] The Lucan emphasis on the totality of renunciation appears in the word "everything" (*panta* in Lk 18.22).

A radical change in this situation occurs with the formation of the Christian community. Assistance is required no longer by those outside the circle of the disciples, but by Christians themselves. Renunciation, therefore, involves care for the Christian poor. The convert contributes to their care by putting his goods at the disposal of the community, which does not imply a single, irrevocable act of renunciation.[22] *Koinonia,* the spiritual oneness of fraternal solidarity, leads to the common use of property (Acts 2.42,44), which Luke conceives as the outward expression of the interior state of mind prevailing within in the community.[23] The unity of the Christian community as a whole was characterized by the general willingness (Acts 4.34) to sell one's property for the benefit of the community whenever the need arose. The alienation of property took place only when necessary, as a means to obviate the danger of material need within the community.[24] Luke does not affirm that all Christians *sold* their property upon conversion. (e.g. Acts 12.10,12).

Only during the Age of Jesus was the renunciation of all property a requirement for discipleship. In the Age of the Church it was replaced by the willingness to part with one's wealth for the good of the community. Jesus' teaching on renunciation (Lk 14.33) applies for both Ages; however, it takes on divergent forms.[25] In the Age of Jesus it demands the im-

---

[21] *Ibid.,* 103.

[22] *Ibid.,* 104. Brown notes that the transition in the form renunciation takes is reflected in the Lucan version of the first beatitude (Lk 6.20), where Jesus praises actual rather than spiritual poverty. Brown holds that this beatitude in its Lucan form does not express a general principle whose validity continues during the Age of the Church, and confirms his view by calling attention to the total absence of the word "*ptochos*" ("poor") in Acts. Within the Christian community, where alone this beatitude might have found application, the practice of Christian solidarity in temporal matters has banished material want(Acts 4.34), in fulfilment of the prophecy in Dt 15.4. Brown affirms that Luke restricts the scope of the first beatitude. It is not a generalized statement as in Matthew (5.3); rather, it is concretely referred to the disciples who are present with Jesus: "And he lifted up his eyes on his disciples and said: 'Blessed are you poor' ..." Thus, only Jesus' followers on his earthly Way are required to practice actual poverty as a prerequisite for entry into the kingdom of heaven.

[23] *Ibid.,* 100.

[24] *Ibid.,* 100.

[25] *Ibid.,* 104.

mediate, irrevocable relinquishment of all one's goods on behalf of the poor. In the Age of the Church it means the repudiation of the proprietary spirit, so that the disciple sells his property when the needs of the community require it, or puts it at the disposal of the community when the common good demands it.[26]

SOME OLD TESTAMENT TEXTS ON POVERTY

Jer. 5.28: Unconcern for the poor is gross heartlessness:
They are grown gross and fat, and have most wickedly transgressed my words. They have not judged the cause of the widow, they have not managed the cause of the fatherless, and they have not judged the judgment of the *poor*.

Hosea 12.9: Wealth leads to pride and self-sufficiency:
And Ephraim said: But yet I am become rich, I have found me an idol.

Amos 2.6-7: Yahweh protests:
... because he has sold the just man for silver and the poor man (ebyon) for a pair of shaes. They bruise the heads of the needy (dallim) upon the dust of the earth and push the poor (anawim) out of their path.

Amos 4.1:
Hear this word, you fat kine that are in the mountains of Samaria, you that oppress the needy and crush the poor. (ebyonim).

Isaiah 10.1-2:
Woe to them that make wicked laws, and when they write, write injustice to oppress the poor in judgment, and do violence to the cause of the humble of my people.

Psalm 81.3-4:
Defend the lowly and the fatherless; render justice to the afflicted (ani) and the destitute. Rescue the lowly and the poor (ebyon); from the hand of the wicked deliver them.

Isaiah 11.4, speaks of the Messiah:
He shall judge the poor (anawim) with justice ...

Proverbs 29.14:
If a king is zealous for the rights of the poor, his throne stands firm forever.

---

[26] *Ibid.*, 105.

Proverbs 29. 7:
The just man has a care for the rights of the poor; the wicked man has no such concern.

Proverbs 29. 17:
He who has compassion on the poor lends to the Lord.

Zephaniah 2. 3, an invitation to spiritual poverty, to faith, humility and absolute confidence in God:
Seek Yahweh, all you poor (anawim) of the earth, you that have wrought his judgment: Seek the just, see the poor: if by any means you may be hid in the day of Yahweh's indignation.

Isaiah 49. 13, praises Yahweh upon the return from exile:
Give praise, O you heaven, and rejoice, O earth; you mountains, give praise with jubilation: because Yahweh has comforted his people and has shown mercy to his poor ones (aniyyim).

Isaiah 57. 15, illustrates the spiritual aspect of poverty:
For thus says the High and the Eminent that inhabits eternity. And his name is Holy, who dwells in the high and holy place and with a contrite and humble spirit, to revive the spirit of the humble and to revive the heart of the contrite.

Psalm 149. 4:
For Yahweh loves his people, and he adorns the poor (anawim) with victory.

Isaiah 66. 2:
Thus says Yahweh: But to whom shall I have respect, but to him that is poor and little and contrite of heart, and that trembles at my words?

Psalm 9. 13, 17:
... he has not forgotten the cry of the *anawim*
The desire of the anawim you hear, O Yahweh.

Psalm 21. 27:
The poor shall eat their fill; they who seek Yahweh shall praise him: "May your hearts be ever merry!"

Psalm 68. 33-34:
See, you who are poor, and be glad; you who seek God, may your hearts be merry! For Yahweh hears the poor, and his own who are in bonds he spurns not.

NOTES

H.-W. Bartsch, "Feldrede und Bergpredigt. Redaktionsarbeit in Luk. 6," *Theologische Zeitschrift* 16 (1960), 5-18, distinguishes between the Matthean and Lucan accounts of the beatitudes, maintaining that the literary form of Matthew's sermon is primitive Christian exhortation and that Luke's is closer to the early preaching. Luke's redactional work represents a stage in the development from one form to the other. In the Lucan account, the sermon is addressed to the crowds (cf. 6. 17-19; 27 ff; 6. 20a refers only to the Beatitudes), whereas in Matthew it is directed to the disciples (5. 1f). This change in audience marks a shift of emphasis from preaching to parenesis. The second person in Luke's Beatitudes (and woes) distinguishes them as a direct address to those present; another indication of the preaching form. According to Bartsch, Mt 6. 2-18 shows knowledge of the "woes," but Matthew has made a parenetic redaction of what appears in Luke as eschatological preaching. Bartsch does not believe that a common *Grundschrift* lies behind Mt 5. 3-12 and Lk 6. 20b-23, or Mt 6. 2-18 and Lk 6. 24-26. Antithesis is employed to express the Matthean teaching on love of enemies and on retaliation: the Lucan parallel is composed of two originally independent units (6. 27-31; 32-35). The latter context concerns reward in the coming judgment, whereas Matthew's antitheses are involved with the present behavior of the Christian community. Mercy is the unifying theme of Lk 6. 36 and the logia which follow; Luke gives them a different meaning from that of their parallels in the First Gospel: Lk 6. 40 teaches that the disciple must not set himself above the merciful Lord in judging others; Mt 10. 24f. teaches that the disciples can expect no better treatment than their Master has received. Both drew from an oral tradition. Bartsch rejects the hypothesis that a common written document was the basis of their work. He calls attention to the closely knit character of the Lucan sermon in which the Beatitudes constitute a promise of entrance into the kingdom of God and threaten exclusion from it (i. e. the woes). The conduct of those who accept the offer of entrance is described under the aspect of refusal to judge others, and love of neighbor. The Third Gospel integrates this material into the theme of the preaching of the kingdom of God.

M. M. Bourke, "The Historicity of the Gospels," *Thought* 39 (1964), 37-56. To illustrate the modern biblical approach the author studies the Beatitudes in detail (Mt 5. 3-12 = Lk 6. 20-23). He refers to the work of J. Dupont, *Les Béatitudes: Le problème littéraire* (2nd ed., 1958). He argues that the Beatitudes originally numbered four, of which three were influenced by Isa 49. 8-13; 61. 13. In these three Jesus declared to the poor, the hungry and the afflicted that in him the kingdom is being inaugurated. After the Church was established these Beatitudes would have lost their immediate revelance. Therefore, both Synoptics modified their original meaning to make them relevant to the particular ecclesial context. Thus, Matthew presents the Beatitudes as the image of the moral perfection demanded by the Sermon on the Mount. The Lucan version insists on actual poverty and on the danger of riches, reflects the teaching of the Parable of Dives and Lazarus (Lk 16.19-31) and of the Rich Fool (Lk 12.16-21).

R. E. Brown, "Le 'Beatitudini' secondo San Luca," *Bibbia e Oriente* 7 (1965), 3-8. In contrast with Matthew, the Lucan Beatitudes emphasize actual poverty, hunger, suffering and persecution. Luke reflects the social conditions of the early Christians, most of whom were slaves. Luke does not limit his condemnation to excessive attachment to riches. He condemns riches in themselves and glorifies that poverty which is accepted out of love of God.

J. Cantinat, "Le mauvais riche et Lazare (Luc 16, 19-31)," *Bible et Vie Chrétienne* 48 (1962), 19-26. The parable of Lazarus and the Rich Man is an instruction on the obligations of the rich to the poor. The use of this world's goods determines man's state after death. God provides the rich with the means for salvation, despite the dangers of wealth.

R. Koch, "Die Wertung des Besitzes im Lucasevangelium," *Biblica* 38 (1957), 151-169. In the Old Testament riches were regarded as a sign of the divine favor. The same belief persists in Matthew and Mark. Luke seems to disagree, but the disagreement is only apparent, as it consists in a different viewpoint. In the Lucan account Jesus does not condemn riches, but only their bad use and the obsessive striving for them. Such striving disregards God's dominion over all creatures. Man has the right to use creatures; he does not enjoy the right of absolute ownership. He who has made the search for wealth his life's desire serves Mammon. Luke is the Evangelist of the poor. Christ was born of poor parents and came to preach the gospel to the poor.

F. J. Moore, "The Parable of the Unjust Steward," *Anglican Theological Studies* 47 (1965), 103-105. To the Parable of the Unjust Steward (Lk 16: 1-7 or 8a) Luke seems to have added his own lesson (v. 9). Elsewhere his Gospel contains a number of sayings with the same theme. Together they imply that Luke believed that "the Gospel was a gospel to the poor; and that Kingdom was a kingdom for the poor." He had given the beatitude on poverty (6.20-21) and the Parable of the Foolish Rich Man (12.16-21). To underscore this point, he immediately followed the Parable of the Unjust Steward with a comment on the Pharisees "who were lovers of money" (16:14) and the story of the Rich Man and Lazarus (16:19-31).

12.

PRAYER

Introduction

Luke emphasizes prayer more than any other synoptic.[1] He records nine prayers of Jesus, of which all but two are found in no other Gospel.[2] Luke associates prayer with the most important moments of Jesus' life.[3] Jesus prays at his baptism (3.21), and after a day of working miracles (5.15-16). Before choosing the Twelve Jesus spends the night on the mount in prayer (6.12). Before Peter's confession of faith and his first prediction of the Passion, Jesus prays alone (9.18; cf. 5.16).[4] Jesus goes to the Mount of the Transfiguration to pray (9.29). He prays with gladness and thanksgiving after the mission of the seventy disciples because of his Father's revelation to the little ones (10.17-21). His example leads the disciples to ask him

---

[1] The Greek verb "to pray" (*proseuchesthai*) occurs in the following texts which occur in the Lucan Gospel alone: 1.10; 3.23; 5.16; 6.12; 9.18; 11.1; 18.1, 10, 11; and in common texts: 6.28 = Mt 5.44; 11.2 = Mt 6.9; Lk 20.47 = Mk 12.40; Mt 23.14; 22.41 = Mt 26.36; 22.44 = Mk 14.39; in Acts: 1.24; 6.6; 8.15; 9.11; 10.9, 30; 11.5; 12.12; 13.3; 14.23; 16.25; 22.17; 28.8.

[2] The parallel texts of the Synoptics do not mention Jesus' prayer in the following instances:

—the baptism (3.21 = Mt 3.13 = Mk 1.9)
—The selection of the Twelve (6.12 = Mt 10.1 = Mk 3.7)
—Peter's confession of faith (9.18 = Mt 16.13 = Mk 8.27)
—the Transfiguration (9.28 = Mt 17.1 = Mk 9.2)
—before the teaching of the Lord's prayer (11.1 = Mt 6.9)
—at the Crucifixion (23.34, 46 = no parallel tezt)

[3] D. Guthrie, *New Testament Introduction* (Chicago, 1965), 86. Jesus' prayer of exaltation at the return of his disciples is found in Mt 11.25-27 and that of Gethsemane occurs in all the Synoptics.

[4] A. Hastings, *Prophet and Witness in Jerusalem* (New York, 1958), 90, conjectures that it might have been to this prayer that Jesus was referring when at the Last Supper he declared "Simon, Simon . . . I have prayed for you, that your faith might not fail" (22.31-32).

to teach them to pray (11. 1). Jesus prays during his agony on the Mount of Olives (23. 39-46),[5] and during his Crucifixion (23. 34-46).

Luke alone relates two special parables about prayer: the friend at midnight (11. 5) and the unjust judge (18. 1-8). He alone presents the story of the Pharisee and the Publican at prayer in the Temple (18. 9-14), and states that Jesus exhorted his disciples to pray during his agony in Gethsemane (22. 40).[6]

Infancy Narrative

The Holy Spirit, who has fully and actively present at the conception of Jesus, descends upon all those who are intimately associated with his coming.[7] The Spirit inspires the jubilant prayers of Zachary, Mary, Elizabeth and Simeon.[8] Insight into the Holy Spirit's saving activity leads the protagonists of the Infancy Narrative to prayer and thanksgiving.[9]

The Baptism of Jesus

From the moment of his conception (1. 35), the whole of Jesus' life is characterized by an intimate union with the Holy Spirit which is first publicly revealed at the moment of his bap-

---

[5] E. Rasco, *Synopticorum Quaestiones Exegeticae* (Rome, 1965-66), 205-230, presents an excellent study of this prayer as well as a fine bibliography.

[6] H. Conzelmann, *The Theology of St. Luke*, tr. G. Buswell (New York, 1967), 180, states that the Baptism, the Transfiguration and the Agony in the Garden are three scenes which mark the main stages of Jesus' ministry and that they are assimilated to one another. On each of these three occasions a divine revelation is depicted as the answer to prayer. W. C. Robinson, *The Way of the Lord* (Dissertation for Univ. of Basle, 1962), 41, notes that these three "epiphanies" introduce respectively the rejections of Nazareth, of the Samaritan village and of Jerusalem with the trial and Cross. The three rejections introduce respectively three distinct sections of Luke's work (4. 16ff.; 9. 51ff.; Acts).

[7] Cf. R. Laurentin, *Structure et théologie de Luc* I-II (Paris, 1957). The *magnalia Dei* of the Infancy Narrative are the occasion for jubilant prayer.

[8] A. George, "Jesus Fils de Dieu dans l'évangile selon saint Luc," *Revue Biblique* 72 (1965), 190, notes that the Spirit descends upon Mary as a source of life in much the same creative role that was his in Genesis (1. 2) and in the expectation of that new creation whose principle shall be the resurrection of Jesus (1 Cor 15. 45; Rom 1. 4; 8. 11, 23); the overshadowing of Spirit is like that of the cloud which covered the tabernacle in the desert both to manifest and yet to conceal the divine presence.

[9] Cf. J. P. Audet, "L'annonce à Marie," *Revue Biblique* 63 (1956), 346-374.

tism, when the Holy Spirit descends upon him. Luke emphasizes the operation of the Spirit more than Mark, when describing the descent of the dove, by the insertion of the phrase "in bodily form". The messianic anointing of Jesus with the Spirit is an important aspect of the early apostolic preaching (e.g. Acts 4.26).

Luke alone of the Evangelists notes that Jesus was praying at the time of the Spirit's descent. This circumstance introduces the Lucan theme of the complementary character of prayer and the Spirit's effective action. The Spirit's effectivness in Luke-Acts is generally associated with the prayerful attitude of his recipients.

The descent of the Spirit upon Jesus and the accompanying pronouncement of the Father, "You are my beloved Son, in you I am well pleased" (3.22), are a clear reference to Isaiah 42.1: "Behold my servant: I will uphold him; he shall judge the Gentiles." Thus, it is while praying that Jesus is revealed as the Servant of the Lord, the Messiah, and the Son of God.[10]

Jesus' coming and manifestation inaugurates the new age, the New Israel, and the new creation. By having taken Jesus' genealogy back to Adam, and not only to Abraham as in the Matthean account, Luke suggests an association between the Spirit's creative activity in Genesis and at the baptism of Jesus.[11] As the Spirit moved over the waters from which came the first earth, so now the same Spirit descends on the head of the new creation as he rises from the Jordan. Jesus' prayer is, therefore, linked with the Spirit's creative action.

Filial Prayer

All the prayers of Jesus begin with "Father" in Luke's Gospel.[12] This is no definitive indication of divine sonship, because

---

[10] Prayer is a condition for the Spirit's effective action. Jesus promises that the heavenly Father will give the Holy Spirit to those who pray for it (11.13). Jesus' prayer at his baptism suggests that he is disposed for the Holy Spirit, and that he receives it in answer to his prayer. If the Spirit reveals that he is the Servant of the Lord, then this too may be in answer to his prayer.

[11] A. Hastings, *Prophet and Witness*, 84.

[12] A. George, *art. cit.*, 203. In fact all the prayers of Jesus in all the Gospels begin with "Father", except that starting with the psalm text in Mk 15.34 (Mt 27.46). This theme appears in W. Marchel, *Abba, Père* (Rome, 1963).

every disciple must address God in prayer as "Father"; however, these prayers contribute to an understanding of Jesus' sonship.[13]

Five references to God as Father occur in Jesus' prayer of thanksgiving for the revelation of his Father to the little ones (10. 21-22 = Matt. 11. 25-27).[14] After having addressed God directly as "Father", Jesus refers to him as "my Father" before his disciples. His prayer proclaims the cosmic sovereignty and liberty o fthe Father in the accomplishment of his plan (10. 21). The prayer not only reveals Jesus' unique filial relationship with God, but also his capacity for extending that relationship to his disciples (10. 21-22):[15]

Unlike Matthew, Luke introduces this prayer with the theme of joy: "He rejoiced in the Holy Spirit" (10. 21).[16] This is the only text in the Gospel where we read of Jesus' rejoicing. His joy is analogous to that of Mary and Elizabeth who rejoice because of their insight into and participation in God's effective plan of salvation (1. 14, 47). In both cases joy is associated with the Holy Spirit.

The prayers and words of Jesus about his Father are remarkably original in the Lucan account. Their appearance at the beginning and end of the Gospel indicates their importance, as well as Luke's particular interest in the sonship of Jesus as

---

[13] *Ibid.* 204.

[14] Cf. H. F. D. Sparks, "The Doctrine of the Divine Fatherhood in the Gospels," in *Studies in the Gospels, Essays in Memory of R. H. Lightfoot*, ed. D. E. Nineham (Oxford, 1955), 246-247.

[15] Studies of the revelatory character of Jesus' prayer in Lk 10. 21-22 are: A. Feuillet, "Jésus et la Sagesse divine d'après les évangiles synoptiques," *Revue Biblique* 62 (1955), 161-196; H. Mertens, L'hymne de jubilation chez les synoptiques (Grembloux, 1957); W. Marchel, *Abba, Pere* (Rome, 1963), 147-177.

[16] A. George, *art. cit.*, 195, affirms the messianic character of this revelation and of the disciples' joy which distinguishes the Lucan version from that of Matthew. Jesus invites his disciples to rejoice that their names are written in heaven (10. 17-20); he congratulates them for having received the grace to see what the prophets and kings of the Old Testament had longed for (vv. 23-24). In Matthew's account the text has a controversial character because of its context in which Jesus speaks against the cities unmoved by his miracles (11. 20-24), and against the Pharisees (12. 1-14).

The Lucan insertion, "He rejoiced in the Holy Spirit," possibly refers to the charismatic prayer Luke knew in the Church (Acts 10. 46; Rom. 8. 26-27; Eph. 6. 18), and whose origins were to be found in the prayer of Jesus. Thus, the prayer of the Church is that of Jesus and likewise reveals the Father in the joyful expression of gratitude for the accomplishment of his salvation plan in Jesus.

a unique relationship which is especially revealed in his prayers (10.21; 23.34, 46).

In prayer Jesus is closest to the Holy Spirit and to his Father (10.21-22). At such times, he leaves his disciples and remains alone with God. His are not only prayers of petition but also of union.[17] Although Jesus is apparently solitary in prayer, it is then that he is actually in the society of his equals.[18] Prayer is the most divine of his activities in the sense that it shows him as the equal of the Father, the beloved Son.

The Transfiguration

Jesus' public ministry begins with the prayer of the Jordan and closes with the prayer of the Cross (23.46). The Transfiguration, which occurs in the middle of the public ministry, is a moment of intense prayer when the glory of Jesus is revealed as at once that of the beloved Son and of the prophet to whom all must listen. Seldom does Jesus appear nearer to his Father than in this manifestation of his glory. As the Father's beloved Son he wholly transcends Moses and Elias in his union with God.[19]

The glory of the Mount of the Transfiguration and the agony of the Mount of Olives bracket the redemptive work of Jesus with two mysterious moments of intense prayer in which Luke presents Jesus as fully human and fully divine. As human, Jesus could be a prophet, could be filled with the Spirit, could be encouraged by an angel and could feel the need of prayer; as the Son of God, Jesus could send the Spirit, could be transfigured, and could speak as an equal of the Father.

Jesus' Teaching on Prayer

The two exclusively Lucan parables about prayer, the friend at midnight (11.5) and the unjust judge (18.1-8), encourage persistence and confidence in prayer. The exclusively Lucan story of the Pharisee and the Publican at prayer in the Temple (18.

---

[17] A. Hastings, *Prophet and Witness*, 88.

[18] S. Garofalo, "La Preghiera solitaria di Gesù, *Euntes Docete* (1955), esp. 166-169.

[19] A. Hastings, *Prophet and Witness*, 90, 95. ....

9-14) is an instruction on the proper spirit of prayer, teaching that man has no claims on God. Prayer with a humble and contrite heart, and not self-righteousness, is pleasing to God.

Prayer at Gethsemane

Luke alone affirms that Jesus exhorted his disciples to pray during his agony at Gethsemane (22. 40). This pericope has been linked with that of the Temptation (4. 13-22. 3) on the assumption that both pericopes depict Jesus as the model of human victory over temptations.[20] Jesus appears as the new Adam, the prototype of every Christian in temptation and in victory over it.[21] Luke, in these parallel pericopes, instructs Christians to pray in temptation. However, despite the genuine parallelism between the situations of Christ and Adam confronting temptation, there is no evidence in the text which proves that Luke had this in mind.[22]

The Crucifixion

Jesus utters two prayers at his Crucifixion which are found in the Lucan account alone. The first is the prayer in which Jesus intercedes for those who are responsible for his death (23. 34): "Father, forgive them; they know not what they do". The prayer of the Son expresses the infinite mercy of the Father, so often affirmed by Luke. It verifies the words of Jesus: "Love your enemies" (6. 35). Stephen echoes these words during his martyrdom (Acts 7. 60); and the apostles also exonerate the people of Jerusalem and their leaders because they had acted in ignorance (Acts 3. 17; 13. 27).

The second prayer is a citation of Ps. 31. 5: "Father, into your hands I commend my spirit" (23. 46). This text does not

---

[20] E. Rasco, *Synopticorum,* 228, notes that Jesus, as once the people of God, is comforted by an angel in time of crisis. In the Old Testament tradition God cared for his people through angels. The angel on the Mount of Olives serves as the representative of the new people of God in a gesture analogous to that of the angel at the Temptation and to those mentioned in the Epistle to the Hebrews (1. 6). Cf. H. Aschermann, "Zum Agoniegebet Jesu, Lk 22. 43-44," *Theologia Viatorum* 5 (1953-54), 145 and n. 8.

[21] A. Feuillet, "Le recit Lucannienne de la tentation (Lc. 4. 1-13)," *Biblica* 40 (1951), 613.

[22] I. de la Potterie, *Excerpta Exegetica Ex Evangelio Sancti Lucae,* class notes mimeographed (Rome 1963-64), 115.

correspond with its counterpart in the other Synoptics which cite Ps. 22. 1. The Greek words of the Lucan text suggest the writer's familiarity with the parallels, at least in their source; nevertheless, he quotes Ps. 31. 5, the traditional evening prayer of Judaism which Jesus certainly would have known. This prayer expresses the confidence of the Jews in God who would guard their lives from peril. Thus, Luke has Jesus speak of his Father in both his first (2. 49) and last words (23. 46).

The Prayer of the Church

In the Book of Acts Luke shows the correspondence of the Church's prayer life with that of Jesus. Like Jesus at his baptism, the disciples are gathered in prayer before the descent of the Holy Spirit (1. 14). They pray with confidence because their prayer is united with the efficacious prayer of their risen Lord who had commanded them to pray (21. 36) and had assured them that their heavenly Father would give them the Holy Spirit (11. 13; Acts 1. 8). The Lucan Gospel teaches that Jesus' prayers are always answered: he receives the Holy Spirit at his baptism (3. 22); he receives the Twelve after his night of prayer (9. 20); he receives Peter's confession of faith after his prayer (9. 20); his glorification at the Transfiguration follows upon his prayer (9. 29); the disciples learn to pray the Lord's Prayer after his prayer (11. 1); Peter repents (22. 62) because Jesus has prayed that his faith would not fail (22. 32); the apostles preach the forgiveness of sins to the people of Jerusalem (Acts 2. 38, etc.) which Jesus had requested of his Father at the Crucifixion (23. 46). Luke implies that what follows upon Jesus' prayer is the answer to his prayer and the sign of its efficacy.

While at prayer the disciples receive the Spirit which empowers them to speak the word of God with great courage and impact (2. 42; 4. 31). Prayer is the special obligation of the Twelve (6. 4). It accompanies the ordination of the Church's ministers and the commissioning of its missionary preachers (6. 6; 13. 3; 14. 23). Through prayer and the imposition of hands the Samaritans receive the Spirit (8. 15, 17). Prayer precedes the miracles of the apostles (9. 40; 28. 8). Through prayer are communicated the divine power, inspiration and guidance of the Holy Spirit.

In the life of the early Church prayer is associated with the reception of revelations through dreams and angelic visitations (9. 11; 10. 4; 12. 5), which Luke indicates are related to the activity of the Holy Spirit.[23]

Because prayer enables men to become subject to the dynamic influence of the Holy Spirit, Luke regards the gift of the Spirit as the answer to "prayer" (Luke 11. 13). The Christian community carried on the constant prayer of Jesus, according to his command (Luke 21. 36). Like Jesus, it prayed above all at the decisive moments of its life. Peter and John, after having been released by the chief priests, return to their people and pray; all are filled with the Holy Spirit and speak the word of God with confidence (Acts 4. 23-31). Prayer also preceded the election of Matthias (1. 15).

The Spirit, known as the "Spirit of Jesus" (16. 7), is the gift which enabled Christians to share his character and witness to him. Jesus had promised that his gift of the Spirit would make them his witnesses (1. 8). The prophets had also given witness to Christ (10. 43). Through his Spirit, Jesus transmits his own prophetic power to bear witness to the fulfilment of the divine promises (4. 33), and to perform the same signs which he had performed.

Praise and Blessing

The prayer of praise occurs more frequently in Lucan writings than in the rest of the New Testament together. This prayer is expressed by three main words.[24]

'Ainein, "to praise", is used of the angels (2. 13), of the shepherds (2. 20), and of the crowds when Jesus rode into Jerusalem in triumph (19. 37).

Doxazein, "to glorify", is used of the shepherds (2. 20), of the paralyzed man after he has been healed (5. 25, 26). Others who "glorify" God are the people of Naim (7. 16), the bent woman (13. 13), the grateful beggar (17. 15), the blind man who has received his sight (18. 43).

---

[23] G. W. H. Lampe, "The Holy Spirit in the Writings of St. Luke," in *Studies in the Gospels* (Oxford, 1955), 169-170.

[24] W. Barclay, The First Three Gospels (Philadelphia, 1966), 293, notes that the phrase "praising God" occurs oftener in Luke's writings than in all the rest of the New Testament together. Luke's Gospel begins and ends with people praising God in the Temple (1. 9; 24. 53).

Eulogein, "to bless", is used of Zachary after his cure (1. 64) and of Simeon when he saw the infant Jesus (2. 28). It describes the activity of the disciples in the Temple after the Ascension of Jesus (24. 53). Zachary declares that the Lord who has delivered his people is *eulogetos;* Mary is called *eulogemene* by Elizabeth (1. 68, 42). God blesses men and men bless God. All semitic peoples believed that the gods blessed them; however, only the Hebrews blessed God. R. Meir estimates that the faithful Jew pronounced one-hundred blessings upon God daily. [25]

The Exile and Restoration reminded the People of God of their complete dependence upon God and his promises. They realized that their infidelity was matched only by God's fidelity (Neh. 9. 33). They reminded God of his blessings in order that He repeat them. [26] The prayer of Esdras (Neh. 9) summarizes sacred history: the favours of God are enumerated from Abel to Judith, from Esther to the Macchabees. The blessing declared the favors of God and appealed to his fidelity. His past blessings were interpreted as his gracious and gratuitous commitment to the future of his people.

After the Exile, the blessing becomes the preface to a petition (1 Kings 8. 56), introducing a series of reasons for praising God and concluding with a request. [27] In the Septuagint the word *eulogein* means "to speak well of", to glorify God by declaring and praising his wonderful works with the confidence that he will remain eternally faithful to his people who can survive only in virtue of his continued blessings. [28] The Jews were taught to bless God both for good and bad fortune.

The Jews blessed God before their prayer, or request (*proseuchē*). [29] Thus, thanksgiving for what God had already done preceded the prayer for his present assistance. The blessing is a grateful commemoration; the prayer which follows is a hopeful petition.

---

[25] Cf. E. J. Bickermann, "Bénédiction et prière," *Revue Biblique* 69 (1962), 524. Most of the Jewish background for understanding the concept of blessings and prayer in Luke's Gospel is taken from this article.

[26] *Ibid.*, 530.

[27] *Ibid.*, 531.

[28] *Ibid.*

[29] *Ibid.*, 529.

The Emmaus account combines the declarative aspect of the traditional Jewish blessing with the eucharistic prayer.[30] Christ's recollection of God's great works and past favors corresponds to Israel's blessing of God; the self-revelation of Christ in the consequent blessing and breaking of the bread corresponds to God's blessing of the New Israel.[31] The blessing of the bread before the disciples at Emmaus (24.30) occurs in a eucharistic, joyous context of Christ's self-revelation, after his interpretation for them of everything in the Scriptures referring to himself (24.27). Christ's remembering forms an integral part of an action which terminates in the blessing and breaking of the bread.

In the worship of the early Church eucharistic prayer is accompanied by the joyful praising and thanking of God (Acts 2.47). Just as the Jewish blessing looked to the past and Jewish prayers looked to the future, the Church's eucharistic worship was both commemorative and eschatological: "As often as you eat this bread and drink the cup, you proclaim the Lord's death until he comes" (1 Cor. 11.26).[32] The Church blesses God for the redemptive Passion, death, and Resurrection of Christ, which constitute God's continuing blessing of the Church and the basis of its eschatological hope.[33]

The verb "to give thanks" (*eucharistein*) is synonymous with "to bless" (*eulogein*).[34] It is found in the account of the Last

---

[30] J. A. Grassi, " Emmaus Revisited (Luke 24,13-35 and Acts 8.26-40)," *Catholic Biblical Quarterly* 26 (1964), 463-464, cites a passage from R. Orlett, "An Influence of the Early Liturgy Upon the Emmanus Account," *Catholic Biblical Quarterly* 21 (1959), 216-217:

> ...the early Christian experienced the effects of both the Holy Spirit and of the Eucharist above all during their liturgical gatherings. Thus, for those Christians who had never seen Jesus alive on earth, the experience of the two disciples epitomizes what they experienced at these early liturgical meetings from the readings and explanations of the Scriptures, and from the agape, climaxed, as it was by the celebration of the Eucharist.

[31] J. A. Grassi, *art. cit.*, 467, asserts that the Emmaus account represents Christ manifesting himself to those who receive him with hospitality and listen with faith to his word in the explanation of the Scriptures; this occurs especially in the eucharistic celebration of the liturgy.

[32] H. Flender, *St. Luke Theologian of Redemptive History,* tr. R. H. and I. Fuller (London, 1967), 80-84, treats the table scenes in Luke, underscoring their eschatological, christological and soteriological aspects.

[33] W. C. Robinson, *The Way,* 114-117, treats of history and eschatology in Luke, presenting the polarity of the past and future in the life of the Church.

[34] M. H. Shepherd, "Eucharist" in The *Interpreter's Dictionary of the Bible,* II (New York, 1962), 179.

Supper (Matt. 15. 36; Mk. 14. 23; Luke 22. 17, 19; 1 Cor. 11. 24). Eucharistic prayer is characterized by proclamation and community. Jesus' discourse at the Last Supper ends with his intercessory prayer to the Father and with his injunctions for the life of his community in the world (22. 31-38). Strife and temptation lie ahead; however, Jesus promises his disciples that he will pray for them. This is their hope. The intercessory prayer of Jesus for his community, God's new creation, preserves it for the fulfilment of its task in the world. The prayer of Jesus, preceding the selection of the Twelve (6. 12 = Matt 10. 1 = Mk. 3. 7), is answered by the creation of the community; his intercessory prayer is answered by the Church's continued existence.

The prayer of Jesus is essentially that of the Son with his Father. It is both creative and communitarian because it is the prayer of the community of Jesus, created and preserved in virtue of the response to Christ's effective intercession. The Christian community is one of prayer, carrying on the constant prayer of Jesus, according to his command (21. 36). Its prayer is accompanied by the Spirit which descended upon Jesus while praying at the Jordan and upon his disciples while praying in the upper room.

The continuity of the Spirit's presence during the prayers of Jesus and those of his disciples is in each case characterized by the creative opening of a ministry which inaugurates a new age, a new Israel, and a new creation. [35] The mission of the New Israel, like that of its Lord, is achieved in prayerful responsiveness to the same Holy Spirit. Thus, the risen Christ continues his work of salvation through the gift of his Spirit to his disciples. [36]

The eucharistic prayer of Jesus is that of his Church. It combines the elements of the traditional Jewish blessing and petition, of the past and the future, of proclamation and invocation, of eucharistic thanksgiving and praise for the wonderful works which God has done and of eschatological hope and petition for their final accomplishment. Thus, Luke begins and ends his Gospel with prayers of rejoicing at God's wonderful saving deeds (1. 47; 24. 52, 53). With the spirit of eucharistic joy and

---

[35] H. Flender, *St. Luke*, 83.
[36] *Ibid.*, 84.

confidence in the intercessory prayer of their risen Lord, the disciples embark on their mission to the ends of the earth.

Conclusion

The mission of Jesus is accomplished in a spirit of filial dependence on God, which is expressed in prayer.[37] Discipleship requires that union with God which Jesus manifested in his prayer; and this must be learned from Jesus himself (11. 1).[38] Jesus' precepts on prayer imply that we must pray to the Father because He is good and will give us the Holy Spirit, the fulness of His gifts (11. 9-30) and the source of Christian joy (10. 21).[39] The gracious acceptance of the Father's gifts characterizes the openness to God expressed by prayer; this includes the acceptance of the Father's will, the cause of Christian joy,[40] which caused Jesus to rejoice in prayer (10. 21-22).[41] Jesus and his Father

[37] Cf. L. Legrand, "L'arrière-plan néotestamentaire de Lc. 1. 35," *Revue Biblique* 70 (1963), 179. The same Spirit that overshadowed Mary, and through whom she brought forth her son, is called "The Spirit of the Son" which cries out from within us "Abba, Father", an echo of the preferred prayer of Jesus (Lk. 9. 2; 23. 34, 46; Mk. 14. 36; Matt. 9. 25).

[38] Cf. M. Zerwick, "Oratio Dominica," *Verbum Domini* 28 (1950), 176-180, affirms that this prayer implies the recognition of God by reasoning, loving creatures in faith and charity, in word and works. Such recognition constitutes the Kingdom of God and his glory, which are identical with our happiness. We are created for that profound joy which expresses the loving will of God for our sanctification in Christ. Prayer, as Christ taught it, expresses the loving recognition of God as source of our peace and joy. To share in the peace and joy which exist first in God is to enter into his kingdom of heaven.

[39] Cf. M. Zerwick, "Perseverante Orare (11. 5-13)," *Verbum Domini,* 28 (1950), 243-247, states that living according to the word of God means living by what it says and the spirit it expresses. If it says "Pray", I pray; if it says "Trust", I trust. The Word promises to give more than man imagines: God Himself. Luke says the Holy Spirit (11. 13). All genuine prayer seeks God himself, his own best gift. Its efficacy is assured if we pray for the will of God, for that love which is His. For all those who love God, all things are seen as a grace and understood in terms of his love and saving perspective. Prayer enables our openness to seeing all His way.

[40] Cf. M. Zerwick, "Exultatio Domini (10. 21-22)," *Verbum Domini* 26 (1948), 229-233, notes that the Father's will, his love for the little ones, is Jesus' joy. Jesus receives joy as a gift from the Father and rejoices with the Father in virtue of it. Only the Father's gift, associated with the Spirit, causes Christian joy. The Father's joy becomes that of Jesus; and the joy of the Father and of Jesus is that of all Christians.

[41] Cf. M. Zerwick, "Diliges Deum Tuum ex Toto Corde Tuo (19. 25-29)," *Verbum Domini* 26 (1948), 365-369, affirms that Jesus commands us to love and to rejoice in and with the Lord. Dependence upon God, which charac-

sanctify with joy. Jesus points the way to a higher joy when he tells his disciples to rejoice that their names are written in heaven (10. 20), in their communion with God, rather than in their power to cast out devils.[42]

Prayer is the basis for hope in the struggle which leads to peace and joy for some and to eternal unrest for others (10. 17-20).[43] It guarantees victory over temptation (22. 46).[44] Jesus' victory over temptation (4. 3, 9) is the unique work of the Son of God, whose prayer and example enable Christians to overcome temptation in their own lives.[45] The kingdom of God does not come without a struggle; and prayer overcomes the obstacles to the benevolent reign of God.[46] Consequently, the early Church had a special interest in the prayers of Jesus:

> The earliest church always appreciated the historical side of its exalted Lord, the time and the circumstances of his earthly life. The gospel narratives leave no doubt about this. Nothing could be more historical, real or earthly than the way Jesus prays in the synoptics.[47]

---

terizes the religious man, means dependence upon Him for our love and joy: we love and rejoice in what He loves and enjoys. He loves our existence, the result of His creative loving and divine concern. Thus, in accepting ourselves and our need for salvation in Jesus, we can share in God's joy and love.

[42] Cf. M. Zerwick, "Vidi Satanam Sicut Fulgur de Caelo Cadentem (10. 17-20)," *Verbum Domini* 26 (1948), 110-113, notes the warfare between the creator and anticreator, between peace and unrest, between joy and unhappiness. Jesus can point the way to a higher joy because he was with God frof the beginning of creation and can explain what lies at the heart of this conflict. Just as the Creator saw Satan fall, so too he knows whose names are written in heaven.

[43] Cf. M. Zerwick, "In Beelzebub, principe Daemoniorum (11, 14-28)," *Verbum Domini* 29 (1951), 44-48, comments that Jesus provokes diverse responses. Admiration for his work and character is one from which much good originates. Sin is the abuse of our minds and hearts, the ultimate abuse of our humanity, in rejecting the traces of God's wisdom and love in our lives. It is the blackout of the soul confronting the Light of the World.

[44] H. Flender, *St. Luke*, 55.

[45] Cf. J. Jeremias, *TWNT*, I, 141, cited in H. Flender, *St. Luke*, 55, n. 2.

[46] Cf. A. Salas, *Discurso Escatologico Prelucano*: Estudio de Lc. XXI, 20-36 (Monasterio-Escorial, 1967), 95-117 treats of the theology of destruction in the Third Gospel and affords background material for the concept of the Christian struggle.

[47] H. Greeven, *Gebet und Eschatologie im NT* (Berlin, 1931), 11.

NOTES

R. Leaney, "The Lucan Text of the Lord's Prayer (Lk xi 2-4)," *Novum Testamentum* 1 (1956), 103-111. A long series of references to the New Testament indicates that Luke may have learned the Lord's prayer from the early liturgy, where it probably was used after baptism and in the Lucan origin of "May the Holy Spirit come upon us and cleanse us" as found in 162,700, Gregory of Nyssa and elsewhere. Individual words of Gregory's text are found in Lk 11. 13; Acts 10. 15; 11. 8; 15. 8-10, and Gregory's its authenticity against Mt "May they kingdom come" (PG 44 1157 C). Luke distinguished the two comings, of the spirit and of the kingdom, and considered the first a preparation for the second.

13.

PROPHET

Matthew presents Jesus as the new Moses, the legislator of the new law. Jesus appears as the Son of God in the Fourth Gospel. Luke, however, depicts Jesus especially as a prophet. Luke attributes the title of prophet to Jesus more often than Mark.[1] He never employs this title in the narrative parts of his Gospel, as if he had to affirm Jesus' prophetic character. It is the people and Jesus himself who acknowledge this title.[2]

I. The Prophetic Spirit in the Life of Jesus

The prophetic Spirit manifests itself at the most important moments of Jesus' life. At his baptism, Jesus' prophetic mission is designated by the descent of the Spirit in the form of a dove and by the words of the heavenly voice: "You are my Son, the Beloved; my favor rests on you" (3. 22).[3] Nearly the same words describe the Servant of Yahweh and his prophetic mission (Isa 42. 1):

> Here is my servant whom I uphold
> my chosen one in whom my soul delights.
> I have endowed him with my spirit
> that he may bring true justice to the nations.

In the first words of his public ministry, Jesus asserts that he has received the Spirit of the Lord for the accomplishment

---

[1] The title prophet appears in Lk 4. 24; 7. 16, 39; 9. 19; 13. 33; 24. 19.

[2] In his narratives Luke frequently calls Jesus "Lord" (e. g. 7. 13, 19; 10. 1, 39, 41).

[3] I. de la Potterie, *Excerpta Exegetica ex Evangelio Sancti Lucae,* informally published class notes (Rome, 1963), 76-97, exegetes the theophany after the baptism of Jesus. The Spirit anoints Jesus for his *prophetic* mission of proclaiming the Good News in word and deed. The anointing is not kingly or priestly.

of his prophetic mission as the spokesman of God who shall reveal the way of salvation by word and deed (4. 18 = Isa 61. 1):

> The Spirit of the Lord has been given to me,
> for he has anointed me.
> He has sent me to preach the good news to the poor,
> to proclaim liberty to captives
> and to the blind new sight,
> to set the downtrodden free,
> to proclaim the Lord's year of favor.

The Spirit of prophecy which Jesus has received was traditionally associated with the Messiah and his time, with the last days and the new Covenant.[4] The general outpouring of the prophetic Spirit represented the historical fulfillment of Israel's messianic hopes. Jesus is faithful to his messianic mission. He is led by the Spirit into the desert where he is tempted (4. 1). The desert was the place of the prophets in their formative years. Moses, Elijah and the Baptist had been there. After his temptation Jesus begins to preach in Galilee where the Spirit led him (4. 14). When the crowds try to prevent his leaving them, he declares: "I must proclaim the gospel of the kingdom of God to the other towns too, because that is what I was sent to do" (4. 43).

Jesus promises the prophetic Spirit to his disciples on several occasions. It is the Father's gift (11. 13): "... how much more will the heavenly Father give the Holy Spirit to those who ask him" (instead of the "good things" of Mt. 7. 11, because the Spirit is the best of all the "good things"). The disciples must not worry about what they must say when they are brought before synagogues, magistrates and authorities (12. 12): "because when the time comes, the Holy Spirit will teach you what you must say." Luke distinguishes between the Spirit's internal activity and the disciples' external testimony, between the teaching of the Spirit and the speaking of the disciples. The phrase, "when the time comes," suggests the "kairos" or the eschatological moment of the Spirit's arrival. At the end of the Lucan account, Jesus commissions his disciples to preach and to confer the Holy Spirit (24. 49).

---

[4] G. W. H. Lampe, "The Holy Spirit in the Writings of St. Luke," in *Studies in the Gospels*, ed. D. E. Nineham (Oxford, 1955), 163.

Luke underscores the prophetic character of Jesus and his mission because the time of salvation begins with him. Luke regards the outpouring of the Spirit as the great eschatological event and as the sign which authenticates Jesus as the Messiah. The messianic age arrives with the outpouring of the prophetic Spirit (Joel 3.1-5 = Acts 2.16-21): [5]

> In the days to come — it is the Lord who speaks —
> I will pour out my spirit on all mankind.
> Their sons and daughters shall prophesy ... (Acts 2.17)

II. Jesus as Foreshadowed by the Prophets

Luke draws attention to the ancient prophets as an adumbration of the work of Jesus. In the Nazareth sermon the mission to the Gentiles and the rejection of the gospel by Jesus' countrymen are prefigured in the stories of Elijah and Elisha. [6] "All the prophets" (13.28), as well as Matthew's "Abraham, Isaac, and Jacob" (8.11) shall attend the feast in the Kingdom of God, to which the Gentiles will be admitted but into which the unbelieving Jews cannot enter. Jesus' persecution and martyrdom of the Jews of Jerusalem verifies his prophetic mission; for a prophet cannot perish outside Jerusalem (11.33).

Jesus' journey to Jerusalem fulfills the prophetic predictions of the Son of Man. The ultimate significance of the journey is revealed on the way to Emmaus in the context of "all that the prophets have spoken," beginning from Moses and "all the prophets" (18.3; 24.25-27). The slaying of Jesus corresponds to the treatment which the prophets have traditionally experienced at the hands of the Jews (Acts 7.51; cf. Lk 11.50, where Luke speaks of "the blood of all the prophets" in contrast with Matthew's "all righteous blood"). All the prophets had proclaimed the age of fulfillment which Jesus' death and exaltation inaugurated (Acts 3.25); they had testified to the remission of sins through faith in him (Acts 10.43). Ignorance of the prophecies explains why the people of Jerusalem and their leaders condemned Jesus (Acts 13.27). Jesus fulfills the prophecy of Deut. 18.15:

---

[5] U. Luck, "Kerygma, Tradition und Geschichte bei Lukas," *Zeitschrift für Theologie und Kirche,* 57 (1960), 51-60.

[6] G.W.H. Lampe, *Studies,* 173.

"The Lord your God will raise up a prophet for you ... like myself (Moses): you must listen to him" (Acts 3. 22-23; 8. 37).

III. Jesus Climaxes the Prophetic Tradition

An outburst of prophetic activity pervades the first two chapters of the Third Gospel. The Baptist is filled with the Spirit from his mother's womb (1. 15). The Spirit inspires Elizabeth's salutation of Mary (1. 41), and Zachary's *Benedictus* (1. 67). Inspired insight into the divine plan of salvation is manifest in the prophetic utterances of he *Benedictus,* the *Magnificat* and the *Nunc Dimittis.* Jesus grows and is strengthened by the Spirit (1. 80).

The last and greatest of Israel's prophets proclaims that Jesus is the climax of the prophetic tradition, excelling all who have preceded him (3. 15-18). At his baptism Jesus is anointed by the Spirit with the prophetic power for his preaching the word of God (3. 22). Empowered with the same Spirit, he preaches in the synagogues of Galilee (4. 14-15). In the synagogue of Nazareth he proclaims himself the servant of the Lord in the words of Isaiah (61. 1-2). He is endowed with the prophetic Spirit to inaugurate the messianic age (4. 18).[7]

Although his prophetic preaching is inspired by the prophetic Spirit, his fellow countrymen drive him out of the synagogue. Jesus comments: "No prophet is ever accepted in his own country" (4. 24). After having declared his mission in terms of a prophet's vocation, Jesus is described as a prophet by those who witness his raising the dead at Naim (7. 16): "A great prophet has appeared among us".

Simon the Pharisee cannot believe that Jesus is a prophet because he permits a sinful woman to approach him. Simon reasons: "If this man were a prophet ..." (7. 39). The Codex Vaticanus reads: "If this man were *the* prophet ..." For Pilate's soldiers Jesus is a mock king; whereas, for their Jewish counterparts in the palace of the High Priest he is a false prophet, and "Come, prophesy" is the tenor of their mockery (22. 64). The disciples on the road to Emmaus describe Jesus as the "great prophet by the things he said and did in the sight of God and of the whole people" (24. 19).

---

[7] A. Hastings, *Prophet and Witness in Jerusalem* (London, 1958), 62-63.

IV. The New Elijah

Luke interprets Jesus in terms of Elijah, the prophet who ascended into heaven.[8] Although Luke is aware that the Baptist is the Messiah's forerunner "in the Spirit and power of Elijah" (1. 17), he avoids copying the Marcan identification of him with Elijah *redivivus*. Elijah is explicitly mentioned in Jesus' programmatic address (4. 25-26):

> There were many widows in Israel, I can assure you, in Elijah's day, when heaven remained shut for three years and six months and a great famine raged throughout the land, but Elijah was not sent to any one of these: he was sent to a widow at Zarephath, a Sidonian town. And in the prophet Elisha's time there were many lepers in Israel, but none of these was cured, except the Syrian, Naaman.

Jesus chose his disciples as Elijah chose Elisha and raised the widow's son at Naim as Elijah raised the widow's son at Zarephath. The miracle-worker, in both cases, is acclaimed a prophet (Lk. 7. 16 = 1 Khs 17. 24; Lk. 7. 15 = 1 Kgs 17. 22-23).

The disciples implicitly recognize Jesus' resemblance with Elijah when they expect him to call down fire from heaven on the unhospitable Samaritan villagers (9. 54). Jesus' words, "I came to cast fire on the earth" (12. 49) recalls Elijah, "the flame, his word flaring like a torch" (Eccl 48. 1), whose prophetic word could both illuminate and punish. This twofold aspect of Jesus' prophetic mission had been adumbrated in Simeon's prophecy, where he is described as having come "for the fall and the rising of many in Israel" (2. 34-35).

The Baptist had prophecied that Jesus would baptize with the Spirit which is fire (3. 16),[9] and that he would "burn the chaff in a fire is associated with the purifying and chastising fire of the eschatological judgment which divides mankind into two groups: those who shall be rewarded and those who shall be punished.

The prophecy of Joel described the event as "the great and manifest day of the Lord" (Acts 2. 20 = Jl 3. 4). In the Hebrew

---

8 G. W. H. Lampe, *Studies*, 176-177.

9 I. de la Potterie, *Exerpta*, 26; Cf. P. Van Imschoot, "Baptême d'Eau et Baptême d'Esprit Saint," *Ephemerides Theologicae Lovanienses* (1936), 653-666.

text the equivalent of "manifest" is "terrible"; consequently, the outpouring of the Spirit at Pentecost is simultaneously the terrible moment of the judgment and the baptism of the Spirit with fire.[11] Thus, the prophetic Spirit descends upon the disciples and inspires the apostolic preaching of the word of God which judges mankind, dividing it into those who lovingly accept it as their salvation and those who reject its power for salvation.

Elijah is mentioned in other texts. Herod hears that Elijah has reappeared (9. 8). Moses and Elijah appear at the Transfiguration (9. 30, 33). The "exodus" of which they speak may have symbolical affinities with that of Elijah and his disciple when they passed through the divided waters before the former was taken up in the chariot of fire (2 Kgs 2. 8).[12] The Transfiguration prefigures the Ascension. The word used for Elijah's ascent (*analambanesthai*) is that which Luke employs to describe the Ascension of Jesus (2 Kgs 2. 9-11; Ecclus 48. 9).[13] The Elijah theme returns at the beginning of the journey to Jerusalem (9. 51): "And now the time was approaching for him to be *taken up* to heaven." This assumption (*analempsis*) suggests that of Elijah (4 Kgs 2. 1): "And now the time had come when the Lord would have Elijah carried up by a whirlwind to heaven." In both cases a last journey leading to a solemn ascension and glorification is indicates (Lk 24. 51: Acts 1. 9-10).

Pentecost and the Ascension manifest Jesus as the new Elijah who endows his disciples with his Spirit after they have seen him going up to heaven. Elijah gave his spirit to Elisha in a similar scene. The gift of the Spirit, in both cases, enables the disciple to do the work of his master.[14] Elisha raises the dead son of the Sunamitess and Peter raises Tabitha from the dead (4 Kgs 4. 8-37 = 9. 36-43). Both women never tired of doing good and giving in charity. The intervention and conversion of

---

[10] A. Hastings, *Prophet*, 73.

[11] I. de la Potterie, *Excerpta*, 27. See texts in which the Spirit of prophecy and of the word preserve their judicial character which separates men into good and bad, into those to be rewarded and those to be punished in terms of their response to the word of God (Eph 6. 17; Hb 4. 12; Jn 12. 48; Apoc. 1. 16);

[12] G. W. H. Lampe, *Studies*, 176.

[13] *Ibid.*, 177.

[14] A. Hastings, *Prophet*, 74.

Gentiles followed both miracles: Namaan and Cornelius, both foreign officers (4 Kgs 5.1-15 = Acts 10.1-48).[15]

Although Elijah permits Elisha to take leave of his parents before following his master (3 Kgs 19.19-21), Jesus will not make this concession to one who wished to follow him: "No one who looks behind him, when he has once put his hand to the plough, is fit for the kingdom of God" (9.61).[16] The spiritual character and demands of Jesus' work exceeds that of Elijah in a transcendentally original way.

V. Preaching the Prophetic Word of God

The preaching of the word of God is a prophetic theme, because the prophetic Spirit is revealed in the words of God. The word *euaggelidsasthai* represents the preaching of Jesus: "He sent me *to preach the good news* to the poor" (4.18). The Spirit of prophecy empowers the prophet to become God's spokesman on behalf of the kingdom of heaven, the object of that favorite Lucan word, *euaggelidsasthai* which recalls the prophet's mission of Isaiah 61.1 (Cf. Isa 40.9; 52.7; 60.6 and Joel 2.32). This word distinguishes the prophetic preaching of Jesus from that of John (16.16): "Up to the time of John, it was the Law and the prophets: since then, the good news of the kingdom of God has been preached". With the preaching of the good news the messianic time has begun.[17]

Conclusion

Jesus' promise of the prophetic Spirit to his disciples is fulfilled in the Book of Acts where the Spirit inspires their testimony. The apostolic preaching of the good news of salvation

---

[15] *Ibid.*

[16] *Ibid.*

[17] The concept of "preaching the Gospel" in the sense of proclaiming the arrival of the day of salvation derives from the Second Isaiah where it refers to the proclaming of the day of salvation, whether from the Babylonian captivity or in a deeper messianic sense (Isa 40.9; 41.27; 52.7; cf. Lk 2.10). This is the Isaianic eschatological conception of the mission of the Servant which Luke ascribes to Jesus and his Church.

is impelled by the Spirit (16. 6-9) which enables them to speak the word of God in Christ courageously and with great impact (4. 29-31).[18]

NOTES

A. Feuillet, "Les perspectives propres à chaque évangeliste dans les récits de la transfiguration," *Biblica* 39 (1958), 281-301. Luke relates the Transfiguration with the Ascension. Moses and Elijah speak with Jesus about his impending "departure" (*exodus*), a word signifying the entire period from the Passion to the Ascension, corresponding to that of the Israelites' wanderings in the desert before entering into the Promised Land. Moses and Elijah announce the future glory of Jesus. In the Third Gospel the Transfiguration prefigures the Ascension.

A. George, "La predication inaugural de Jésus dans la synagogue de Nazareth. Luc 4, 16-30," *Bible et Vie Chrétienne* 59 (1964), 17-29. Luke has Jesus explain his prophetic mission and the principal themes of his preaching. Jesus begins in the synagogue, and the apostles later first preached in synagogues (Acts 9. 20; 13. 5; etc.). The Lord's preference is for the poor, suffering and oppressed. Salvation demands faith in Christ. The people of Nazareth, representing Israel, rejects and expels Jesus.

J. Manek, "The New Exodus of the Books of Luke," *Novum Testamentum* 2 (1957), 8-23. The word "exodus" of which Moses and Elijah speak at the Transfiguration had a special meaning for Luke. (9. 31). Luke alone designates the two prophets as "two men," a phrase which reoccurs when the women see "two men" at the tomb (24. 4). These two men are not angels, but the same Moses and Elias of the Transfiguration. They had spoken of Christ's death, and Resurrection and the New Exodus. The original Exodus was historical and prophetic; similarly the Church considered Christ's death and Resurrection in the prophetic sense, as did Christ himself (24. 27). Luke associates the Exodus with the Passion and Jerusalem, which he compares with Egypt. The earthly city of Jerusalem is related to the heavenly one as the passage through the Red Sea is related to the Promised Land. Christ's New Exodus is an act of God, enabling all to believe, and by which the enemies of God, like the Egyptians, would be punished. The post-resurrectional appearances of forty days correspond to the forty years' journey to the Promised Land. At Jesus heavenly entrance the two men were present. The Egypt-Palestine antithesis is contrasted with the earthly-heavenly Jerusalem

---

[18] The prophet speaks (lalein) what God commissions to communicate. The word *lalein* expresses the prophetic utterance of the Magnificat (1. 55), the Benedictus (1. 70). Anna speaks her prophetic words (2. 38). Jesus reveals the wisdom of God in his prophetic speaking (9. 11; 24. 32).

or sin—holiness antithesis. The New Exodus marks the transition from the earthly to the heavenly city. Jesus' entrance into heaven corresponds to that of the people of God into the Promised Land. The two men are types of the new leader of the New Exodus.

J. A. T. Robinson, "Elijah, John and Jesus. An Essay in Detection," *New Testament Studies* 4 (1958), 263-281. John preached Jesus as the Elijah who was to come with fire (as a judge), and Jesus in the beginning accepted this identification. Later John sends messengers to confirm whether Jesus will fulfill the role of Elijah. Jesus answers that he will fulfill the role of the Isaian Servant of the Lord, as the comforter and healer: "I have come to cast fire on the earth (i. e. role of Elijah), and what do I care if it be accomplished. Instead I must undergo the baptism of suffering (Lk 12. 49-53). In Acts 3. 12-26 Jesus is the new Moses, the prophet who restores all things, and therefore Elijah in all but name.

J. B. Soucek, "La prophétie dans le Nouveau Testament," *Communio Viatorum* 4 (1961), 221-231. The content of New Testament prophecy is not the Christian message itself, but rather words of edification, exhortation and consolation for the community. These prophecies cope with concrete situations rather than with the revelation of the fundamental mystery of God in Christ. Prophecy preached love rather than faith and expressed the communitarian orientation of the Christian community towards the basic problems of life. Thus, the prophets of the early church were depositories of particular gifts of the Holy Spirit for strengthening and instructing the Church.

14.

SALVATION

Salvation is a characteristically Lucan theme *expressed by four Greek words*: *soter* (savior), *sozein* (to save), *soterion* and *soteria* (salvation).[1] Luke alone of the Synoptics uses the words *soter* and *soteria.* Mary rejoices in God her savior (1. 47); and the angels proclaim the birth of a savior to the shepherds (2. 11). Peter and the apostles preach that God has raised Jesus up to be leader and savior (Acts 5. 31). At Antioch in Pisidia Paul preaches that God has kept his promise to the Jews and has raised up for Israel Jesus, the savior (Acts 13. 23). *Soteria* occurs three times in the Benedictus when Zachary proclaims that God has raised up a power for salvation (1. 69) through whom the people of God shall be saved from their enemies (1. 71) and shall enjoy the knowledge of salvation (1. 77). Zacchaeus is told that salvation has come to his house (19. 9).

Soterion is found only once outside Luke's Gospel (i. e. Eph 6. 17). Simeon declares that his eyes have seen the salvation which God has prepared for all the nations to see (2.300: and the Baptist affirms that all mankind shall see the salvation of God (3. 6).

*Sozein a*ppears 30 times in the Lucan writings (13 times in the Gospel and 17 times in Acts). It occurs 14 times in Matthew. and 14 times in Mark.

The Lucan concept of *salvation embraces the Passion, death, Resurrection and Ascension* of Jesus, as well as the preaching of the Gospel (Acts 13. 47; 28. 28). Luke does not restrict the saving activity of Jesus to his death. Paul and Barnabas assert that they had to proclaim the word of God to the Jews first and later

---

[1] A. Schmoller, *Handkonkordanz zum griechischen Neuen Testament* (13th ed., Stuttgart, 1963).

to the pagans because the Lord had commanded them to do this when he said: "I have made you a light for the nations, so that my salvation may reach the ends of the earth" (Acts 13.47). Paul later declares to the Roman Jews that salvation has been sent to the pagans because they will understand it (Acts 28.28).

Salvation is accomplished according to the divine plan (*boule*) which includes the Passion and Crucifixion (Acts 2.23; 4.28; 20.27).[2] The abundance of *pro*-compounds in the Lucan writings indicates that God is directing everything in the salvation process according to his plan.[3] Peter proclaims that the death of Jesus was according to the *divine* foreknowledge (Acts 2.23); that the death of Jesus had been *fore*told (Acts 3.18); that Jesus' final struggle had been *pre*determined (Acts 4.28). The frequency of the verb *orizein* (to decree, define, predetermine) in Lucan writings affirms that salvation is achieved according to the divine design (Lk 22.22; Acts 2.23; 10.42; 17.26, 31).[4] On the eve of the Crucifixion Jesus affirms that the Son of Man goes to his already determined fate (Lk 22.22). The necessity of fulfilling the divine plan of salvation is emphasized by the verb *dei* (must, to be necessary). It is necessary for Jesus to be on his way to Jerusalem (13.33), to suffer (17.25), to remain at the house of Zacchaeus for his salvation (19.5), to enter into his glory by means of his suffering and death (24.26).

Luke seems to have recognized *the continuity of salvation history in terms of "the way of the Lord"* (3.6) which leads to the Gentiles: "therefore be it known to you that this 'salvation of God' is sent 'to the Gentiles' — and they will listen" (Acts 28.28).[6] The fulfillment of the eschatological kingdom of God is not accomplished with the beginning of Jesus' ministry. The fulfillment begins with Jesus' ministry: "Know that the kingdom of God is near" (21.31). It takes place in stages and culminates

---

[2] W. C. Robinson, *The Way of the Lord* (dissertation for University of Basle, 1960), 66. The whole divine economy of salvation is designated by this term.

[3] H. Flender, *St. Luke Theologian of Redemptive History,* tr. R. H. and I. Fuller (London, 1967), 143.

[4] K. L. Schmidt, *art.,* "orizo", *TWNT* V, 453.

[5] E. Stauffer, *New Testament Theology,* tr. J. Marsh (London, 1963), 26. This verb occurs 44 times in Luke, out of 102 times in the entire New Testament.

[6] W. C. Robinson, *The Way,* 61; See also A. Feuillet, "Les grands étapes de l'église," *Sciences Ecclésiastiques,* (1959), 243.

in the Church. The history of salvation as the evolving plan of God has universal scope from the creation of all things (Acts 17. 24; cf. 14. 15, Lk 3. 38) to the restoration of all things which God had foretold through his prophets (Acts 3. 21).

It is in Jerusalem where the great salvation events occur: the Passion, death, Resurrection and Ascension of Christ, as well as the descent of the Holy Spirit at Pentecost. Luke's Gospel begins and ends in the Temple of Jerusalem (1. 5; 24. 63). Jesus' journey to Jerusalem (9. 51-19. 28) is a literary device by which Luke underscores the role of the Holy City in the drama of salvation (9. 31; 13. 33; 18. 31; 19. 11).[7] Jesus journeys to Jerusalem to accomplish his mission of salvation.[8] After the Ascension, the way of salvation history will be one "beginning from Jerusalem" (Lk 24. 47) and extending to Rome (Acts 1. 8; 23. 11) The message of salvation comes to the world from Jerusalem, the Holy City in which the saving events were enacted.[9]

Luke considers *the redemptive death of Christ* more in terms of a transition from death to exaltation.[10] Through his death, Jesus enters into his glory (24. 26); he becomes the "author of life" (Acts 3. 15) and "Savior" (Acts 5. 31). Luke tends to see salvation as a process, as a succession of events, in which death leads to life and glory. Matthew (20. 28) and Mark (10. 45) place greater emphasis on the expiatory sacrifice constituted by Christ's death.[11] In the Lucan account Jesus finishes his course on the third day (13. 32). The context of this affirmation implies the integral unity of Christ's Passion, death, Resurrection and Ascension.[12]

The saving life and mission of Christ is paralleled by that of the Church.[13] The genuine organic unity of the Third Gospel

---

[7] *The Jerusalem Bible*, tr. A. Jones, "Introduction to the Synoptic Gospels," (London, 1966), 13.

[8] Cf. W. Grundmann, *Das Evangelium nach Lukas* (Berlin, 1961), 456.

[9] Cf. H. Conzelmann, *The Theology of Saint Luke*, tr. G. Buswell (London, 1960), 164-65.

[10] I. de la Potterie, *Excerpta Exegetica ex Evangelio Sancti Lucae*, informally published class notes (Rome, 1963), 10. The author also explains the eschatological nature of the kingdom in relation to the beginning of Jesus' ministry, (p. 7).

[11] S. Lyonnet, *De Peccato et Redemption*, II, *De vocabulario redemptionis* (Rome, 1955), 49-67 .

[12] R. Laurentin, *Jésus au Temple* (Paris, 1966), 101-102; I. de la Potterie, *Excerpta*, 9.

[13] W. C. van Unnik, "The Book of Acts the Confirmation of the Gospels,"

and Acts enables Luke to underscore how the messianic gifts of Christ are verified in his Church. Both Jesus (3. 21) and his Church (Acts 2. 1) undergo a baptism of the Spirit. The inaugural sermons of the ministries of Jesus (4. 16-19) and of Peter are based on Old Testament prophecies concerning the eschatological outpouring of the Spirit for the accomplishment of the prophetic mission of preaching the good news of salvation. Jesus (4. 29), Stephen (7. 58), Paul and Barnabas (13. 50) are "cast out" by their hearers. Jesus (4. 14) and Peter (4. 8, 33) are filled with the Spirit and speak in virtue of him. Jesus (4. 40-41) and Peter (2. 43; 5. 16) work miracles of healing. The Transfiguration (9. 28-36) prefigures the Ascension (1. 9-11). Stephen's martyrdom parallels Jesus' death. He sees Jesus at the right hand of God (Acts 7. 56 = Lk 22. 69). Stephen commends his spirit to Jesus (Acts 7. 59 = Lk 23. 46); he too forgives his executioners (Acts 55. 60 = Lk 23. 34).

Among the Synoptics, *Luke alone entitles Jesus "savior"*. God has raised Jesus up to be "leader and savior" (Acts 5. 31). He is savior because he leads to life (Acts 3. 15). The Lucan concept of salvation does not stress the expiatory aspect of Christ's death so much as indicate it as a means for the attainment of eternal life.

Salvation is a central theme of the Infancy Narrative.[14] The appearance of the word in the Magnificat (1. 47) is not specifically related to Christ; however, its significance in the angels' message to the shepherds (2. 11) is christological. *Soter, soteria* and *soterion* would all seem to allude to the name of Christ. "Jesus" derives from the root *yascha,* which means "to save"; thus, Jesus, or *Yeshua,* means savior. The position of Christ's name in the very introduction to Luke's Gospel implies its great importance in the Lucan perspective of salvation history.

Novum Testamentum 4 (1960), 26-59. The article affirms that Luke-Acts sets forth God's eschatological plan of salvation which came to the world in gives an excellent etymological account for all the words related to salvation came to the world and Jesus and how it built a bridge between the saving activity of Jesus and those who did not see him incarnate. The leading ideas of Acts are thus *soteria* or *sozein* and *martys,* the witness proclaimed by man and brought by God himself. Acts is the sequel and complement of Luke's Gospel; it is its confirmation and verification.

[14] R. Laurentin, *Structure et theologie de Luc I-II* (Paris, 1967), 124-27, gives an excellent etymological account for all the words related to salvation (esp. "Jesus") in the first two chapters of Luke's Gospel. Cf. also his article, "Traces d'allusions étymologiques en Luc I-II," *Biblica* 37 (1956), 435-456.

In his Gospel, Luke systematically avoids using the word "to save" with reference to cures and the liberation from purely physical evils.[15] In these cases, he employs the verb *diasozein* (e.g. in the healing of the centurion's servant, Lk 7. 3). In the account of the storm on the Sea of Galilee, the disciples exclaim "Lord, *save* us, we perish!" in Matthew's version: whereas, they cry out "Master, Master, we perish!" in Luke's version (Mt 8. 25 = Lk 8. 24).[16] Because there is a question of purely physical salvation, Luke avoids *sozein*; he reserves this verb for the expression of Jesus' soteriological significance in a context which is more directly related to faith (*pistis*). In the cure of the woman with a hemorrhage (Mt 8. 22; Mk 5. 34; Lk 8. 48), Luke concurs with the other Synoptics in using *sozein* because there is a direct connection with faith: "... your faith has saved you".[17] Luke speaks of salvation in cases of cures only when the event has an explicitly spiritual aspect which expresses Man's attitudes of faith, praise, thanksgiving and love with regard to God. The word "faith" embraces all these attitudes. Thus, in the Lucan edition of the Parable of the Sower, we read that the devil removes the word of God *"from their hearts lest believing they should be saved"* (8. 12).[18] The Marcan version reads "The devil comes and removes the word" (4. 15). Luke's editing of this text underscores his basic theme of salvation through faith, in which salvation results from the presence of the word of God in one's heart.

The theme of salvation in the Benedictus is found in Zachary's traditionally Jewish prayer for "salvation from our enemies" (1. 71), and in the more typically Christian plea for the remission of sins through the "knowledge of his salvation" (1. 77).

In Jesus' public life, Luke employs the expression "your faith has saved you" four times. In every case, *faith is the fundamental condition for salvation.* Two pericopes are common to the other Synoptics. In the first of these, the cure of the woman with the hemorrhage (8. 48), the Lucan version reveals

---

[15] I. de la Potterie, *Excerpta,* 31, 33.

[16] Cf. E. J. Tinsley, *The Gospel according to Luke* (Cambridge, 1965), 91.

[17] Cf. P. Bonnard, *art.,* "Salvation", in *Vocabulary of the Bible,* ed. J.-J. Von Allmen, tr. H. M. Wilson, (4th ed. London, 1961), 385.

[18] Cf. H. Mehl-Koehnlein, *art.* "Man", *Vocabulary of the Bible,* ed. J.-J. Von Allmen, 251-252. *b*

a distinctively kerygmatic aspect, inasmuch as the miracle is proclaimed "before all the people". The second text concerns the cure of the blind man near Jericho (18. 42). Although the Lucan version shares some elements common to the other versions (e.g. "Your faith has saved you."), it is distinctive in noting that after his cure the blind man followed Jesus, praising God and that "all the people who saw it gave praise to God" (18. 43).

The other two texts are proper to Luke and are therefore especially indicative of his use of *sozein*. The sinful woman at the home of Simon the Pharisee is told that her faith has saved her (7. 50). There is no question of a physical cure. The forgiveness of her sins is her salvation (7. 48).[19] The second text concerns the ten cured lepers of which only one returns to thank Jesus. To him alone Jesus gives the assurance that his faith has saved him (17. 19). Salvation, in this case, does not consist in the miraculous cure; rather, it is achieved in the particular way that the recipient accepts it.

In these four pericopes drawn from the public life of Jesus, *salvation is associated with the public expression of gratitude* for Jesus' publically performed acts of mercy. His mere presence at the home of Simon is such an act; and the sinful woman's reaction tells us that she recognizes it as such. In these four cases, Luke clearly shows that the "faith" which has saved is not restricted to a purely internal conviction. As an inference from the Parable of the Sower, where the proper place for the word of God is in the heart (8. 12), it may be affirmed that genuine "faith" is manifested in the public expression of gratitude evoked by the saving words and acts of Jesus which have changed the human heart.

Salvation is associated with *healing* in a particularly Lucan way in the account of Peter and the lame man (Acts 4. 9-12).[20] There is a remarkable transition from the physical to the soteriological and messianic significance of the event. The healing is mentioned (v. 8) and proclaimed as the work of Jesus (v. 10); finally, Peter declares that there is no other name by which we can be saved (vv. 11-12).

---

[19] Cf. G. W. H. Lampe, "The Holy Spirit in the Writings of St. Luke," in *Studies in the Gospels*, ed.. D. E. Nineham (Oxford, 1955), 179.

[20] I. de la Potterie, *Excerpta*, 34.

Salvation is linked with *deliverance from death* in the account about Jarius' daughter where Luke explicitly associates faith with salvation (8. 50). The soteriological dimensions of saving and destroying life appear in the pericope about the man with the whithered hand (6. 9), where Jesus clearly implies his power to save.

Salvation is associated with *deliverance from diabolical possession* (8. 36); and with the remission of ins in the case of the sinful woman (7. 50) and Zacchaeus (19. 10).

Salvation appears in an eschatological context (9. 24; 18. 26, common to the other gospels ,and in 13. 23 and 23. 35-43, found in Luke alone).[21] *It involves losing one's life* to save it (9. 24) and entering the kingdom of God (18. 26). When the question of eternal salvation (= life) is raised (13. 23), it is in the eschatological context of entrance into the kingdom of God. The "saved" are they who are in the process that leads to salvation and who are making salvation their own (cf. Acts 2. 47).

Jesus assures the Good Thief of salvation because of his confession of faith and conversion (23. 40-43). His prayer that Jesus remember him is a plea for salvation. It is in the tradition of Israel's complaint psalms which ask Yahweh to "remember" his people, because this is their salvation (Ps. 74. 2, 18; 79. 8; 105. 8; 106. 45; 137. 7).[22] *The divine remembering* is one way in which salvation is traditionally expressed in the prayers of Israel. (e.g. 1 Chr. 16. 15).

With a crescendo of contempt, three groups at the Crucifixion tell Jesus to save himself.[23] The elders scoff (23. 35; the soldiers ridicule (vv. 36-37); the first thief blasphemes (v. 39). The context of this pericope is messianic. The soldiers' expression "king of the Jews" (v. 37) refers to a purely temporal messianism. The elders speak of Jesus in messianic terms as "the Christ of God, the Chosen One" (v. 35). In the same verse, Luke refers to a messianic psalm (21. 8). The first thief also uses the messianic title of "the Christ".

The Good Thief's words, "when you enter into your kingdom," have an authentically messianic significance that is recognized in

---

[21] *Ibid.*, 36.

[22] B. S. Childs, *Memory and Tradition in Israel* (London, 1962), 35-41.

[23] A. Plummer, *A Critical and Exegetical Commentary on the Gospel According to St. Luke* (4th ed., Edinburgh, 1901), 135.

the promise of Paradise which Jesus makes to him. Luke contrasts the purely temporal interpretation of the messianic kingdom, which characterizes those who tell Jesus to save himself, with the genuinely spiritual interpretation of the man who, despite the apparent hopelessness of the situation, asks to be remembered (i.e. saved).

Salvation consists in the eschatological reality of entering into the kingdom of God (13. 23; 18. 24, 25), and of receiving eternal life (18. 26, 30). In the pericope of the Good Thief the promise of entrance into the kingdom of God is the ultimate and supreme realization of salvation. Luke rejects the merely temporal concept of messianic salvation (23. 35-39); he shows that it is a religious and an essentially eschatological concept (23. 40-43). In the pericope of the Good Thief, Luke teaches that salvation consists in undergoing death with a spirit of faith and repentance, and of being led into the kingdom of God by Christ. Salvation ultimately consists in being with Christ in Paradise.

Luke, above all the Synoptics, underscores Jesus' mission as savior. He has come to save what was lost (19. 10). Faith is the condition of salvation. It is a transition through suffering and death to life and the kingdom of Christ (Acts 3. 15; 5. 31).[24] *Salvation is the acquisition of eternal, eschatological life with Christ.*[25]

NOTES

H. Holstein, "Serviteurs inutiles? (Luc 17. 10)," *Bible et Vie Chrétienne* 48 (1962), 39-45. The Pharises believed that they had special claims on God because of their observance of the Law. Jesus corrects the notion that these observances were "useful" to God. There is only one merit, that of Christ, in which the justified Christian participates by his free cooperation.

B. Meyer, "'But Mary Kept All These Things...' (Lk 2, 19. 51)," *Catholic Biblical Quarterly* 26 (1964), 31-49. The object of Mary's reflection in 2. 19 is the titles given her child by the angel: *soter* and *christos Kyrios.* In 2. 15 it is the whole Infancy story as pregnant with salvific mysteries to be accomplished. 2. 19 has structural parallels in 1. 65; 2. 33; 2. 50. All four texts underscore the coming of messianic salvation as a divine work surpassing human understanding.

---

[24] G. W. H. Lampe, *art. cit.,* 180.
[25] I. de la Potterie, *Excerpta,* 37-38.

E. Trocmé, "'Avec Jésus' et 'en Christ': les Évangiles comme miroir de la différenciation croissant entre deux thèmes religieux primitivement confondus," *Revue d'Histoire de la Philosophie Religieuses* 42, (1962), 225-236. The author notes that in Luke-Acts the theme of being "with Jesus" is relegated to the past and to the distinct future of the eschatological end-time, while the actual meeting with the risen Lord is described solely in terms of spiritual communion. Even the apparitions of the risen Lord are only exceptional variants of his spiritual presence. It expresses the Christian's life founded on communion with the risen Lord.

J. Winandy, "Simon et la pécheresse (Luc 7,36-50)," *Bible et Vie Chrétienne* 47 (1962), 38-46. Salvation is not achieved by the minute observance of the Law, but from God's grace through faith in Christ.

D.M. Stanley, "The Conception of Salvation in the Synoptic Gospels," *Catholic Biblical Quarterly* 18 (1956), 345-363. Peculiar to Luke is the introduction of a Christian vocabulary of salvation: *soteria* (1.69,71,77; 19.9), *soter* (1.47; 2.11), to *soterion* (2.30; 3.6); as also his insistence upon the universalist nature of the redemption. He approaches Johannine soteriology by regarding Jesus' death and resurrection as an "assumption" (9.51) and as an "exodus" (9.31) (cf. Jn 13.1). Like the other Synoptics Luke relates Jesus' public ministry to salvation (4.13; 12.49-50; 19.11).

R. Zehnle, "Jesus' Death in Lucan Soteriology," *Theological Studies* 30 (1969), 420-444. The death of Jesus has a soteriological significance for Luke. (1) Becaus eof his life of obedience that led Him on His way to the cross, Jesus has been established Christ and Lord, and has poured forth the Spirit upon His Church, which is now the locus of salvation. His life and death have constituted Him an active cause of salvation for men. (2) Through the life and death of Jesus the graciousness of God, His love for man, has been made known. God does not hate man; He awaits only man's turning to Him to forgive him all his sins and grant him salvation. (3) This turning to God (*metanoia*) means a profession of faith in the Name of Jesus. It involves becoming a member of His Church by baptism and following His "way," His life of obedience to the Father, no matter what contradictions and sufferings such obedience may entail. What is true in the position of Wilckens, Käsemann, Conzelmann, and Dodd is that Luke does not employ the doctrine of satisfaction to explain the meaning of the death of Jesus, a doctrine which historically has relied heavily on certain passages of the Pauline epistles for its scriptural foundation. In scholastic terms, Luke explains the link between the death of Jesus and the salvation of the individual Christian along the lines of formal (exemplary) causality rather than efficient causality. But that his lack of agreement with Paul on this point means that his own theological viewpoint should *ipso facto* merit an inferior note is a totally unwarranted conclusion. Zehnle concludes that whatever position we may adopt on the much-debated question of the relationship of Paul to the author of Luke-Acts, we misunderstand it unless we realize we are dealing with two creative theological geniuses, and that the latter deserves a fair hearing on his own terms and in his own right. Recent Lucan study of the last fifteen years invalidates the remark of C. H. Dodd, *According to the Scriptures* (London, 1952) p. 110: "Among Christian thinkers of the first age known to us there are three of genuinely creative power: Paul, the author of Hebrews, and the Fourth Evangelist."

15.

THE HOLY SPIRIT

Only the first and third Gospels describe the birth of Jesus. Both writers agree in denying that Joseph or any other human being fathered Jesus, and in affirming that Mary's pregnancy was inaugurated by the Holy Spirit (Matt. 1. 18-20; Luke 1. 35). The conception and birth of Jesus result from the creative activity of the Holy Spirit.

1. The *Creator Spiritus* in the Old Testament

In the Old Testament the Spirit acts creatively only at the creation of the world and man, and in the redemption and formation of the people of God. The Spirit of God, along with the creative word of God, is the agent by which the existing world was brought out of the primeval void in the creation story of Genesis (1. 2). In Ezek. 37. 1-14, God promises to bring his people up out of their graves, to reconstitute Israel: "And I will put my spirit in you, and you shall live." This is a striking form of the recurring prophecy that God would visit and redeem his people.

Redemption would be a new creation. Just as God had once breathed into dust and made man a living soul, he would breathe again into a people who had forfeited their life, and make them live again. The new life of the redeemed Israel, of the Israel of the New Age, is God's life because it results from his creative Spirit. In both creations the Spirit is *Creator Spiritus.*[1]

Just as the Spirit of God was active at the foundation of the world, so that same Spirit was also to be expected at its

---

[1] C. K. Barrett, *The Holy Spirit and the Gospel Tradition* (London, 1947) 23-24.

renewal. The Spirit of God is spoken of as the recreating, revivifying power of the days of the Messiah. The entry of the redeemer upon the stage of history would therefore be the work of the Spirit; its significance would be grasped in terms of the messianic and eschatological prophecies concerning the new creation.[2]

The role of the Holy Spirit at the birth of Jesus is the fulfilment of God's promised redemption in a new act of creation. Luke proclaims the conception and birth of Jesus through the agency of the Holy Spirit. He implies that the conception and birth of Jesus are messianic because they are the product of that activity of the Spirit which was expected to break forth at the inauguration of the New Age, at God's new act of creation.[3]

For the faithful of Israel the Spirit is a guide and leader (Ps. 143. 10) whose activity is an integral part of the covenant relation between God and the people. The thought of a renewal of this activity is not surprisingly associated with Israel's eschatological hope, and in particular with the expectation of a new Covenant and of a New Age.[4] In a future age of blessedness the Spirit will "be poured upon us from on high", bringing an era of judgment and righteousness (Isa. 32. 15-16). Isaiah foresees that the faithful remnant will be cleansed by "the Spirit of judgment and the Spirit of burning" (4. 4), a prophecy the Baptist echoes with his words concerning the coming baptism of Spirit and of fire. In those days the outpouring of the Spirit will be directly connected with devotion to the Name of the Lord (Isa. 44. 3-5), which would seem to foreshadow the close connection between the outpouring of the Spirit and salvation by the Name (now that of Jesus as Lord and Messiah) which characterizes Acts.

The prophecy of Joel 2. 28, of such cardinal importance in Lucan theology, conceived the bestowal of the Spirit in terms of a universal outpouring of the prophetic gift, so that all Israel would be possessed by the Spirit in the days of the renewed Covenant. This is especially associated with Israel's leader, who will possess the fullest endowment of the Spirit as her Spirit-

---

[2] *Ibid.*, 23.

[3] *Ibid.*, 25.

[4] G. W. H. Lampe, "The Holy Spirit in the Writings of St. Luke," in *Studies in the Gospels: Essays in Memory of R. R. Lightfoot*, D. E. Nineham, ed. (Oxford, 1955), 161-162.

possessed Messiah (Isa. 11.1-5). He will be truly anointed with the inward unction of the Spirit of God. In Second Isaiah's figure of the Servant the ideas of Spirit-possession and Covenant relationship are already united in the person of an individual redeemer (Isa. 42.1 and 66; 49.8). The notion of a Spirit-possessed Messiah was closely associated with the eschatological hope of a universal outpouring of the Spirit.

2. The Holy Spirit and the Messiahship

The events of Luke-Acts are interpreted against the background of the Old Testament view of the Spirit whose outpouring would mark the historical fulfilment of Israel's messianic hopes as well as the time of the New Covenant and the last days. The Lucan Infancy Narratives present Jesus as the messianic king, the on of the Most High, who is to receive the throne of David and rule over his house forever. [5] The conception and birth of Jesus are messianic, in the broad sense of the term, because they result from that activity of the Spirit which was expected to break forth at the inauguration of the New Age. [6] The work of the Holy Spirit is to call into being the new creation of the messianic days. [7] Thus, the messianic conception of Jesus underlies the whole significance of the Lucan account.

Three important texts identify Jesus' divine sonship with his messiahship (1.32 and 35; 3.22; 9.35), according to A. George; however, they reveal the total newness of his messiahship. Jesus is also the Servant, and he is Son because holy, born of a special action of the Spirit and of the divine power and united to God at the deepest level of his being. [8] The devils recognize Jesus' divine sonship (4.3 and 9; 4.41; 8.28); but no man proclaims Jesus as the Son of God in Luke — the centurion's confession is replaced by Jesus' final invocation: "Father, into thy hands..." The words of Jesus speaking to or of his Father show that his sonship is not merely a solemn title, or a privilege, but a depend-

---

[5] *Ibid.*, 163.

[6] Barrett, *The Holy Spirit*, 25.

[7] *Ibid.*, 45.

[8] A. George, "Jésus Fils de Dieu dans l'Evangile selon saint Luc," *Revue Biblique* 72 (1965), 185-209.

ence, an intimacy, a total communion. Jesus lives by and for his Father.

The Annunciation (1. 32 and 35) reveals two stages in the revelation of the divine sonship.[9] The first stage (1. 31-33) describes Jesus as the traditional Messiah hoped for by the Jews. In the second, Mary's question forces the angel to explain the uniqueness of this divine sonship. Luke then gives the unusual divine act of the virginal conception by the Holy Spirit as the source and sign of Jesus' divine sonship and holiness. Luke will use these same stages of understanding in the two questions posed by the Sanhedrin (22. 67 and 70). Jesus is "son of God" (1. 35) in a sense which surpasses any conception had by the Old Testament or Judaism.

3. The Holy Spirit and the Power of God

The text announcing the conception of Jesus embraces three Lucan themes: the Holy Spirit, the power of God and the divine sonship. Mary is told that "The Holy Spirit will come upon you, and the power of the Most High will overshadow you; therefore the child to be born will be called holy, the Son of God" (1. 35).

Although the word "spirit" (*pneuma*) occurs 5 times in Matthew and 4 times in Mark, it is especially Lucan.[10] The Third Gospel is called the Gospel of the Spirit because it emphasizes the role of the Spirit in the life of Christ more than any other Gospel. The expression "Holy Spirit" occurs 13 times in Luke's Gospel and 41 times in Acts.[11]

The word "power" (*dunamis*) is also Lucan. It is found 10 times in his Gospel and 7 times in Acts; whereas, it appears only 3 times in Matthew and 2 times in Mark.[12]

Another Lucan peculiarity is that of calling God the "Most High" (*hupsistos*). The expression occurs 5 times in Luke and 2 times in Acts. It is found once (a doubtful text) in Mark and

---

9 *Ibid.*

10 Cf. H. von Baer, *Der Heilige Geist in den Lukasschriften* (Stuttgart, 1926).

11 Cf. J. C. Hawkins, *Horae Synopticae* (Oxford, 1909), 27; A. Plummer, *The Gospel according to St. Luke* (ICC) (Edinburgh, 1896), 24.

12 Cf. W. Grundmann, *art.* "dunamis" in *TWNT*, II, 302.

once in the rest of the New Testament where it is a citation from the Old Testament (Heb. 7.1 — Gen. 14.17).[13]

The relationship between the Holy Spirit and the power of God is one of parallelism in which the terms are practically synonymous. The relation between the Spirit and the power of God, on the one hand, and the divine sonship, on the other hand, is one of cause and effect; it is because of (*dio kai*) the activity of the Spirit and of the power of God that the child shall be called the Son of God.[14]

The relationship between the Spirit and the power of God is a peculiarly Lucan leitmotiv. The two themes appear 3 times together in his Gospel (1.17 and 35; 4.14. and 3 times together in Acts (1.8; 6.8; 10.38). In every case, except Luke 1.17, the two themes appeared together in important contexts where they dominate the development of the plan of salvation. Thus, in 4.14, at the beginning of Jesus' public ministry, Luke underscores the fact that all that Jesus is about to achieve will be done through the "power of the Spirit" received on the day of his baptism.

More than the other Synoptics, Luke stresses (4.1) the role of the Spirit in inspiring Jesus to confront and defeat the devil in the desert before his ultimate victory on the cross.[15] Thus, the ministry of Jesus is contained within an inclusion marked by the words "filled with the Holy Spirit" (4.1). Luke repeats this phrase in his redactional note at the beginning of the Galilean ministry: "Jesus went to Galilee in the power of the Spirit" (4.14). The subsequent teaching and miracles of Jesus therefore appear as the manifestation of the power of the Spirit at work in Jesus. The theology of Acts 10,38 also teaches that after his baptism Jesus was "anointed with the Spirit and power" before setting out upon a determined mission in which his miracles would be signs of the salvation which he brings.

The work of the apostles in Acts is similarly described. Their activity is marked by *dunamis* and their teaching is characterized by *exousia*. The power of their impact derived from the gift of

---

[13] H. von Baer, *Der Heilige Geist*, 127.

[14] A. Plummer, 24.

[15] L. Legrand, "L'arrière-plan néotestamentaire de Lc, I, 35," *Revue Biblique* 70 (1963), 164.

the Spirit at Pentecost, just as that of Jesus had derived from his union with the Spirit manifested at the Jordan.[16]

In the Lucan perspective of salvation, power and spirit are intimately linked. According to W. Grundmann, power is the essence of God and the gift of power goes with that of the Spirit.[17] In showing their role in the conception of Jesus, Luke proclaims the forces which have brought the divine infant into existence.

Luke carefully avoids giving the impression that the Spirit is an agent over Jesus.[18] Mark (1. 12) states "The Spirit cast him out into the wilderness"; whereas, Luke 4. 1, in contrast, states that "Jesus being full of the Holy Spirit returned ... and was led in the Spirit into the wilderness". Luke is not satisfied with the Old Testament idea of the power of God falling upon a man. Instead, Jesus becomes the agent — "in the Holy Spirit". He is not merely a spiritual man, but Lord of the Spirit. In 4. 14, Luke again introduces the Spirit and from then on the dominant description of Jesus is that of one who possesses the power of the Spirit. Jesus is not the mere object of the Spirit's activity.

W. Grundmann makes an analogous observation on the theme of *dunamis.*[19] He notes that for Luke Jesus is more than a prophet endowed with power. His very existence is especially characterized by the power of God. In the Lucan account, the Spirit and power do not come upon Jesus as charismatic force; rather, because Jesus is conceived by the power of the Spirit of God, he is penetrated by them to the deph of his being.

4. The Holy Spirit and the divine sonship

Spirit and power make Jesus the Son of God, at least in his humanity. This basic element of Lucan theology is reaffirmed in the baptism narrative which underscores the relationship between the Spirit and power, on the one hand, with the divine sonship of Jesus, on the other hand.[20] The Spirit and the power which

---

16 *Ibid.*, 164.
17 *art. cit.*, 301.
18 E. Schweizer, "pneuma", in *TWNT* VI, 420.
19 *art. cit.*, 301.
20 L. Legrand, *art. cit.*, 166.

are manifestly operative within Jesus are the Spirit and the power of the Son of God who shares in the fulness of the divine life because of his intimate relationship of "well-beloved son" with his Father.

Though the other Synoptics give importance to the heavenly proclamation of Jesus' divine sonship at his baptism, Luke ascribes greater importance to it. He centers his entire account on this one point, avoiding the theological allusion of the other lengthier Synoptic accounts. The descent of the Spirit and the proclamation of Jesus' divine sonship constitute the central interest in the Lucan account of the baptism.[21]

The "western" text of Luke 3. 22 offers a perfect parallelism between Luke 1. 35 and the baptism account: "You are my Son; today I have begotten you" (Ps. 2. 7) is applied to the baptism. In both the Annunciation and the Baptism is described a type of "generation" for Jesus which is the work of the Holy Spirit communicating the power of God.[22] Even if the variant reading is rejected, the parallelism remains. The words of the angel and the heavenly voice announce the coming of the Son of God because the divine Spirit has marked him and the power of God is at work within him.

Luke locates the genealogy of Jesus after his baptism. The genealogy runs from David through Abraham to Adam, who, in a striking and enigmatic conclusion, is called the Son of God (3. 38). The universal salvation effected through Christ is correlated to the universal state of sin which originated in Adam (Rom. 5. 12-19). In this Lucan text, it is not the origin of Adam which explains the divine sonship of Jesus, but the inverse. It is not Jesus who is like Adam; rather, Adam, in a certain way, prefigures the image of Jesus, Son of God.[23] The Lucan genealogy orchestrates the words of the heavenly voice and extends the doctrine of 1. 35.[24] Adam was the son of God, made in the divine likeness (Gen. 1. 26). Human history culminates in Jesus, the new Adam, who realizes within himself all that had been merely adumbrated in Adam. Jesus' humanity is the perfect revelation

---

[21] Cf. H. von Baer, *Der Heilige Geist*, 59-62.

[22] J. Dupont, "Filius meus es tu, L'interpretation de Ps., ii, 7 dans le Nouveau Testament," in *Revue des Sciences Religieuses* 35 (1948), 522.

[23] Cf. J.M. Lagrange, *Evangile selon saint Luc* (Paris, 1948), 126.

[24] L. Legrand, *art. cit.*, 169.

of the divine sonship, which Luke explains in terms of the Spirit and power of God both in his presentation of the Annunciation and the Baptism of Jesus. Thus, the mystery of Jesus' origins is the underlying Lucan principle of interpretation for comprehending the work of Jesus. His divine sonship, the core of this mystery, derives from his complete possession of the Spirit and power of God from the moment of his conception; it is innate to him. He is the incarnation of the divine power.

Jesus is "Son of God" from his conception. The Baptist and has parents are "full of the Holy Spirit". From Pentecost on this expression characterizes important Christian leaders: Acts 2, 4 (Pentecost); 4. 8 (Peter); 6. 5 (Stephen); 11. 24 (Barnabas); 13. 9 (Paul); also, Acts 4. 31 and 13. 52). In the Third Gospel the phrase is used in 1. 15. 41. 67 and 4. 1. After 4. 1 only Jesus is so described. J. E. Yates conjectures that this phrase for Luke is connected with the idea of the persons so "filled" have a plenary inspiration which expresses, as the *dunamis* of the Spirit (Luke 14. 4), effects upon others.[25] Although Jesus is in full possession of the Spirit from the beginning, it is only after the resurrection that he becomes the donor of the Spirit (24. 49; Acts 2. 33). The risen Lord is encountered in his gift, so that either the Spirit or the risen Lord can be referred to interchangeably (12. 12; 21. 15; Acts 10. 14; 19; 16. 7).[26]

5. The Holy Spirit and Jesus' Baptism

The conception of Jesus through the Holy Spirit and his baptism are considered by H. Flender as representing two parallel traditions which Luke connects by the term "Holy Spirit".[27] According to the first tradition (1. 35), the life of Christ proceeds from the creative power of God of which he is in full possession. The story of the baptism serves to protect the story of the conception from misunderstanding. Jesus has not been provided with a non-human, supernatural kind of body; he receives the Holy Spirit as a gift, "in bodily form" (3. 21). The baptism narrative affirms that Jesus' genuine humanity has been endowed

---

[25] J. E. Yates, *The Spirit and the Kingdom* (London, 1963), 190.

[26] E. Schweizer, *art. cit.*, 420-421.

[27] H. Flender, *St. Luke Theologian of Redemptive History*, tr. R. H. and I. Fuller (London, 1967), 136.

with the Holy Spirit it has been "adopted". In the Lucan perspective, Jesus' baptism is the historical recognition of what he had been from birth. Conversely, 1. 35 protects the baptism narrative from an adoptionist interpretation: Jesus was not elected to be the Son of God at his baptism. By means of this complementary parallelism Luke keeps intact the mystery of Jesus' person.[28]

Because Jesus bears the Holy Spirit he is at once unique and comparable to other men. He states: "The Spirit of the Lord is upon me because he has anointed me" (4. 18). The anointing took place at his baptism and implies that he is unique (Acts 10. 38); however, in 4. 1, in 4. 1, Jesus is described as being "full of the Holy Spirit" whem he returns from the Jordan. This same formula is used to designate other faithful men in both the old and new covenants; consequently, in one respect, Luke implies Jesus' equality with them. Thus, the Lucan statements about Jesus' endowment with the Holy Spirit were to distinguish Jesus as one who enjoys a unique relationship of union with God and a unique mission; they also describe him as a man who like other men receives the Holy Spirit as a gift.[29]

6. The Holy Spirit and the (Jesus') Temptation

The Temptation narratives in both Matthew (4. 1-11) and Luke (4. 1-13) begin with a reference to the Holy Spirit. Jesus faces his opponent fully and manifestly equipped with the divine power of the Spirit. The Lucan account alone emphasizes Jesus' perfect possession of the Spirit, with his characteristic phrase "filled with the Holy Spirit". Jesus is the messianic leader prophecied by Isaiah (11. 1-5) who, in full possession of the Spirit, would overcome the forces of evil, as well as exercise wisdom and judgment.[30] Luke often associates the activity of the Spirit with the conflict against the adversary (10. 21). The devil is defeated but not destroyed. The messianic kingdom is marked by an activity that is neither unrestricted nor unopposed.[31]. J. Dupont notes that the Lucan redaction accords more importance to the

---

[28] *Ibid.*, 137.
[29] *Ibid.*
[30] G. W. H. Lampe, *art. cit.*, 170.
[31] G. K. Barrett, *The Holy Spirit*, 52.

devil's words and to his departure until the "opportune time".[32] The Lucan stress on the devil's role in both the temptations and in the Passion account implies the close relationship between these two events. The mention of a later "opportune time" adumbrates the devil's reappearance at the Passion and the final messianic conflict (4. 13; 22. 3).

Jesus' temptations are messianic because they are those of his nationalist compatriots: they are the temptations of the Messiah, not of an ordinary individual.[33] The Messiah is in full possession of the Spirit. The course he will follow for the establishment of his kingdom is that of the Spirit and not of men.

After his temptation in the desert, Jesus returns to Galilee with the power of the Spirit. He enters the synagogue at Nazareth on the Sabbath and reads from Isaiah: "The Spirit of the Lord is upon me; he has anointed me, and sent me out to preach the gospel to the poor... to proclaim a year when men may find acceptance with the Lord" (4. 18-19). Luke indicates in this way that Jesus was beginning his ministry as prophet and Messiah anointed by the Spirit, as the servant of the Lord foretold by Isaiah (61. 1-2). His ministry will always be characterized by the "power of the Spirit" (4. 14), visibly and historically manifested at his baptism. The entire impact of his mission is achieved in virtue of the Spirit.

7. The Holy Spirit and the "dunamis" and "exousia" of Jesus

In the description of the healing of the paralytic, the Lucan account states: "the power of the Lord was with him to heal" (5. 17). The equivalence of the Spirit and power would seem to be implied in Jesus' healing which occurs just after Luke has quoted Isa. 61. 1, "The Spirit of the Lord is upon me... he has sent me to proclaim... recovery of sight to the blind."[34] Power (*dunamis*) is linked with Jesus' role as earthly prophet; his miracles are acts of prophetical power.[35] They indicate his messiahhip: "Go and tell John what your own eyes and ears have wit-

---

[32] Cf. J. Dupont, "Les tentations de Jesus dans le récit du Luc (*Luc* 4, 1-13) *Sciences Ecclésiastiques* 14 (1962), 7-29.

[33] C.K. Barrett, *The Holy Spirit*, 48.

[34] *Ibid.*, 76.

[35] A. Hastings, *Prophet and Witness in Jerusalem* (London, 1958), 66.

nessed; how the blind see, and the lame work, and the lepers are made cleant, and the deaf hear, how the dead are raised to life, and the poor have the gospel preached to them. Blessed is he who does not lose confidence in me" (7. 22-23); thus the program announced in the synagogue of Nazareth (4. 18-19) is fulfilled.

Although Jesus' power will ultimately be revealed at his second coming, he still employs it while on earth. In slight contrast with "authority" (*exousia*), which belongs to him more as the heavenly Son of Man, "power" characterizes his prophetic role and miracles, whereby he exercises compassion, reveals his authority and manifests signs of the mysteries he has come to teach.[36] He power is particularly associated with the Holy Spirit in the same way as his function of prophet: "Jesus came back to Galilee with the power of the Spirit upon him" (4. 14).

8. The Holy spirit and Jesus' Prophetic Vocation

At Nazareth Jesus declares his mission in terms of a prophet's vocation. The special Lucan material affords three instances in which Jesus is held as a prophet. After raising the widow of Naim's son from the dead (7. 16), the people declare that a great prophet has risen among them, and that God has visited his people. Simon the Pharisee rejects the view that Jesus is a prophet (7. 39); however, the disciples of Jesus maintain that he is a prophet (24. 19).

When the spectators at Naim exclaim that a great prophet "has been raised up" among them, Luke has them employ an expression (*egerthe*) which recalls the raising up of the Judges as Spirit-possessed saviours and God's raising up of Cyrus to be his agent (Isa. 41. 25; 45. 13).[37] At the Transfiguration (9. 28-36) Luke implies that the prophetic line has achieved its culmination in Jesus, now revealed in the glory into which he was to enter through his "exodus" at Jerusalem. Thus Jesus "was found alone"; the great figures of the old dispensation having disappeared from the scene "when the voice came" (9. 36).[38] Jesus

---

[36] *Ibid.*
[37] G. W. H. Lampe, *art. cit.*, 174.
[38] *Ibid.*

had already followed their example in his fast of forty days (Cf. Deut. 9. 9; 1 Kings 19. 8). Moses and Elias, with whom Jesus speaks at the Transfiguration, are the two men who had seen God on Horeb. They are now witnesses to Jesus, who is revealed as the prophet "like unto me" foretold by Moses in Deuteronomy. Of this prophet Moses had said "It is to him you must listen" (Deut. 18. 15). On the Mount of the Transfiguration the disciples hear the heavenly voice saying "This is my beloved Son; to him, then, listen" (9. 35). The command is now renewed, the prophet like Moses is identified. This concept develops in Stephen's speech before the Council. He argues that because Jesus was the prophet like Moses foretold in Deuteronomy that he could be, like Moses, both rejected by Israel and at the same time her true ruler and saviour (Acts 7).[39]

Luke prefers to interpret Jesus more in terms of Elias, the prophet who ascended into heaven, and of the Servant, the Spirit-possessed sufferer and redeemer, rather than of Moses the Lawgivert.[40] The Servant is preeminently a Spirit-possessed prophet (Isa. 42. 1), commissioned to redeem men by the power of God (Isa. 42. 7), to be a light to the Gentiles (Isa. 42. 6; 49. 6), and to glorify God (Isa. 49. 3). Jesus sets out on the road to Jerusalem (9. 51) and to his death, as Luke alone relates, in fulfilment of the prophecy of the Servant who was to be counted among the lawless (22. 37; Isa. 53. 12). When the Servant Jesus has been exalted, according to the promise of Acts 1. 8, the disciples will receive the Spirit at the beginning of their ministry just as Jesus had enjoyed it at the start of his ministry (4. 14 and 18). Like the Servant they shall be witnesses in virtue of the Spirit "unto the ends of the earth" (Isa. 49. 6).

The prophetic Spirit appears at the most important moments of Jesus' life. At his baptism (3. 22), the Spirit descends upon Jesus to anoint him with the prophetic power for the task of preaching the word of God. After the Temptation (4. 18), with the power of the Spirit, Jesus returns to Galilee to undertake his prophetic ministry of preaching the word of God in the synagogue at Nazareth (4. 18). During his public life, the only mention of the Spirit in relation to Jesus occurs in an exclusively Lucan

---

[39] A. Hastings, *Prophet*, 68-69.
[40] G. W. H. Lampe, *art. cit.*, 176.

text, where Luke relates "Jesus rejoiced in the Holy Spirit" (10. 21). Joy is a Lucan theme which belongs to the apocalyptic literary genre employed in the revelation of mysteries, and is inspired by the Holy Spirit.[41]

After Jesus' sermon in the synagogue at Nazareth (4. 18) there are fewer references to the Holy Spirit in the Lucan Gospel. A. Hastings remarks that there is no need of them, and that this lack is good evidence of the Lucan account's historical value.[42] In spite of the early Christians' great Spirit-consciousness, they resisted the temptation to fill their accounts of Jesus' teaching with references to the Holy Spirit. All the Gospels agree that Jesus' human career was inaugurated by the Spirit's messianic anointing and that Jesus promised his disciples the help of the Spirit in future trials. Thus, prior to Jesus' final instructions there was no need to say more about the gift the disciples were soon to receive.

9. The Holy Spirit and Prayer

A good number of the Third Gospel's references to the Holy Spirit are linked with the prayer of Jesus. The theme of the Holy Spirit and prayer enters into the account of Jesus' baptism. Luke alone notes that Jesus was praying when the Holy Spirit anointed him (3. 21-22). Jesus' joyful prayer of gratitude at his Father's self-revelation to the little ones (10. 21) is inspired by the Holy Spirit. The Christian community's prayer is also accompanied by the Holy Spirit (Acts 4. 23-31); and it carries on the constant prayer of Jesus, according to his command (Luke 21. 36).[43]

10. The Holy Spirit and the Apostolic Preaching

Jesus promises the Holy Spirit to his disciples (11. 13; 12. 12). He sends his disciples to preach and confer the Holy Spirit (24. 49). The disciples receive the power of Jesus which was especially the prophetical power of the Spirit. Jesus' prophetical

---

41 L. Cerfaux, *Recueil Cerfaux,* vol. 3, (Paris, 1956), 145.
42 A. Hastings, *Prophet,* 87.
43 *Ibid.,* 88 and 96.

power, transmitted by the Holy Spirit, enables his disciples to become witnesses (Acts 1. 8; 4. 33) and to perform the same mighty acts and signs which he had performed.[44] The Holy Spirit inspires the testimony of the disciples (Acts 1. 8). He impels their preaching and directs it (16. 6-9); He gives the disciples the courage to speak out on behalf of Christ and the kingdom (4. 29-31).

The Holy Spirit is revealed in the preaching of the prophetic word of God and in miracles. Luke perceives a relationship between the infusion of the Holy Spirit and the prophetic preaching of the Gospel: "He has sent me to preach the Good News to the poor" because "The Spirit of the Lord is upon me" (4. 18).[45] The theme of "preaching the Good News" (*euaggelizesthai*) is characteristically Lucan (ten times in Luke, and only once in the other Synoptics, in Matt. 11. 5) and indicates the division of messianic time after the Baptist and before Christ in the exclusively text: "The law and the prophets were until John; since then the Good News of the kingdom of God is preached" (16. 16).[46]

The apostolic preaching followed the reception of the Spirit. During the ministry of Jesus, the activity of the Twelve was relatively limited. This is not surprising because the disciples needed time to penetrate the message of their master and the mystery of his person. All the evangelists associate the Apostles' awareness of their preaching mission to the apparition of the risen Christ. Luke is within the common tradition; however, he gives it particular attention.[47] Luke edits the paschal message in terms of the apostolic preaching (Luke 24. 44-48). He links all the characteristics of the apostolic preaching to the appearance of the risen Christ to the apostles: the preaching of the death and resurrection of Christ as the fulfilment of the Scriptures (vv. 46. 44-45; Acts 2. 23-32; 3. 13-15; 4. 10-11; 5. 30-31; 10. 39-40; 13. 28-30 26. 22-23); the call to conversion for the forgiveness of sins (v. 47a; Acts 2. 38; 3. 19; 5. 31; 10. 43; 13. 38-41; 26. 18); the mission to all nations on departure from Jerusalem (v. 47b; Acts 1. 8; 2. 39; 3. 25; 13. 46-47; 26. 17, 23); the role of witness which the apostles inherit from Jesus (v. 48; Acts 2. 32; 3. 15; 5. 32; 10. 41;

---

[44] *Ibid.*, 94-95.
[45] I. de la Potterie, *Excerpta Exegetica ex Evangelio Sancti Lucae*, private notes for student use (Rome, 1963), 22.
[46] *Ibid.*
[47] A. George, *art. cit.*, 125.

13. 21; 22. 15; 26. 16); the coming of the Spirit which will enable them to give witness (v. 49; Acts 1. 4; 5. 2, 8, 31; 5. 32; 10. 19, etc.). Thus, the gift of the Spirit creates the apostolic Church through its inspiration of the apostolic preaching.

The Lucan vocabulary emphasizes the novelty of the apostolic preaching, which more than 20 times is described as witness.[48] Of the three instances in the Third Gospel where there is question of witness on the part of the disciple, two concern their future mission (21. 13; Mark 13. 9; Matt. 10. 18; Luke 12. 14, 48 in Luke alone). Before Pentecost, Luke only once speaks of the Twelve as preaching the gospel in the course of their brief Galilean mission (9. 6); however, he applies this word 14 times to their missionary activity in Acts (5. 4; 8. 4, 12, 25 35, 40; 11. 20; 13. 32; 14. 7, 15, 21; 15. 35; 16. 10; 17. 18). The word "gospel" occurs twice in two other texts (15. 7; 20. 24), and the title "evangelist" is given to Philip (21. 8). Only after Pentecost does Luke speak of "the teaching of the apostles" and of their collaborators (Acts 2. 42; 5. 28; 13. 12; 17. 19); of their being engaged in teaching (Acts 4. 2, 18; 5. 21, 28, 42; 9. 26; 25. 1, 35; 18. 11, 25; 20. 20; 21. 21, 28; 28. 31).[49]

The apostolic preaching is marked by the use of Scripture. Luke notes that the risen Christ "opens the Scripture" to Emmaus disciples (24. 25-27, 32); he "opens the spirit" (of the Eleven) to an understanding of the Scriptures (24. 44-45). Until now, to speak of tradition, the disciples had only applied Ps. 113, 25-26 to Jesus to celebrate his entrance into Jerusalem (Matt. 21. 9; Mark 11. 9; Luke 19. 38) and this was a temporal understanding of messiahship.

11. The Holy Spirit and the Church

The existence of the Church is not constituted by its origin in Judaism, but on the basis of the Holy Spirit and consequent obedience to him. U. Luck maintains that the Gospel of Luke is a recognition of the facts concerning Jesus as the deeds of God, and the eyewitnesses of Luke 1. 1 are those who have wit-

---

[48] The term "testimony" (Acts 4. 33; 22. 18), "to witness" (2. 40; 8. 25; 10. 42; 18. 5; 20. 21, 24; 23. 11; 26. 22; 28. 23), "witness" (1. 8, 22; 2. 32; 3. 15; 5. 32; 10. 39, 41; 13. 31; 22. 15, 20; 26. 16).

[49] A. George, *art. cit.*, 126.

nessed from the beginning (the baptism of Jesus) the effect of the Holy Spirit on the history of Jesus.[50] Consequently, Luke does not use the fulfilment of Scriptures as we find it in Matthew. For Luke the history of Jesus stands under the "must" (*dei*) of the divine will, which manifests itself through the Spirit. From this vantage point the Old Testament is understood. In the Old Testament the Spirit speaks as a prophetic witness and thereby relates the present community to itself. Luck concludes that in his Gospel Luke has attempted to understand the past history of the ever present effect of the Holy Spirit as God's history (*Gottesgeschichte*). "Now" is the *"Mitte der Zeit"*, not "then".

The gift of the Holy Spirit to the disciples characterizes the life of the Church.[51] Luke had already shown in his Gospel's Infancy Narratives the men who were inspired by the Spirit: John the Baptist is filled with the prophetic Spirit from his mother's womb (1. 15, 41); Elizabeth is inspired by it when she blesses Mary (1. 41, 45); Zachary is inspired by the Spirit when he pronounces his Benedictus (1. 67); Simeon undergoes its influence when he welcomes Jesus in the Temple and utters his prophecies about him (2. 25-35). However, in the Lucan perspective, all these persons still belong to the Old Testament which shall end with the Baptist (16. 16). They received the Spirit by the same title as the prophets.

The Lucan Gospel similarly reports the relationship of Jesus with the Spirit. Just as Matthew (1. 18, 20), Luke shows Jesus as conceived by the Spirit (1. 35;[52] as Matthew (3. 16 and 4. 1) and as Mark (1. 10, 12), Luke sees Jesus as endowed with the fulness of the Spirit at his baptism (3. 22; 4. 1). Unlike them, however, Luke carefully notes that Jesus sends the Spirit (24. 49;

---

[50] U. Luck, "Kerygma, Tradition und Geschichte Jesu bei Lukas," *Zeitschrift für Theologie und Kirche* 57 (1960), 51-66.

[51] On the Spirit in the work of Luke, see H. von Baer, *Der Heilige Geist in den Lukasschriften* (Stuttgart, 1926); C.K. Barrett, *The Holy Spirit in the Gospel Tradition* (London, 1966, new ed.); H. Conzelmann, *Die Mitte* der *Zeit* (Tübingen, 1954); H. Flender, *Heil und Geschichte in der Theologie des Lukas* (Münich, 1965): C.W. Lampe, "The Holy Spirit in the Writings of Luke," in *Studies in the Gospels* (R.H. Lightfoot), (Oxford, 1955), 159-200; E. Schweitzer, *Pneuma,* in *TWNT* VI (1956). 402-410; U. Luck, "Kerygma, Tradition und Geschichte Jesu," *Zeitschrift für Theologie und Kirche,* 57 (1960), 51-66.

[52] Luke does not say that Mary was inspired to pronounce the Magnificat (1. 46). This may have been his way of implying that the Spirit came upon her in a special way.

Acts 2. 33); therefore, he is not subordinated to the Spirit.[53] Luke stresses the action of the Spirit within Jesus (4. 14, 18; 10. 21). Jesus possesses the Spirit; therefore, he is able to send it, a fact which Luke alone relates. The prophets of the Old Testament, on the other hand, were possessed by the Spirit at different moments of their lives. They were subordinated to it. The Spirit was not their abiding possession.

Jesus' sending of the Spirit to the disciples constitutes in the Lucan scriptures the first event in the life of the Church.[54] Jesus had promised to send it at the moment of his departure (24. 49; Acts 1. 4-5). He makes good his promise at Pentecost, when the Spirit becomes an ever-present reality within the Church (which Luke mentions 55 times in Acts). The Spirit is given to the Twelve for preaching the Word (Acts 2. 4, 14; 4. 31), for witnessing Jesus (4. 8; 5. 32), for directing their activity (5. 3, 9; 10. 10-29; 11. 12). He is given to preachers and missionaries for the same purposes (6. 10; 7. 55; 8. 29, 39; 13. 4, 9; 16. 6-7). He inspires the prophets (11. 28; 21. 4, 11). He is especially given to the faithful to constitute the messianic people foretold by the prophets (2. 38; 6. 3, 5; 8. 15-17; 9. 17, 31; 10. 44-47; 13. 52; 19. 6). Before Luke, the gospel tradition promised this gift of the Spirit to the disciples, in the announcements of the Baptist (Mtt. 3. 11; Mark 1. 8; Luke 3. 16) and in the words of encouragement which Jesus speaks on behalf of his witnesses who will be taken before the tribunals (Matt. 10. 29; Mark 13. 11; Luke 12. 12). Luke, however, adds to these promises in his Gospel: the gift of the Spirit is the supreme good that can be granted in response to prayer (11. 13, different from Matt. 7. 11); the blasphemy against the Spirit shall not be forgiven (12. 10, in the context of confessing Christ before the tribunals);[55] the promise of the Spirit in the final word of the pascal message (24. 49).

Luke was profoundly impressed by the gift of the Spirit to the Church. The place which he gives to the Spirit in his book of Acts indicates the key position occupied by this event in the life of the Church and in the perspective of Luke. It was clearly a sign of the divine intervention in the apostolic preaching; it was

---

[53] Cf. H. Conzelmann, *Die Mitte,* 168; E. Schweitzer, *art. cit.,* 402.

[54] A. George, "Tradition et rédaction chez Luc la construction du troisième évangile," *Ephemerides Theologicae Lovanienses,* 43 (1967), 123.

[55] Cf. H. Conzelmann, *Die Mitte,* 167; G. W. H. Lampe, *art. cit.,* 190.

evidence of the risen Jesus' activity within his Church.[56] This sign united the time of the Church with the time of Jesus and with the time of the prophets. He distinguished these three epochs because the action of the Spirit differs within each: the inspiration of the prophet, the fulness of the Spirit in Jesus, the charisms.[57] Luke's experience of the Spirit within the life of the early Church is an important source for his division of salvation history.

Luke teaches that the Church lives under the rule of Jesus Christ the Lord, who works through the Holy Spirit. G. K. Barrett observer that it is better to express the matter this way than in terms of the Spirit only, for not only is the Lord said to have poured forth the Spirit (Acts 2. 33). He is himself directly operative in the work of his people, so that the heavenly voice can say to Saul, "Why persecutest thou me?" (9. 4).[58] Luke assumes that Christians obey the orders of their Lord (9. 10-17); and that the Lord will not leave His people without the direction and support they need (18. 9). The usual agent of admonition and consolation is the Holy Spirit. Barrett remarks that Luke's conception of the Trinity is one in which the Father sends the Son, and the Son sends the Spirit; however, the operations of the Holy Spirit never bear any valuation lower than the operation of God.[59] He too is the Lord, in that when he commands men must obey (10. 19). It is characteristic of Acts that the activities of the Holy Spirit are especially outgoing. They convey the Gospel to new fields, both in impelling and directing evangelism (8. 29; 16. 6), and in equipping the evangelist (4. 8; 6. 5; 13. 9).

Through testimony to Christ in preaching the Word of God the Holy Spirit extends the kingdom God in Christ. The disciples and the evangelists proclaim the Word of God (*euaggelizethai*); those who hear and believe their preaching are said to receive the Word of God. When the Church is prospering Luke says that

---

[56] In Acts 16. 7, Luke writes of "the Spirit of Jesus" (the expression "the Spirit of the Lord" occurs in Acts 5. 9 and 8. 39). This unity of action between Jesus and the Spirit appears in Luke 21. 15 where there is attributed to Jesus the same role which is given to the Spirit in the traditional logion of Mt 10. 20 and Mk 13. 11, reproduced in Lk 12. 11-12.

[57] A. George, *art.cit.*, 124.

[58] C. K. Barrett, *Luke the Historian in Recent Study* (London, 1961), 68.

[59] *Ibid.*

the Word of God grows and multiplies.[60] Those who hear the message can be sure about it, because it is guaranteed by the prophets as a promise of the coming salvation and by the actuality of the resurrection by those who were eyewitnesses to the risen Christ (1.22; 3.15; 5.32).[61] The gift of the Holy Spirit leads the disciples to missionary work they had not planned. It is not man's design but God's that will be realized through the agency of the Holy Spirit.[62]

NOTES

R. H. SMITH, "History and Eschatology in Luke-Acts," *Concordia Theological Monthly* 29 (1958), 881-901. The mission of the Church is an eschatological sign. It bears witness to Christ before mankind. Now the Spirit is unleashed and is transforming the world. The Second Coming will effect the *apokatastasis,* the Messianic re-creation, as found in Acts 3.20.21.

---

[60] *Ibid.,* 69. The word occurs 32 times in Acts in this context.

[61] W. C. van Unnik, "The Book of Acts, the Confirmation of the Gospels," *Novum Testamentum* 4 (1960), 54.

[62] *Ibid.,* 57; V. Taylor, *The Person of Christ in N.T. Teaching* (London, 1958), 9, 12. "Like St. Mark, St. Luke also believes Jesus to be the Messiah. In fact, he uses the name "Christ" more frequently than Mark, but he rarely introduces it into the sayings of Jesus. In 24.26 and 46 he connects the title with suffering and death. This fact, together with the note of universalism in his Gospel, shows how decisively the Lucan idea of Messiahship has broken from its Jewish moorings. For St. Luke Jesus is a Saviour." (10)

Jesus is the Son of God because He is born of, and possessed by, the Spirit in a manner and to a degree never recorded in the Old Testament concerning the Patriarchs and Prophets. The Spirit plays an essential part in his birth, (1.35), baptism (3.22), desert experience (4.1), return to Galilee and Nazareth (4.18), prayer (10.21) and is ultimately promised to his disciples (24.49).

16.

THE TEMPTATION ACCOUNT IN ST. LUKE (4, 1-13)

Justin, Ireneaus, Tertullian and Origen interpreted the Temptation account in terms of the entire history of salvation. [1] Jesus is the New Adam. Unlike the first Adam, Jesus is victorious in his encounter with Satan. The Church Fathers gave greater importance to the Adam typology than to the Exodus typology. They also interpreted the Temptation as an adumbration of the Passion and of the future temptations of the Church. [2]

Chrysostum, Ambrose, Augustine, Jerome and Gregory the Great explained the Temptation from a moral and psychological perspective. [3] Jesus is an example for Christians in time of temptation. The temptations were concretized. Gluttony, vain glory, and ambition were respectively symbolized by the temptation to change stones into bread, to leap from the pinnacle of the Temple, and to acquire the kingdoms of this world.

Today, R. Bultmann, [4] G. Bornkamm [5] and W. Grundmann [6] deny the historicity of the Temptation; whereas, V. Taylor, [7] J. Jeremias, [8] and T. W. Manson [9] affirm it. For Bultmann the temptations are similar to those ascribed in other religious litera-

---

1 Cf. M. Steiner, *La tentation de Jésus dans l'interprétation patristique de Saint Justin à Origène* (Paris, 1962).

2 The patristic exegesis is especially typological and theological; it remains faithful to the basic sense of the Temptation. The messianic interpretation, common among contemporary exegetes, was the exception. It is found in Origen, Cf. Steiner, 154-158.

3 Cf. J. M. Vosté, *De baptismo, tentatione et transfiguratione Iesu* (Rome, 1934), 100-104.

4 *Die Geschichte der synoptischen Tradition* (2nd ed., Göttingen, 1931), 270-74.

5 *Jesus von Nazareth* (Heidelberg, 1956), 158.

6 *Die Geschichte Jesu Christi* (2nd ed., Berlin, 1959), 271.

7 *The Life and Ministry of Jesus* (London, 1955), 52-54.

8 *Die Gleichnisse Jesu,* (Göttingen, 1958), 105-106.

9 *The Sayings of Jesus* (London, 1949), 45.

ture to other holy men. A. Plummer asserts that the temptations arise from a natural mental reaction to the events of the preceding narrative of the baptism, inasmuch as times of spiritual exaltation are commonly followed by occasions of special temptation.[10]

In all three Gospels Jesus at the time of the Temptation is under the influence of the Holy Spirit. All the Gospels agree in using the word *peirazo* to describe the temptation;[11] in attributing the temptation to the devil (or to Satan, in Mark); in making the desert the location of the temptation; and in designating a forty-day duration, which is probably a reference to the fasts just mentioned, recalling the forty years of the temptation which Israel underwent in the desert.[12]

In the tradition common to Matthew and Luke, Jesus fasts during the temptations. The detail suggests the motivation for the first temptation and recalls the fasts of Moses (Ex. 34.28; Dt. 9.9) and of Elias (1 Kgs. 19.8). The threefold temptation is common to this tradition, although the order of the temptations is different. The third temptation in Matthew becomes the second in Luke and vice-versa.

Elements found in the Matthean account that are not found in the Lucan version include the "forty nights" (4.2) and the "high mountain" (4.8). Elements of the Marcan account lacking in the Lucan presentation are the "wild beasts" (1.15) and the ministering angels (1.13). Luke omits mention of the angels found in both Matthew and Mark because of his different perspective.

Luke alone employs the expression "full of the Holy Spirit" (4.1), a typically Lucan phrase (Acts 6.5; 7.55; 11.24).[13] The concluding verse distinguishes the Lucan edition from the others (4,13); it is the key to understanding the special purpose for which he recounts this story. Luke relates the story to the

---

[10] *Exegetical Commentary on St Matthew* (London, 1909), 35.

[11] This word is used in the LXX as an equivalent of *nissah*; thus, both the Greek and the Hebrew words mean to "test" or to "try" a person. God tests Abraham (Gn 22.1). The Hebrews put God to the test (Ex 17.2; Num 14.22; Dt 33.8).

[12] C.K. Barrett, *The Holy Spirit and the Gospel Tradition* (London, 1947), 51; W. P. Du Bose, *The Gospel in the Gospels* (London, 1911), 35-41.

[13] The seven deacons, Stephen and Barnabas (Acts 6.3-5; 7.55; 11.24) were also "filled with the Holy Spirit"; also, the beneficiaries of Pentecost, Peter and the first Christians and Paul receiving baptism (Acts 2.4; 4.8,31; 9.17).

Passion. He explicitly mentions that the devil departed from him for *"a while"* (4. 13), namely, until "the hour" of his passion, death and resurrection. Satan returns at the hour of the passion: "this is your hour, and the power of darkness" (22. 53; Acts 26. 18, where the power of darkness is identified with the dominion of Satan). The insistent demands for a sign which begin with the Temptation, continue to the end of Jesus' life with the mocking cry, "if you are the King of the Jews, save yourself!" (23. 37). The cry echoes Satan's "if you are the Son of God ..." (4. 3; 9).[14]

A. Feuillet believes that the Lucan account of the Passion points out the exemplary character of Jesus' temptation.[15] Jesus is the New Adam, the prototype of every Christian in temptation and in victory over it. This makes Jesus the antitype of the first Adam, who fell when tempted in paradise (Lk. 3. 38). Satan tempts Jesus less as Messiah than as an ordinary man. The temptation becomes an example for all the baptized, depicting Jesus as the model of human victory over temptation.

Much of Feuillet's argument is based on the genealogy of Jesus which in the Lucan edition (3. 23-38) appears immediately before the Temptation, and after the Baptism of Jesus.[16] Luke universalizes the genealogy more than Matthew, and extends it back to Adam. This links Jesus with the creation of the first Adam. Just as Adam represented a beginning for mankind, Jesus analogously represents a new beginning. Adam in 3, 38 is man made in the image of God; his derivation from God points to this divine image (Acts 17. 26) and to the true humanity of Jesus which corresponds to this creation. Luke does not conclude the genealogy with Adam as sinner but points to his divine origin. Thus, if the baptism of Jesus is the point of departure for a new

---

[14] C. B. Caird, *Saint Luke* (Pelican Gospel Commentary) (London, 1963), 79, notes another "echo" when he comments that the Temptation is a sequel to the Baptism. Jesus knows his unique vocation and rejects all unworthy interpretations of his baptismal experience in which he had heard the heavenly voice saying, "You are my beloved Son." Now Jesus hears another voice, "If you are the Son of God . . ." and he must discern whether it comes from the same source. Three times he concludes that the voice which prompts him to action is that of the devil.

[15] A. Feuillet, "Le récit Lucanien de la tentation (Lc 4, 1-13), *Biblica* (1959), 613-631.

[16] Several other biblical scholars have noted and argued from the unique-position of the genealogy. Cf. A. Hastings, *Prophet and Witness in Jerusalem* (London, 1958), 24; E. J. Tinsley, *The Gospel According to Luke* (Cambridge Bible Commentary) (London, 1965), 49-50.

humanity in which Jesus is the prototype of the baptized, Feuillet would conclude that the temptation of Jesus represents the divine exemplar of the baptized in their victory over the devil. If Jesus as the "beloved Son" (3. 22) has a unique dignity (Baptism), as true man he is comparable with others and can become an example to his own.

Feuillet's attempt to explain the Lucan edition of the Temptation in terms of the Adam typology assumes that the Temptation is formally related to the temptation of Adam and to those of Christians.[17] Luke gives no description of the Baptism and its circumstances that would substantiate the assumption that the Temptation account formally represents Jesus as the exemplar of the newly baptized in their struggle against the devil. Nor does the one explicit reference to Adam in the genealogy (3. 38) justify employing the Adam typology as the key to interpreting the Lucan Temptation account. I. de la Potterie's study of the literary structure of these pericopes clearly indicates that the genealogy is linked the Baptism pericope and not with the Temptation pericope.[18] The closeness of Adam's name to the Temptation pericope and the genuine parallelism between the temptation of Adam and that of Jesus explain why the Adam typology appealed to the Fathers as a means of interpreting this pericope. Paul explicitly expresses this typology in Rom. 5. 19, where he speaks of the opposition between the "disobedience of one man" and of "the obedience of one"; however, even if there is a true parallelism between the situations of Adam and of Christ, there is no evidence in the Lucan text that Luke had this in mind.

The main elements absent from the Lucan edition of the Temptation that are characteristic of the other editions are: (1) the fast of 40 days and *40 nights* (Mt. 4. 2); (2) the high mountain (Mt. 4. 8); (3) "He was with wild beasts" (Mk. 1. 13); (4) the ministering angels (Mt. 4. 11; Mk. 1. 13). The two Matthean elements suggest the Moses typology; the last two suggest a messianic interpretation. The high mountain is not a visionary conception as in Apoc. 21. 10, but suggests Pisgah, the mountain

---

[17] I. de la Potterie, *Excerpta Exegetica ex Evangelio Sancti Lucae,* informally published class notes (Rome, 1963-1964), 114, rejects Feuillet's interpretation of the Lucan Temptation account on this basis.

[18] *Ibid.,* 115.

from which Moses viewed the Promised Land.[19] So from this mountain Jesus views a possible kingdom which he rejects: the Messianic Kingdom would not be established in collaboration with Satan and his methods. Because the Messiah's kingdom is different, it is established in a completely different way. The wild beasts may represent a reminiscence of the friendly relation between Adam and the beasts in Paradise before the Fall.[20] The Messiah's victory over Satan would re-establish the idyllic conditions of primeval times, before the entry of sin into the world. The dominion over wild beasts is associated with conquest over Satan. The Messianic prophecies in Is. 11.6; Ez. 34.21; are important in this context, as well as Ps. 91, 11-13 and Job 5.23. In all these passages the wild beasts have, in different ways, ceased to be dangerous.[21] The theme of the ministering angels appears to be derived from Psalm 91, which in the Matthean context has a messianic sense. In his struggle against Satan, Jesus is attended by angels (Mt. 26.53). Both cases recall the miraculous feeding of Elias by angels (1 Kgs. 19.5).[22]

Furthermore the order of the temptations in the Lucan account of (1) stones, (2) kingdoms, (3) temple, does not correspond to the temptations of Israel in the desert; whereas, as J. Dupont has noted, the Matthean order of the temptations inverts that of Deuteronomy and corresponds perfectly with the order of the real Exodus events (Ex. 16; 17; 23.24).[23] The Israel typography is not suggested. In this respect the Lucan edition of the Temptation differs from that of Matthew, which interprets the temptations in the light of Israel's history.

Though all three Gospels agree that Jesus is under the influence of the Spirit at the time of the Temptation, the expressions in Mark and Matthew suggest that Jesus was constrained by the Spirit to go into the desert.[24] Mark 1.12 reads: "The

---

19 E. Klostermann, *Das Matthäusevangelium* (Berlin, 1927), 29.

20 J. Jeremias, *art.* "adam" in *Theologisches Wörterbuch zum neuen Testament*, I. ed. by G. Kittel (Stuttgart, 1933), 141.

21 C. K. Barrett, *The Holy Spirit*, 50.

22 *Ibid.*

29 J. Dupont, "Les tentations de Jésus dans le désert (Mt 4.1-13)," *Assemblées du Seigneur* 26 (1962), 37-53. "Les tentations de Jésus dans le récit de Luc (Lc 4.1-13)," *Sciences Ecclesiastiques* 14, (1962), 7-29.

24 E. Schweizer, *art.*, "Spirit of God" in *Bible Key Words* III, tr. D. Barton, P. Ackroyd, A. Harvey (New York, 1960), 37.

Spirit cast him out into the desert"; in contrast, the Lucan version reads: "Jesus being full of the Holy Spirit returned ... and was led in the Spirit into the desert." Luke avoids giving the impression that the Spirit is an agent set over Jesus. He is not satisfied with the Old Testament idea of the Spirit seizing a man. As Lord and agent "in" (not "by") the Holy Spirit, Jesus goes into the desert under the inspiration of the Holy Spirit. Luke introduces the Spirit again in 4. 14, and from then on the dominant description of Jesus is that of one who possesses the power of the Spirit. This is the first instance of the Holy Spirit's being a power in the struggle against Satan. Luke's use of *plērēs,* as opposed to *plestheis,* indicates that Jesus is continually full of the Holy Spirit (4. 1-2).[25] The descent of the Spirit upon Jesus at the Baptism (3. 22) is a great eschatological reality which inaugurates the final conflict between the "power" of the devil (4. 6), or the "power of the enemy" (10. 19) and the "power" of the Spirit (4. 14) which motivates Jesus. These three texts on power in the context of the eschatological struggle between Jesus and the devil are found in Luke alone.

G. W. H. Lampe notes that Luke alone emphasizes the completeness of Jesus' Spirit-possession in connection with the Temptation, and so brings the struggle with the devil within the scope of the Spirit's operation.[26] Victory over the forces of evil, as well as the exercise of wisdom and judgment, was part of the work of the Spirit-possessed messianic leader prophesied by Isaiah, and the activity of the Holy Spirit is often associated by Luke with the conflict against the adversary (e. g. 10. 21). The Lucan text indicates that both the action of the Spirit and the temptations extended over a period of forty days.[27]

In the first temptation (4. 3-4) two Lucan peculiarities stand out. Jesus is tempted to turn a stone into bread; in the Matthean version he is tempted to turn stones into loaves. The Lucan temptation offers the solution to one man's hunger; whereas Matthew's use of the plural suggests the Israel typology and Dt. 8. 2, which refers to the forty years of trial in the desert and

---

[25] *Ibid.*

[26] G. W. H. Lampe, "The Holy Spirit in the Writings of St Luke," in *Studies in the Gospels in Memory of R. H. Lightfoot,* ed. D. E. Nineham (Oxford, 1955), 170.

[27] I. de la Potterie, *Excerpta Exegetica,* 116.

the miracle of the manna. The Temptation in Matthew suggests a repetition of the miracle of the manna, which was expected in messianic times; in Luke, the Temptation has a more personal character. Secondly, in the first two temptations, the citation of Deuteronomy in Christ's response is briefer in Luke than in Matthew; whereas the devil's conversation is longer in Luke than in Matthew.

In the second temptation (4. 5-8) the Lucan text differs from Matthew's in several ways. Luke makes no mention of the mountain from which all the kingdoms of the world are seen. The omission can be explained by the phrase "in a moment of time", which implies that Christ was not physically transported to a high place, and that he did not actually view with his eyes all the kingdoms of the world. This would be clearly impossible. The devil tempts Jesus with an internal, imagined, ecstatic view. [28] Grundmann believes that the expression "he took him up" (*anagagon*) suggests the apocalyptic and visionary character of the event. [29]

The Lucan expression "of the world" (*oikoumenēs*) (2. 1; 21. 26; Acts 11. 26; 17. 6. 31; 19. 27; 24. 5) designates the inhabited universe and suggests the political character of the devil's offer of world dominion. [30]

Luke's editing of this pericope is also noteworthy for the addition of the world "authority" (*exousia*). [31] The devil claims authority over the world. This authority, he claims, has been committed (*paradedotai*) to him, and he can apparently hand it on to whomsoever he wishes. The word *exousia* often occurs in Luke in the context of political power, (7. 8; 12. 11; 19. 17; 20. 20; 23. 7). Political authority is offered to Jesus. Luke alone, of all the Synoptics, speaks of the "power" of the devil. It is a power which "has been given" to him, the "power of darkness" mentioned in the Passion account (22. 53), and described in Acts 26. 18 as "the power of Satan". It is the apocalyptic and eschatological concept of the opposition of two kingdoms which was common in Judaism and the primitive Church. John writes of "the prince of this world" (12. 31; 14. 30; 16. 11). Luke would

---

[28] *Ibid.*, 117.
[29] W. Grundmann, *Das Lukas Evangelium* (Berlin, 1961), 116.
[30] I. de la Potterie, *Excerpta Exegetica*, 117.
[31] *Ibid.*

seem to have had contact with the Johannine tradition, which might explain the literary similarity of this text with Apoc. 13. 1-8, where the "dragon" (12. 9) represents Satan and gives authority (*exousian*) to the "beast", to the Roman Empire, and is "adored" by men (12. 4. 12).[32]

Of all the verses of the Temptation account these two have undergone the greatest transformation in the Lucan edition. In these verses Luke underscores the *political power* which the devil offers Jesus, and the *apocalyptic* and *eschatological aspect* which is grounded in Satan's universal world power.

In the third temptation (4. 9-12) Luke alone mentions that Jesus is taken "to Jerusalem". In Lucan theology the city has especial importance. I. de la Potterie, noting the contrasts in the literary structure of the Lucan and Matthean accounts, concludes that Luke focuses the temptations on Jerusalem.[33]

The entire verse 13 is a Lucan addition: "And when the devil had ended every temptation, he departed from him for a while." The victory of Jesus is definitive: the devil could not really "tempt" him. The devil's retreat is merely temporary; he will return at the Passion. Luke alone cites the moment of Satan's return: "Satan entered into Judas" (22. 3); and, when Jesus is apprehended at Gethsemane (22. 53), he declares "This is your hour and the power of darkness". H. Conzelmann[34] and R. Schnackenburg[35] do not believe that Jesus underwent temptations in a moral sense; rather, he experienced trials.

Luke situates the last temptation in Jerusalem to stress the close connection between the desert episode and the Passion. In both cases Jesus is attacked by the devil. The Passion, in the Lucan account, is especially the devil's "hour". The Temptation prefigures the Passion in Jerusalem and underscores its importance.

In contrast with Luke, Matthew stress the messianic aspect of the Temptation, interpreting it with the typology of the Old

---

[32] M. E. Boismard. "Rapprochements littéraires entre l'Evangile de Luc et l'Apocalypse," in *Synoptische Studien A. Wikenhauser dargebracht* (Berlin, 1950), 53-63.

[33] Cf. *Excerpta Exegetica,* 118.

[34] *Die Mitte der Zeit* (Gottingen, 1964), 22.

[35] R. Schnackenburg, "Der Sinn der Versuchung Jesu bei den Synoptikern," *Theologische Quartalschrift* 132 (1952), 324-325.

Testament, and endowing it with a parenetic tone.[36] Luke, on the other hand, directs attention to the future events of Christ's Passion, and endows the Temptation with an eschatological and apocalyptic orientation.[37] Jesus opposes the "power" of the devil. His interpretation is more soteriological: Jesus' victory over the devil is our salvation. There is nothing in his account which directly suggests a parenetic orientation. Both Synoptics situate the Temptation in the wider framework of salvation history: Matthew links it with the past phase and Luke with a future phase. In each case the insertion of the Temptation pericope into the overall context of salvation history endows it with a deeper significance.

The concept of the devil which underlies the Temptation account corresponds to the reality of Jesus' life and to his experience (Mk. 1. 23-24; Mt. 12. 29; Lk. 10. 18). His mission involved a genuine struggle against the power of Satan. The early Church believed that Jesus had defeated Satan through his suffering, death, and resurrection (10. 13. 31; 16. 11; 1 Jn. 3. 8; Apoc. 20. 2-10).[38]

The three temptations do not correspond to the temptations of Christians as described in the epistles of the New Testament. They are genuinely messianic: they are the temptations of the Messiah, not of an ordinary individual.[39] They occur after Jesus has received his mission from his Father (Baptism), and before the beginning of his mission. This position suggests the close connection of the Temptation with the mission of Jesus and its messianic character, in the Matthean account, and its soteriological character in the Lucan account.

The *fact* of the Temptation cannot be convincingly explained unless it corresponds to an historical reality.[40] It could only be known if Christ himself had related it; and this is not unlikely, especially since Christ was careful to correct the messianic views of his disciples.[41] The *way* in which the Temptation took place

---

[36] I. de la Potterie, *Excerpta Exegetica,* 119.
[37] *Ibid.*
[38] *Ibid.*, 123.
[39] C. G. Montefiore, *Synoptic Gospels* I (2nd ed., London, 1927), 20.
[40] I. de la Potterie, *Excerpta Exegetica,* 124.
[41] V. Taylor, *The Person of Christ in the New Testament Teaching* (London, 1958), 10, comments: "Like St. Mark, St. Luke also believes Jesus to be the Messiah. In fact, he uses the name 'Christ' more frequently than

should not be interpreted in a literal sense. The event was by all means a real, interior experience, more profoundly significant than the more externalized, literal interpretation in which Jesus would actually have been taken up to the high mountain and to Jerusalem's Temple pinnacle.

CONCLUSION

The temptation of Christ (Lk 4. 1-13) has a unique sense. Although the passion represents the devil's renewed attack against Jesus, it is not a new temptation. Luke's deletion of Satan's designation as "the tempter" (cf. Mt 4. 3) emphasizes the uniqueness of the scene, indicating that the devil is not exercising here his typical function which he also exercises with regard to the faithful (I Thes 3. 5).[42] This temptation does not have any counterpart in the life of the Christian; rather, it is the unique experience of the son of God (Lk 4. 3). Form critics, in line with typical patristic exegesis, understood Jesus conduct as an example for the faithful. Recent scholarship stresses the exclusively messianic character of the temptation,[43] which is conceived as a cosmic event in which Satan attempts to impede the accomplishment of the divine plan of salvation.[44] It is not a crisis of faith in Jesus' personal religious life. Instead of obstructing the divine plan, the devil's attack occasions the opposite effect: Jesus sets out on his Way from Jerusalem to Galilee (4. 14a), his fame spreads throughout the entire region (4. 14b), his teaching receives universal acclaim (4. 15) and culminates in the proclamation of his messianic program in the synagogue in Nazareth (4. 16-21).

Mark, but he rarely introduces it into the sayings of Jesus. In xxiv. 26 and 46 he connects the title with suffering and death. This fact, together with the note of universalism in his Gospel, shows how decisively the Lukan idea of Messiahship has broken from its Jewish moorings."

[42] S. Brown, *Apostasy and Perseverance in the Theology of Luke* (Rome, 1969), 17.

[43] R. Schnackenburg, "*Der Sinn der Versuchung Jesu bei den Synoptikern,*" *Theologische Quartalschrift* 132 (1952), 298, 312.

[44] B. Noack, *Satanas und Soteria* (Copenhagen, 1948), 85-86.

NOTE

S. Legasse, "'L'homme fort' de Luc. xi. 21-22," *Novum Testamentum* 5 (1962), 5-9. This parable, connected with the Beelzebul controversy, suggests that there was a tradition in the Church which identified Jesus with the stronger man who overcomes Satan, the strong one. Judaism offers the basis for this tradition (Isa 53.12). There would seem to be a link between the Christology of the "stronger" and the Servant theology in Judaism. Christ gives the Church the results of his victory. In Luke as in the other Synoptics the strong man is Satan; however, in the Lucan account the evil overcome by Christ is riches, possessions which (Acts 4.34) are appropriately distributed to the needy.

A Bibliography for the Temptation Account

Baumach, J., *Das Verständnis des Bösen in den synopsischen Evangelien* (Berlin, 1963).

Charlier, C., "Les tentations de Jésus au désert," *Bible et Vie Chrétienne* 5 (1954), 85-92.

Corbon, J., "Epreuve - Tentation," in Léon-Dufour, ed., *Vocabulaire de Théologie Biblique* (Paris, 1962).

Derousseaux, L., "L'épreuve et la tentation," *Assemblées du Seigneur* 26 (1912), 54-68.

Dupont, J., "L'arrière-fond biblique du récit des tentations de Jésus," *New Testament Studies* 3 (1956-57), 287-304.

—, "Les tentations de Jésus dans le récit de Luc (Luc, 4, 1-13), *Sciences Ecclésiastiques* 16 (1962), 7-29.

—, "Les tentations de Jésus dans le désert (Mt 4.1-11)," *Assemblées du Seigneur* 26 (1962), 37-53.

Duquoc, C., "La tentation du Christ," *Lumière et Vie* 53 ("La tentation") (1961), 21-41.

Fascher, E., *Jesus und der Satan* (Halle, 1949).

Guillet, J., *Thèmes bibliques* (Paris, 1951).

Feuillet, A., "Le récit lucanien de la tentation (Lc 4, 1-13)," *Biblica* 40 1959), 613-621.

—, "L'épisode de la tentation d'après l'Evangile selon saint Marc (1.12-13)," *Estudios Biblicos* 19 (1960), 49-73.

Holzmeister, U., "Jesus lebte mit den wilden Tieren," in *Festschrift Meinertz* (1951), 85-92.

Lohmeyer, E., "Die Versuchung Jesus," in *Zeitschrift für syst. Theologie* 14 (1931); now however in *Urchristliche Mystik.* Neutestamentliche Studien, (Darmstad, 1958), 81-122.

Nestle, E., "The Pinnacle of the Temple," *Expository Times* 23 (1911), 184-185.

Noack, B., *Satanas und Soteria. Untersuchungen zur neutestamentlichen Dämonologie* (Copenhagen, 1948).

Riesenfeld, H., " Le caractère messianique de la tentation an désert," in *La venue du Messie* (Recherches bibliques, VI), (Désclée de Brouwer, 1962), 51-63.

Robinson, J. A. T., "The Temptations," *Theology* 50 (1947)), 43-48.

Sabbe, M., *De tentatione Iesu in deserto, Coll. Brugenses et Gandevenses* 50 (1954), 459-465.

Schnackenburg, R., "Der Sinn der Versuchung Jesu bei den Synoptikern," *Theologische Quartalschrift* 132 (1952), 297-326.

Schulze, W. A., "Der Heilige und die Wilden Tiere," *Zeitschrift für die Neutestamentliche Wissenschaft* 37 (1955), 280-284.

Spitta, F., "Die Tiere in der Versuchungsgeschichte," *Zeitschrift für die Neutestamentliche Wissenschaft* 5 (1904), 66-68.

Steiner, M., *La tentation de Jésus dans l'interprétation patristique de Saint Justin à Origène* (Paris, 1962).

Thompson, G. H. P., "Called-Proved-Obedient," A Study in the Baptism and Temptation Narrative of Matthew and Luke, *Journal of Theological Studies* 11 (1960), 1-12.

Van Iersel, B., "Der Sohn" in den synoptischen Jesusworten: Christus-Bezeichnung der Gemeinde oder Selbstbezeichnung Jesu? (Leiden, 1961), 165-171.

Vosté, I. M., *De Baptismo, Tentatione et Transfiguratione Iesu* (Rome, 1934).

17.

"TODAY" AND "NOW"

The entire Third Gospel is presented as the fulfillment of messianic time. The frequency with which Luke employs the adverbs "now" (*nun*) and "today" (*semeron*) underscores the fact that the time of salvation has begun with Christ. Thus "now" occurs 14 times in the Third Gospel and 25 times in Acts; whereas, in Matthew and Mark it occurs only 3 times. "Today" occurs 11 times in the Gospel and 8 times in Acts; it occurs 8 times in Matthew and once in Mark. Some of the main texts are the following:

2. 11 — Today in the town of David a savior has been born to you.

3. 22 — You are my beloved son, today I have begotten you (= Ps 2. 7).

4. 21 — Today this scripture has been fulfilled even as you listen.

12. 52 — From now on a household of five will be divided ...

19. 5 — Today I must stay at your home ...

19. 9 — Today salvation has come to this house.

23. 43 — Today you will be with me in Paradise.

From the time of Christ's appearance something has been essentially changed in human relationships (12. 52); the "today" of Christ's presence (19. 5, 9) marks the beginning of eschatological time, even though the "parousia" is in some way more distant. Luke clearly distinguishes the successive events within eschatological time. The time of Christ and that of the Church are treated respectively in the Third Gospel and the Acts of the Apostles. Both constitute that eschatological time, inaugurated by Christ and extending throughout history. The life of Christ and that of the Church belong to the time of salvation.

The "today" of which Jesus speaks in his inagural sermon in the synagogue at Nazareth is the time within which a decision must be made for or against him. Flender comments on its threefold significance: (1) it is related to the historical past which it fulfills; (2) to the exalted Christ who speaks today; (3) and to all men who hear the word of God through Christ and his apostles.[1]

The "today" of the inaugural sermon identifies Christ with a past attested by the Old Testament prophecies and which is at this moment being fulfilled as men listen to him. It is the "today" of salvation (4. 18) offered to all who hear Christ. It rivets Jesus to history and remains the continuing "today" of the fulfillment of God's historical promises to his people. It is the "today" which indicates the presence of the kingdom and reign of God in Christ and in his Church. It is the "today" of salvation which is proclaimed in history. Only faith recognizes its arrival and existence.

In the Lucan perspective, Christian life within the Church is in some way anticipated in the life of Christ as it is presented in the Third Gospel. This Lucan parallelism bespeaks the connection between eschatology and parenesis: the baptism of Jesus parallels Pentecost, the baptism of the Church (3. 21-22/Acts 2. 1); the inaugural sermon of Jesus parallels the inaugural sermon of Peter, in that both are largely based on prophetic texts concerning the eschatological activity of the Spirit of God 4. 16-19/Acts 2. 17); Jesus, Stephen and Paul are "cast out" by their hearers (4. 29/Acts 7. 58; 13. 50); the sermons of Jesus and Peter heal many people (4. 40-41/Acts 2. 43; 5. 16); the death of Jesus is paralleled by that of Stephen (22. 69/Acts 7. 56; 23. 46/Acts 7. 59; 23. 34/Acts 7. 60).

The eschatological time of salvation is "Today"; it is "Now". Thus, Luke sometimes gives a parenetic orientation to the more primitive texts of Mark and Matthew, which had a directly messianic and escchatological sense. This follows from the fact that eschatology in the strict sense of the *parousia* became a more remote concern for Luke; in the meantime, he applied these texts

---

[1] H. Flender, *St. Luke Theologian of Redemptive History*, tr. R. and I. Fuller (London, 1967), 151-152.

to Christian life in the present intermediate period.[2] The change in focus from the second coming of Christ to contemporary Christian living appears in the following texts:

6. 21-25 — Happy you who are hungry *now*... Alas for you who laugh *now*.
9. 23 — Let him take up his cross *daily* and follow me.
21. 19 — Your endurance will win you your lives.

The second text (9. 23) is found in Luke alone; however, it is not a primitive text with the dramatic and realistic sense that it had in the life of Jesus.[3] Relevance to daily Christian living endows it with a value that is primarily parenetic. The third text (21. 19), which treats primarily of the Christian virtue of patience, has also undergone a change in focus. In the other Synoptics (Mt 10. 22/Mk 13. 13) the text concerned salvation from eschatological tribulation: "... but the man who stands firm to the end will be saved."[4]

---

[2] I. de la Potterie, *Excerpta Exegetica Ex Evangelio Sancti Lucae,* the informally published class notes (Rome, 1963-64), 39-40.
[3] *Ibid.,* 40.
[4] *Ibid.*

18.

UNIVERSALISM

The Gospel of Mark begins with a quotation from Isaiah 40. 3: "Prepare the way of the Lord." By continuing this quotation two verses farther to include Isaiah 40. 5, Luke emphasizes that "the way of the Lord" leads to the Gentiles: "And all mankind shall see the salvation of God" (3. 6).[1] In his inaugural sermon in the synagogue of Nazareth, Jesus speaks of the non-Israelites who were blessed of old (4. 25-27). At Pentecost representatives of all nations are present (Acts 2. 5-7). The theme of Isaiah 40. 5 is the closing word of the Lucan portrayal of the course of the way (Acts 28. 28): "Understand, then, that this 'salvation of God' has been sent 'to the Gentiles'; they will listen." Thus Luke begins and finishes his Gospel-Acts with a text which underscores the way of God's universal salvation for the Gentiles.

Simeon takes Jesus into his arms at the Presentation in the Temple and prophecies that his eyes have seen the salvation which God has prepared "for all the nations to see' (2. 30). The fulfillment of his prophecy is seen at Pentecost and in Paul's final words at the end of Acts. The revelation of Jesus is "a light to enlighten the Gentiles and the glory of your people Israel" (2. 32). It fulfills the prophecy of Isaiah in which the Lord tells his servant that he has appointed him as a "light to the Gentiles, to open the eyes of the blind, and to free captives from prison, and those who live in darkness from the dungeon" (Isa 42. 6-7).

The history of salvation has a universal scope from the creation of all things (Acts 17. 24-28; 14. 15; *cf.* Lk 3. 38) to the universal restoration which God has proclaimed through his prophets (Acts 3. 21), and to the universal judgment which God has deter-

---

[1] W. C. Robinson, *The Way of the Lord* (Dissertation for University of Basle, 1960), 61.

mined (Acts 17.31; *cf.* 1.7; 10.42).[2] The universalism of the divine plan of salvation is progressively clarified by the course of events "beginning from Jerusalem" (Lk 24.47) and extending to Rome (Acts 1.8).

The universalism of the Christian mission is adumbrated in Jesus' sermon in the synagogue at Nazareth (4.16-30). Jesus is depicted as the prophet in the tradition of Elias who is rejected by his own people, who thrust him out of the city.[3] Jesus will perform his miracles elsewhere just as Elias performed his outside of Israel. His reference to Naaman and the widow of Sarepta adumbrates the calling of the Gentiles, just as the behavior of Nazareth implied the behavior of Israel. Tihs incident is paralled by that of the Apostles who are rejected by the Jews and turn to the Gentiles (Acts 13.50).

The Samaritans occupy a special place in Lucan writings. Jesus corrects his disciples for wishing to punish the Samaritans (9.52). A Samaritan is an example of goodness in the Parable of the Good Samaritan (10.13). Only the Samaritan leper returns to thank him for his miracle (10.18). Luke omits Jesus' injunction forbidding entry into Samaritan towns (Mt 10.5). Samaria is the locus of transition between the apostolic preaching to the Jews and to the Gentiles (Acts 1.8; 4.25; 9.31).

Luke shows special concern for pagans. He remarks that Tyre and Sidon shall not be judged so severely as Chorazin, Bethsaida and Capernaum (10.13-15). He alone narrates the cure of the Gerasene (8.26-39). In the story of the centurion servant (7.1-10), Luke stresses the merits of the centurion more than Matthew (7.2,9). There would seem to be a parallel with the conversion of the centurion in Acts 10.1-3. Luke also omits statements that could offend Gentiles; consequently the story of the Canaanite woman does not appear (Mk 7.24-30 = Mt 15.21-28).

Lucan universalism also appears in the context of Jesus' journey to Jerusalem when the question is asked about those who shall be saved (13.23). Jesus answers that the first (Israelites) shall be last and that the last (Gentiles) shall be first (13.30). The sense of the pericope is eschatological and prophetic "And men from east and west, from north and south, *will come* to

---

2 E. Stauffer, *New Testament Theology*, tr. J. Marsh (London, 1963), 27.
3 A. Hastings, *Prophet and Witness in Jerusalem* (London, 1958), 100.

take their places at the feast in the kingdom of God" (13. 29).[4] This theme is expressed in Ps 106, in Isaiah (45. 14-17; 49. 12), Jeremiah (12. 15-16) and in Malachy (1. 11). The theme concerns the pilgrimage of all peoples, Jews and Gentiles, to Mt. Sion to create the new Jerusalem in which there will be perfect messianic happiness. All nations will assemble with Abraham, Isaac and Jacob to form the messianic kingdom.

Universalism is not the dominant Lucan theme; nevertheless, it is found in Lucan writings to a far greater degree than in those of the other Synoptics. Luke underscores the theme of universal salvation and world mission by his use of prophetic texts from the Old Testament. These texts are found in his Gospel and in Acts, demonstrating that both the mission of Jesus and that of his Church are united in the plan of God for the salvation of all nations. If Jesus did not evangelize the Gentiles, it was not for lack of a universal vision. The evangelization of the Gentiles, with its proclamation of universal salvation, is a great eschatological event for which Jesus had paved the way. The disciples continue on the way of the Lord, "beginning from Jerusalem" (Lk 24. 47) and leading to "the ends of the earth" (Acts 1. 8; 13. 47).

The universal scope of the divine plan for the salvation of mankind is implied by the Spirit which leads the way (Lk 4. 1, 14; Acts 16. 6-10).[5] Both the public ministry of Jesus and the Church are marked by the descent of the Holy Spirit. In the synagogue at Nazareth where the public ministry of Jesus begins, he reads from Isaiah 61 that the Spirit of the Lord is upon him (4. 16-18); at Pentecost the Spirit is poured out on those who are to be Jesus' witnesses even "to the ends of the earth" (Acts 1. 8).

---

[4] I. de la Potterie, *Excerpta Exegetica ex Evangelio Sancti Lucae,* informally published notes (Roma, 1963-64), 16.

[5] C. K. Barrett, *Luke the Historian in Recent Study* (London, 1961), 67-68.

19.

THE WAY OF THE LORD

Luke seems to have viewed the continuity of salvation history as a course (*dromon*) or a way (*'odos*). He may have derived this concept from his reading of Mark (1, 1) "Beginning of the gospel of Jesus Christ. As it is written in Isaiah the prophet... 'A voice of one crying in the wilderness: Prepare the way of the Lord, make straight his paths.'"[1]

The Marcan account began with a citation of Isaiah 40, 3: "prepare the way of the Lord". Luke continues the quotation two verses farther to include Isaiah 40, 5. He thereby emphasizes (30, 6) that "the way of the Lord" leads to the Gentiles: "and all flesh shall see the salvation of God." Further traces of Lucan universalism appear when at Nazareth Jesus spoke of non-Israelites who were blessed of old (Lk. 4, 25ff) and at Pentecost the representatives of the nations were present (Acts 2, 5ff). Isaiah 40, 5 closes Luke's portrayal of the way (Acts 28, 28): "therefore be it known to you that this 'salvation of God' is sent 'to the Gentiles' — and they will listen." Luke begins and ends his presentation with this text which underscores the way of the Lord to the Gentiles.

Luke's terminology reveals that the stages in his history of salvation are defined in terms of times fixed by God and are presented as a way travelled by the protagonists at each stage.[2] Paul's sermon at Antioch (Acts 13, 16ff.) clearly states Luke's

---

1 W. C. Robinson, *The Way of the Lord. A Study of History and Eschatology in the Gospel of Luke,* a doctoral dissertation accepted at the University of Basel (Basel, 1960) questions Conzelmann's interpretation of Luke in *Die Mitte der Zeit* and suggests that Luke's main theme is his notion of "way", which envisages the activity of Jesus as a journey, "the way of the Lord." This concept is treated in a subdivision pp. 61-69, of the dissertation.

2 H. J. Cadbury, *The Making of Luke-Acts* (London, 1958), p. 231f.

theology of history. Lucan terminology portrays the history of salvation as a way: "As John was finishing his course (*dromon*), he said..." (13, 25). John's preaching preceded Jesus' entrance (*eisodos,* 13, 24).

The public ministry of Jesus is depicted as a way (13, 33): "It is necessary for me to be on my way today and tomorrow and the day following, for it is impossible that a prophet should die outside Jerusalem;" and Lk. 22, 22: "The Son of man goes as it has been determined" [3] At the Transfiguration Moses and Elias spoke with Jesus in the terminology of a way (9, 31): "they spoke of his *exodus*." [4] The Christian movement is called "the way" (9, 2; 19, 9 and 23; 22, 4; 24, 14 and 22). Apostleship is defined in terms of a trip (1, 21f.); Paul's farewell address at Miletus refers to the conclusion of his ministry as the completion of his course (*dromon*).

Luke expresses the history of salvation in the terminology of a way. His narrative corresponds to the concept of a way so as to suggest an orderly movement along a way or course. This concept of salvation history appears throughout his Gospel. Luke has schematized the first part of Mark's account of Jesus' ministry in Galilee to present a pragmatic and orderly course of movement. They way began in Nazareth (4, 16), extended to Capharnum (4, 31) and continued "thoughout all Judea" (4, 44). [5] The completeness of Jesus' ministry is expressed spatially by the phrase, "throughout all Judea" (23, 5; Acts 10, 37); it is expressed temporally by the phrase "during the whole time," (Acts 1, 21).

The way of the Lord is the way Jesus has gone as the leader of his people. The way recapitulates the familiar Old Testament pattern of disaster and restoration, and, as the Joseph stories insist, of the contrast between the machinations of evil men and the good counsel of God.

The outline of this theme is already drawn in the episode at Nazareth which Luke has serves as the introduction to the rest of his Gospel and Acts. Jesus announces himself as the

---

[3] F. Hauck and Schulz, art. *poreusma, TWNT,* VI, p. 574.

[4] W. Michaelis, *TWNT,* V, 111 n. 13; B. Reicke, *TWNT,* VI, p. 685, p. 20f.

[5] W. C. Robinson, p. 6 states that Luke does not always express the orderly course of saving events with topographical emphasis. Luke avoids Mark's disjointed collection of episodes and creates a chain of events by modifying the introductions to sections in 5. 17-6, 11 = Mk. 2. 1-3. 6).

prophet sent by God to preach a gospel and to heal, indicates the universal scope of his mission, is rejected and, like Stephen in Acts 7, 48, is thrown out of the city to be killed. Yet he passes through the midst of his would-be destroyers and goes on his way. The word used to describe this (*Poreuomai*) is also used in Luke 22, 22 and 33 of his journey to death, and in Acts 1. 10f. of the ascension to heaven or to the Father.

Luke does not permit the way to return to Galilee after the death of Jesus in Jerusalem, because the next stage of the way must "begin from Jerusalem" (Lk. 24, 47; Acts 1, 8). Consequently. Luke changes the statement to the women at the tomb: Mk. 16, 7 reads "say to his disciples and to Peter that he goes before you into Galilee; there you will see him, as he said to you." Lk. 24, 6 reads "Remember how he spoke to you, while he was still in Galilee, saying the Son of man must be given over into the hands of sinners...." The course of the way in Acts is familiar: "beginning from Jerusalem" (Lk. 24, 47) and extending to Rome (Acts 1, 8).

According to Luke's theological understanding, the way is an actualization of God's purpose. The way of Jesus is laid out for him. The Son of Man indeed goes his designated way (22, 22). The writings of Luke bear witness to the mysterious 'must' (*dei*).[6] God's providence has determined that Jesus must enter into the home of Zaccheus for salvation had come to that house that day (19, 5 and 9). Jesus had to leave Capharnum because he had been sent to preach in all the cities of Israel (4, 42f.). This "must" governs every step on the way of the Lord, which God had ordained from the beginning. The way is foretold in scripture chiefly as a way of suffering (22, 37). The divine plan guarantees that along this way there is neither accident nor chance.

The word *dei* is used with special frequency in Luke, where it occurs forty-four times out of hundred and two times in the whole NT.[7] It expresses submission to the will of God, which personally summons men and which fashions history according to its plan. Jesus is always submissive to this will (4, 43; 13, 33; 22, 37; 24, 44, and, in the context of the passion, 9, 22; 17, 24; 24, 7

[6] G. W. H. Lampe, "The Lucan Portrait of Christ," *New Testament Studies* 2 (1955-56), p. 167.

[7] E. Stauffer, *New Testament Theology*, tr. J. Marsh (London, 1963), p. 26.

and 26). Jesus' witnesses also obey the same divine will (Acts 5, 29; 9, 7; 16:14, 22, etc.).

In this context those Lucan passages should be noted which concern the futility of trying to withstand God. Gamaliel warns the Sanhedrin not to oppose God (Acts 5, 39). Peter defends himself in the case of Cornelius: "Who was I that I could withstand God?" (11, 17). The risen Christ tells Paul: "It hurts you to kick against the goad" (26, 14); nor can Paul resist his vision (11, 19).

Luke's view of the divine purpose applies to Jesus' life prior to his ministry (2, 49). Within his ministry it is applied to his suffering, death and resurrection (9, 22; 17, 25; 24, 7 and 26; Acts 3, 21). Subsequent to Jesus' earthly ministry the will of God includes Jesus' Ascension into heaven until the restoration of all things according to the prophecies (24, 26; Acts 3, 21).[8]

The Lucan statements on the range of Christ's way are rooted in a faith that the historical course which Christ followed has its origin and termination in a world beyond this. Jesus spoke repeatedly about the eschatological future of the Son of Man, whom all peoples will see at the end coming to judge mankind.[9] The way of the Lord stretches from the beginning to the end of time.

God's purpose appears in the term "designate" (*orizo*),[10] (22, 22, Acts 3, 21; 4, 28): "The Son of Man goes his designated way, but woe to that man by whom he is betrayed." Then risen Christ is designated by God as the judge of the living and the dead (Acts 10, 42; 17, 31). Paul's course is also "designated" by the divine purpose (*dei* — Acts 9, 16; 14, 22; 19, 21; 23, 11; *procheirizomai* — 22, 14; 26, 16).

The Spirit leads the way (4, 1 and 14; Acts 16, 6-10), expressing the divine purpose. In the sermon opening his public ministry at Nazareth (4, 16ff.), Jesus read from Isaiah 61 "the Spirit of the Lord is upon me" and said "today the scripture is fulfilled". The Spirit is poured out on those who are to be witnesses in the ministry of the Church, and the prophecy of Joel is fulfilled (Acts 2).

---

[8] H. Flender, *St. Luke Theologian of Redemptive History*, tr. R. and I. Fuller (London, 1967), p. 143 n. 4.

[9] W. C. Robinson, p. 65.

[10] E. Stauffer, p. 27.

Though the Spirit's guidance the divine plan of salvation is realized in the community. The divine economy of salvation is designated by the term *boule* (7, 30; Acts 20, 27 and, with reference to Christ only, Acts 2, 23; 4, 28; 5, 38). Many compounds of this word occur with the prefix *pro-*. One group of these compounds deals with divine predestination. Christ (Acts 3, 20), the witnesses of the resurrection (10, 41), Paul (22, 14; 26, 16), and even Jesus' adversaries (4, 28), are said to be predestined (= designated) by God to do certain things. The other groups refer to the word of God in scripture, which is seen beforehand in vision (2, 31), proclaimed beforehand (3, 18; 7, 52; 13, 24), prophesied (1, 16), and thus associated with divine predestination (= designation).[11]

This does not mean that the course of the history of salvation denies man's freedom of choice. The Jews could have acted differently. The Church is the Spirit-guided community following the way of the Lord. At times the Spirit persuades its members to act otherwise than they would have done. Divine providence stands alongside of blindness to God's ways on the part of his witnesses. They must wait for the Spirit to show them the way (Acts 13, 1f.; 1, 14). The Spirit guides Peter to the Gentile mission, although he had objected three times to it (10. 9ff.). Contrary to the itinerary which he had planned for himself, Paul is guided to Europe (16, 6ff.).

The continuity and unity of history in the divine plan of salvation do not exclude the contingency of history and the element of surprise for those who follow the way of the Lord.[12] The Holy Spirit, guiding the apostolic community, gives continuity to the acts of God in the ongoing course of history. The Spirit creates that history of salvation through the dialectical relation between His own activity and the decisions of His community.

Luke emphasizes prophecy and fulfillment as the expression and realization of God's purpose (*dei* and fulfillment of prophecy 22, 37; 24, 44; Acts 1, 16; 3, 21). At Miletus (Acts 20, 27) Paul said "I did not shrink from proclaiming to you the whole plan of God." Luke himself seeks through his gospel and Acts to declare "the whole plan of God."

---

[11] K. L. Schmidt, art. *orizo*, *TWNT*, V, p. 453f.

[12] H. Flender, p. 143.

The one and only God governing the history of salvation (Acts 17, 23f.; 14, 15), gives it a universal scope, from the creation of all things (Acts 17, 24ff.; 14, 15; Lk. 3, 38; Acts 17, 28) to "the restoration of all" concerning which the prophets had spoken (Acts 3, 21).[13] This universal scope extends from the creation of man and the determining of the external factors of his history (Acts 17, 25ff.) to his final judgment which God has designated for all mankind (Acts 17, 31; also 1, 7; 10, 42). Thus creation and history (Jewish and Gentile) are united in the course of salvation established by God.

Although God had apparently allowed the Gentiles to go their own ways in the past (Acts 14, 16) he did not, however, leave himself without witness. Nature testified of God (14, 17; 17, 26f.), and the possibility of a natural knowledge of God is assumed (17, 27; also 10, 35). The Jews were ignorant of the prophecies of the suffering Messiah (Acts 3, 17; 13, 27) and yet fulfilled them by condemning him. Israel's past, like Gentile history can be conceived as a way. Luke notes (Acts 7, 39) that the Israelites had been guilty of "turning back in their hearts" to Egypt (Ex. 32, 8).

Luke maintains the Septuagint view of history that following God meant keeping his commandments (1, 6; Acts 7, 53) and going in the way which the Lord commanded (Deut. 5, 32f.; Kings 3, 14), not turning aside to the right or to the left (Deut. 5, 32f.; 9, 16; 28, 13f.). False prophets led from the way which God commanded Israel to go (Deut. 5, 32f.; also Acts 20, 30). A Jewish false prophet's opposition to the Christian faith is described as "making crooked the straights ways of the Lord" (Acts 13, 10).[14]

Luke viewed the *present* as a stage along the way of the Lord which had its own meaning within that redemptive-historical context.[15] Luke regarded the apostolic beginnings of the Church and Jesus' ministry as past history continuing into his own age. He wrote during the epoch inaugurated at the beginning of Jesus' ministry. The kingdom of God was still being preached and "everyone" was still entering it (Lk. 16, 16); however, the declaration made at the appearance of the Baptist had not yet been fully realized; "And all flesh shall see the salvation of God" (Lk.

---

[13] *Ibid.*, p. 145.
[14] W. C. Robinson, p. 67.
[15] *Ibid.*, p. 68.

3, 6 from Isa. 40, 5). The "times of the Gentiles" (Lk. 21, 24) followed upon the rejection of Jesus and the destruction of Jerusalem. The Church was engaged in the Gentile mission because it believed that the Spirit of God was leading it to this enterprise.

Luke thought of himself and the Church as living in the time between Jesus' two advents. The *past* assured Christians (Lk. 1, 4) of the legitimacy of Christianity' [16] Luke's writings had shown the orderly progress of the way of the Lord, and Christians understood that the plan of God embraced them. Jesus' purification and taking possession of the Temple for his teaching and for later gatherings of Christians, had shown that the true Israel was the Church rather than the Synagogue. The converse of the Church's temporary possession of the Temple appears in Jerusalem's rejection of Jesus and her consequent destruction.

The authentic apostolic witness assured the legitimacy of the Christian mission. The apostolic community possessed the teaching of Jesus. Luke's travel account emphasized the authentication of the witnesses and the content of their testimony. The Lucan account stressed the power of the Spirit in Christian witness rather than in Jesus' exorcisms (Lk. 12, 12). The parable of the sower (8, 4ff.) interprets the apostolic preaching as the sowing of the word of God and the response of converts as accepting the word (Lk. 8, 15 and 21; also 11, 27ff.).

In the Lucan account Jerusalem is an example of a divine visitation demanding decision. The teaching of Jesus emphasizes the radicality of man's decisions (Lk. 9, 57ff.; 14, 25ff.) and the grace of God inspiring and supporting them (Lk. 10, 29ff.; 15, 11ff.). Jesus' ministry is the paradigm of God's gracious reign (Lk. 4, 18-21; 7, 21f.; Acts 2, 22; 10, 38). Joy (Lk. 2, 10 . . . Acts 2, 46; 8, 8; 13, 52; 15, 3) rather than anxiety about wordly concerns (Lk. 8, 14; 10, 14f.; 12, 11, 22ff., 24f.; 21, 34) should therefore pervade Christian life.

The Christians' assurance for the *future* should free them from fear. [17] Their Father has given them the kingdom (Lk. 12, 32); within which they enjoy the benevolent reign of God. Assurance regarding the end is not attainable by means of apocalyp-

---

[16] *Ibid.*, p. 116.

[17] S. Schulz, *Zeitschrift fur die neutestamentlische Wissenschaft* 54 (1963), p. 104ff.

tic calculation, because the final cosmic signs are not in sequence with preliminary natural and historical signs. The final signs will be clearly recognizable, but for those who are not ready it will be too late (Lk. 17,21; Acts 1,7). The way to be ready is to stay ready through regular participation in the life of the Christian community (Lk. 21,34-36; 12,35-40ff.; 17,26ff.). Luke always restricts the realization of God's redemptive plan to the apostolic community.[19]

Christians are assured that the future is in God's plan, and that they find their place in it as members of the way. The signs and wonders which characterize the ministry of the Church (Acts 4,30; 5,12; 6,8; 14,3; 15,12) show that God is with the Church just as He had been with Jesus during his ministry (2,22; 10,38) and with Israel (8,36). The divine plan continues to realize itself in the history of salvation along the way of the Lord.

Luke views history as a course of events following a schedule of times set by God and moving along a "way" leading to the Gentiles. It can be described by the Septuagint expression which Luke found in the beginning of Mark and underscored in his own work: the way of the Lord. It is the way of the Father's will, of Jesus and his community. Through the transmission of his Holy Spirit the Risen Christ abides with his people and guides them along the way of the Lord for the salvation of all mankind.[20]

---

18 W. C. Robinson, p. 115.

19 *Ibid.*, p. 114.

20 G. W. H. Lampe, p. 167.

S. Schulz, "Gottes Vorsehung bei Lukas," *Zeitschrift fur die Neutestamentliche Wissenschaft* 54 (1963, pp. 104-116, states that Luke is the author of a salvation-history in which, between the creation and the consummation, there are three ages — that of Israel, of Jesus and of the Church. Underlying and directing everything is God's providence and His purpose. Though not explicitly formulated in the Gospel, this viewpoint is manifest in many ways. (1) In the abundance of *pro*-compounds. (2) The subject of these compounds is not God but God's design, His providence and will. (3) The terms *horizein, tithenai, histanei* and *tassein* confirm this view of providence. (4) So also do the words *dei* and *mellein.* (5) Certain key statements support this thesis: it is hard for Paul to kick against the goad (Acts 26,14), a typical *fatum* statement; Paul must first preach to the Jews (Acts 13,46); Peter's vision (Acts 10. 8ff). The Lucan view of history is not the concept of election which is found in the Old Testament and in later Judaism. Schulz believes that it is a providential history interpreted according to Hellenistic and Roman ideas of *fatum* and *anagke.*

However, that God wills all these events Luke makes clear by means of the following devices: (1) the history, geography and biography of the salvation events; (2) miracles and signs; (3) frequent statements about pneuma,

The Lucan conception of the Way is a unity in diversity with shifts in meaning in the Age of Jesus and in the Age of the Church.[21] The Way of the Lord in the Age of Jesus is identical with the Way of Jesus (Lk 3.4, 7.27).[22] It is the earthly journey of an historical personality; salvation is expressed by a spatial relationship to the historical figure of Jesus.[23] The continuation of this spatial relationship inaugurated by the disciple's decision to follow Jesus expresses perseverance in the faith. The welcoming of Jesus into the place where he wishes to stop on his Way expresses the acceptance of his call to repentance. The rupture of this spatial relationship with Jesus expresses apostasy.[24] The refusal to grant Jesus hospitality (Lk 9.53) or welcome (Lk 19.37f.) expresses the rejection of faith.

The participation of the Apostles in Jesus's earthly travels makes them witnesses to a particular section of salvation history. Their "standing by" Jesus on his Way represents their persevering faith in his messianic dignity; whereas, "turning aside" from Jesus signifies the termination of discipleship.[25] Those whom Jesus visits on his Way are offered a share in salvation because the Way of Jesus manifests the Way of the Lord and his salvation.

The initial acceptance or rejection of the faith is symbolized in the Age of Jesus by the acceptance or rejection of Jesus when he stops along his way for a "visitation".[26] In the Age of the Church, when the Way of the Lord is the Christian mission, the initial acceptance or rejection of the faith is symbolized by the acceptance or rejection of the word of the Lord.[27] The concepts of perseverance or apostacy are symbolized in the Age of Jesus by "standing by" or "turning aside" from Jesus as he goes his Way.[28] These concepts hinge on the image of "following".[29] In

---

the angels and visions; (4) proofs from Scripture; (5) preaching, witness, apology. Thus Luke, according to Schulz, shows that salvation is present and only present where God's providence wills it.

[21] Brown, S., *Apostasy and Perseverance in the Theology of Luke* (Rome, 1969), 131.

[22] *Ibid.*, 132.

[23] *Ibid.*, 134.

[24] *Ibid.*

[25] *Ibid.*, 133.

[26] *Ibid.*, 142.

[27] *Ibid*

[28] *Ibid.*

[29] *Ibid.*

the Age of the Church these concepts are symbolized by the relationship to the Way of the Lord in the Christian religion.[30]

Jesus's "way to life" (Acts 2.28) was God's answer to his earthly Way and to its *exodus* in Jerusalem (Lk 9.31).[31] More than the acceptance of a teaching, faith in Jesus involves reception in a distinct phase of salvation history in which alone salvation becomes accessible to the individual.[32] For Luke the apostolic faith links the earthly Way of Jesus with the Way of the Christian religion by far more than mere external witness to the events of Jesus' life.[33] Only believers can summon others to believe. Only if the testimony of the eyewitnesses and ministers of the word (Lk 1.2) is the expression of an unbroken, persevering faith can it guarantee the faith of the Christian.[34] Thus, the "sifting" of the apostles during the passion (Lk 22.31) represents their successful withstanding of temptation in the trial of faith and assures the continuity of "the faith" with its historical roots in the Age of Jesus.[35]

After Pentecost the unbroken apostolic faith is the starting point for the apostolic preaching. The Way of Jesus is succeeded by the Way of the Christian mission. The apostolic faith strengthens the infant churches when the kerygma of the apostles or their legitimate emissaries has been accepted (Acts 16.5). Adherence to the teaching of the apostles grounds the *koinonia* (Acts 2.42) of all who accept the word and Way of the Lord in the Christian religion. The apostolic faith protects Christians against heretics even after the apostles and the first Christian missionaries have ended their course (Acts 20.28-30).[36]

The historical Way of Jesus precludes the Christian faith from grounding itself on a mythological person. Because of the historical mediation of the Way of the Christian religion, divine salvation is prevented from becoming pure subjectivism.[37] The

---

30 *Ibid.*

31 *Ibid.*, 146.

32 *Ibid.* The author notes that the object of Christian faith is the past historical reality of the earthly Jesus, and faith in him is mediated through the present historical reality of the church.

33 *Ibid.*

34 *Ibid.*, 147.

35 *Ibid.*

36 *Ibid.*

37 *Ibid.*

reality of the divine presence in this world is expressed by the Lucan presentation of salvation within the framework of human history.

NOTES

Jerome Kodell, in "Luke's Use of *Laos,* 'People,' Especially in the Jerusalem Narrative, (Lk 19,28-24,33)," *The Catholic Biblical Quarterly* 31 (1969), concludes that Luke's explanation of Christian beginnings takes him beyond the other evangelists to Asia Minor and even to the center of the Empire. The Christian message of salvation is universal. But the act of God in Christ is the fulfillment of promises to Israel, and it is not at the expense of Israel that the Gentiles are called. Luke emphasizes the continuity of God's workings with one People of God in two phases, under two successive dispensations. The Lucan use of *laos* in the Jerusalem Narrative expresses this continuity. He does not deny the fact that the Jewish nation was guilty of the death of Jesus, but he presents the guilt as softened by ignorance, and does not consider the Jewish people cursed or rejected. Blame is placed largely on the leaders rather than on the people as a whole. By using *laos* consistently to make this distinction between the people and their leaders during the account of the Passion, Luke preserves the traditional biblical word and the concept behind for further use in his historical narrative. It may still designate the People of God, but the People as it is now, the New Testament Church of Jew and Gentile.

20.

WITNESS

Introduction

The witness of the Church in the writings of Luke depends on eyewitnesses to the events of Christ's life and resurrection. The apostles were commissioned by Jesus to bear witness to all nations. The Church's witness to the resurrection and to the entire course of Jesus' life is the prolongation of the commission given to the apostles and the disciples. The Church witnesses in her preaching, through the gift of the Spirit, in her suffering, miracles and by her existence as the community of the risen Lord. Her liturgy of the word and sacrament witness to her communion with the risen Christ.

I.

Luke offers his readers assurance that the message of the Church is securely based on the testimony of authentic witnesses (1. 4),[1] who verify his orderly presentation of the course of redemptive history. The witness of the Church, in the Lucan view, is both to the resurrection and to the divine plan according to which the ministry of Jesus was effectively inspired. Witnesses were those who testified to the course of events which constituted

---

[1] The Greek word for witness (*martus*) and its derivatives occur 34 times in the New Testament; 13 times in Acts (1. 8. 22; 2. 32; 3. 15; 5. 32; 6. 13; 7. 58; 10. 39, 41; 13. 31; 22. 15. 20; 26. 16) and 2 times in Luke's Gospel (11. 48; 24. 48). The word derives from a juridical context in which it indicates one who has observed an event and can talk about it, generally before judges, testifying for or against someone. It also signified giving testimony to the truth or to the faith one possessed. Cf. R. Koch, "Testimonianza," in *Dizionario di Teologia Biblica,* tr. L. Ballarini, J. Bauer (Brescia, 1965), 1434-35.

the ministry of Jesus.[2] Luke's Gospel not only proclaims the content of the apostolic preaching, but also offers evidence which guarantees that content.[3]

In the preface to his Gospel, Luke appeals to eyewitnesses (*autoptai*), a word which does not appear elsewhere in the New Testament:

> Seeing that many others have undertaken to draw up accounts of the events that have taken place among us, exactly as these were handed down to us by those who from the outset were *eyewitnesses* and ministers of the word, I in my turn, after carefully going over the whole story from the beginning, have decided to write an ordered account for you, Theophilus, so that Your Excellency may learn how well founded the teaching is that you have received (1. 1-4).

The commission to bear witness is firmly rooted in Jesus' earthly life:

> He then opened their minds to understand the scriptures, and he said to them, 'So you see how it is written that the Christ would suffer and on the third day rise from the dead, and that, in his name, repentance for the forgiveness of sins would be preached to all the nations, beginning from Jerusalem. You are witnesses to this.' (Lk 24. 44-49).

II.

Apostolic witness is focused on the resurrection (24. 48; Acts 2. 32; 3. 15; 4. 33; 13. 31). Jesus is condemned for claiming to be the Messiah (22. 67), the Son of Man (22. 69), the Son of God (22. 70), with all that thee titles implied. The testimony of false witnesses against him enabled the Sanhedrin to condemn him for blasphemy. His resurrection from the dead proved the injustice of his sentence and the truth of his claim: Jesus was Messiah, Son of Man and Son of God. Thus, the preaching of

---

[2] W. C. Robinson, *The Way of the Lord,* Dissertation for the University of Basle (Basle, 1962), 57.

[3] Cf. U. Luck, "Kerygma, Tradition und Geschichte Jesu bei Lukas," *Zeitschrift für Theologie und Kirche* 57 (1960), 56.

the apostles witnessed to the risen Jesus. The apostles were the true witnesses who produced the essential evidence to verify Jesus' claim and disprove his judges.[4] The power of the Spirit enabled them to bear witness: "You will receive the power of the Spirit and you will be my witnesses" (Acts 1.8).

Because the Jews of Jerusalem were already familiar with the facts of Jesus' life, there was not need to stress them.[5] The apostolic preaching had to bear witness to the fact of the resurrection. Thus, Peter addressed the Twelve:

> We must therefore choose someone who has been with us the whole time that the Lord Jesus was travelling round with us, someone who was with us right from the time when John was baptising until the day when he was taken up from us — and he can act with us as a witness to his resurrection (Acts 1.21-22).

In the light of the resurrection the apostles witness to the entire public ministry of Jesus (Acts 1.15; 10.39; 10.41; 13.31). The apostles bear witness to the New Israel where the Spirit is to be poured out "in the last days" (Acts 2.17); they are the embodiment of the true Israel whose eschatological witness is encountered in the Church.[6] The authoritative witness of the apostles governed the development of the gospel tradition; it ensured that the special preoccupations of individual teachers did not pervert but rather enriched the original message.[1]

The apostolic preaching did not limit itself to the resurrection; it extended to Jesus' life and teaching from his Baptism to his Ascension. The apostolic preaching was personal witness given by men who had been eyewitnesses; consequently when Peter wished to replace Judas he needed not only someone who believed in Jesus but also had personal knowledge of his life. Peter looked for someone who could witness (Acts 1.21-22).

Peter's address in the house of Cornelius reveals that the Jerusalem events to which he gives witness include and extend

---

[4] A. Hastings, *Prophet and Witness in Jerusalem* (London, 1957), 27.

[5] Cf. L. Cerfaux, "Témoins du Christ," *Angelicum* 20 (1943), 166-68.

[6] H. Flender, *St. Luke Theologian of Redemptive History*, tr. R. and I. Fuller (London, 1967), 121.

[7] A. Hastings, *Prophet*, 29.

beyond the passion and death of Jesus. Peter verifies his qualifications as a witness in terms of the complete course of events from Galilee to Jerusalem:

> Now I, and those with me, can witness to everything he did throughout the countryide of Judaea and in Jerusalem itself: and also to the fact that they killed him by hanging him on a tree, yet three days afterwards God raised him to life and allowed him to be seen, not by the whole people but only by certain witnesses God had chosen beforehand. Now we are those witnesses — we have eaten and drunk with him after his resurrection from the dead — and he has ordered us to proclaim this to his people and to tell them that God has appointed him to judge everyone, alive or dead. It is to him that all the prophets bear this witness: that all who believe in Jesus will have their sins forgiven through his name (Acts 10, 39-43).

The qualified Lucan witness is one who testifies to the entire course of Jesus' public ministry and post-resurrectional appearances (Acts 10. 37). He testifies to the course of events beginning with Jesus' Galilean ministry to his occupation of the Temple of Jerusalem (23. 5); he testifies to the crucifixion (23. 49) and to the resurrection (Acts 1. 22). The witness is competent to testify to the overall significance of Jesus' life; [8] he comprehends its sense of direction in the context of redemptive history. [9] He must have been with Jesus from the beginning, not so much in the sense of time as in the sense of place. [10] Thus, just as Jesus' ministry was viewed in terms of a journey *to Jerusalem;* it is also understood as a setting out *from Galilee.* The witness testified to the events of the journey from Galilee to Jerusalem; he could verify the Church's account of "the recent happenings in Judaea; about Jesus of Nazareth and how he began in Galilee, after John had been preaching baptism" (Acts 10. 37).

Christian witness is associated with discipleship. With Jesus leading the way, the disciple follows with total dedication; he

---

[8] P. Menoud, "Jésus et ses témoins. Remarques sur l'unité de l'oeuvre de Luc," *Eglise et théologie* (1960), 13-14.

[9] M. Dibelius, "The Speeches in Acts and Ancient Historiography," *Studies in the Acts of the Apostles* (1956), 163: the significance".

[10] W. C. Robinson, *The Way,* 59.

gives witness to redemptive history which he recognizes in terms of Jesus' journey from Galilee to Jerusalem (7. 9, 44; 9. 55; 10. 23; 14. 25; 22. 61; 23. 28).[11]

The link between Christian witness and the journey to Jerusalem appears in Luke's careful use of the verbs "to follow" and "to come after".[12] Luke restricts these terms to the expression of discipleship more than the other evangelists. Jesus alone is followed. The disciples' complaint about the exorcist, "because he was not following us" (Mk 9. 38), is changed in the Lucan account to "because he does not follow *with* us (9. 49). In the Marcan account, the Baptist announces "Someone is following me ..." (1. 7); Luke changes this to say that Jesus "came after" (3. 16) John in time to avoid the implication that Jesus was the Baptist's disciple.

Witness not only implied first-hand knowledge but also an ecclesiastical and theological position. The witness was one of those whom "God had chosen beforehand", preeminently an apostle (Acts 10. 41). The eyewitnesses whom Luke mentions is his preface included the apostles, but were not limited to them. On the other hand, Jesus did not appear before "all the people", but specifically to the apostles (Acts 10. 41).[13]

Luke describes Paul as a minister and witness, in a phrase somewhat reminiscent of the Gospel preface: "For this reason have I appeared to you: to appoint you as my minister and a witness of this vision in which you have seen me ..." (Acts 26. 16). The "ministers of the word" (Lk 1. 2) implied a larger group than the Twelve. Paul speaks of the "ministers of Christ" in a context which would seem to include himself, Cephas and Apollo (I Cor 4. 1). Paul claimed his right to the title of "witness of Christ" (Acts 22. 15; 23. 11; 26. 9-20; Gal. 1. 11-2. 10). Luke makes a subtle distinction according to which Paul is primarily a "minister of the word" and then a "witness" of the glorified Lord (Acts 26. 16), whereas the Twelve had first been eyewitnesses and as a consequence became "ministers of the word" (Lk 1. 2).[14]

---

[11] *Ibid.*, 60.

[12] *Ibid.*, 22-23.

[13] Cf. A. Retif, "Témoinage et Prédication Missionnaire dans les Actes des Apôtres," *Nouvelle Revue Théologique* (1951), 152-4.

[14] R. Koch, *art. cit.*, 1436.

III.

The Apostles gave witness to Christ [15] by their preaching, their suffering and the gift of the Spirit. They were above all "ministers of the word"; they gave witness to the good news, to the word of the risen and exalted Lord. Because the Old Testament concept of a valid court witness required the testimony of two or three witnesses (Num 35. 30; Dt 17. 6; 19. 15; Mt 18. 16; Jn 8. 17; 2 Cor 13. 1; 1 Tim 5. 19) Peter, in his attempt to rehabilitate Jesus before the Jewish tribunal, always gave testimony for the Risen Lord in the name of the apostles:

> It was you who accused the Holy One, the Just One, you who demanded the reprieve of a murderer while you killed the prince of life. God, however, raised him from the dead, and to that fact we are the witnesses (Acts 3. 14-15).

When Paul, on the other hand, spoke to a Hellenistic audience it sufficed for him to give his own personal testimony of his vision of Christ (Acts 22.-15-18; 23. 11; 26. 16).

The impact of the apostolic witness derived from the gift of the Spirit at Pentecost (Acts 2. 4), promised by Jesus (Acts 1. 8). Through the influence of the Spirit of God Peter discovered within the Old Testament the announcement of the messianic lordship of Jesus (Acts 2. 34-35 = Ps 110. 1; 10. 38 = Isa 61. 1), of his prophetic mission (Acts 3. 22-23 = Dt 18. 15, 19), of his passion under the image of the Suffering Servant of God (Acts 3. 13; 4. 27, 30 = Isa 52. 13-53. 12; Acts 8. 32-33), of his glorious resurrection (Acts 2. 25-29 = Ps 16. 18-21). Notwithstanding every difficulty, the apostles are so overwhelmed by the Spirit of God that they proclaim the good news with remarkable courage (Acts 4. 20, 31; 9. 27-28; 13. 46; 14. 3; 18. 9-10, 26; 19. 8). In this respect, they had been prefigured by the prophets of the Old Israel (Isa 6. 8; Jer 1. 18; Ezech 3. 8-9; Mich 3. 8).

Even if some Christians had been able to know the Lord during his life in Palestine, they, nevertheless, needed the gift of the Spirit to give witness to him in word and action. [16] Peter

---

[15] *Ibid.*, 1437-39.
[16] *Ibid.*, 1440.

refers to this type of witness when he appears before the Sanhedrin: "We are *witnesses* to all this (death and resurrection), we and *the Holy Spirit whom God has given to those who obey him*" (Acts 5.32). Thus, even the Spirit gives witness to the exalted Lord through Jews and Gentiles who, having accepted Christ, speak and act under his inspiration (Acts 2.4; 4.8,31; 15.28). At Pentecost the Spirit is poured out on all mankind (Acts 2.17-21 = Joel 3.1-5). The reception of the Spirit inspires witness: "As they prayed, the house where they were assembled rocked; they were all filled with the Holy Spirit and began to proclaim the word of God boldly" (Acts 4.31).

The gift of the Spirit is also given to the Gentiles. This astonished the Jewish Christians who accompanied Peter while ne was speaking in the house of Cornelius. They were amazed to see the Gentiles manifest the effects of the Spirit; they heard them speak strange languages and proclaim the greatness of God (Acts 10.44). The Spirit had enabled the Gentiles to become witnesses. Peter justified his having baptized them by recalling to Jewish Christians that Jesus had promised that the apostles would be baptized with the Holy Spirit; at the home of Cornelius, Peter realized that God was giving the Gentiles the identical gift he had given the apostles when they believed the Lord Christ (11.15,17). The same Spirit that had empowered the apostles to become witnesses had been given to the Gentiles on the occasion of Peter's prophetic witnessing to the risen Christ.

The authenticity of the apostolic witness was confirmed by suffering and persecution. The fate of the Lord (Lk 11.47-51; Acts 3.22-23) is the destiny of the authentic disciple (Lk 21.12-15). The condemnation of Jesus was interpreted as the fulfillment of the messianic prophecy of Ps 2.1-2 (= Acts 4.25-26): "This is what has come true: in this very city Herod and Pontius Pilate made an alliance with the pagan nations and the peoples of Israel, against your holy servant Jesus whom you anointed, but only to bring about the very thing that you in your strength and your wisdom had predetermined should happen".

The power of God had enabled them to follow the Servant of God: "And so they left the presence of the Sanhedrin glad to have had the honor of suffering humiliation for the sake of the name (Jesus)" (Acts 5.41). The truth of the Beatitudes is confirmed (Lk 6.22-23): "Happy are you when people hate you, drive you out, abuse you, denounce your name as criminal, on account of the Son of Man. Rejoice when that day comes and dance for joy, for then your reward will be great in heaven." The apostles are ready to verify their witness with their blood (Acts 5.29; 6.15; 20.24; 21.13).

Just as their Lord, the apostles corroborated their verbal witness with signs (*sēmeion*): "The many miracles and signs worked through the apostles made a deep impression on everyone" (Acts 2.43); and "So many signs and wonders were worked among the people at the hands of the apostles ..." (Acts 5.12). Miracles corroborated the authority of the apostolic witness to the resurrection (Acts 2.22; 3.12; 4.7; 6.8; 8.13; 10.38): "The apostles continued to testify to the resurrection of the Lord Jesus with great power ..." (Acts 4.33).

Christian witness is basically communal. It is the testimony of the Church to its life in Christ which it draws from his word and sacrament. The preaching of the *word* and the acceptance of the *sacrament* are both essential to the witness of the new community.[17] The story of Philip in Samaria illustrates their importance: "He went down to the city of Samaria and preached the Christ to them" (Acts 8.5) ... And when they believed Philip as he preached the kingdom of God and the name of Jesus Christ, they were baptized, both men and women" (Acts 8.12).[18]

Because Christian witness is communal, it is characterized by a concern for *authority*, the seal of approval from the only ones who can give approval and a full share in the riches of the community's life: "Now when the apostles in Jerusalem heard that Samaria has received the word of God, they sent to them Peter and John. Then they laid their hands on them and they received the Holy Spirit" (Acts 8.14, 17).[19]

Paul is a witness to the unchanging word. He considered it his primary duty to witness and to transmit, not to create: "Let a man so account us, as servants of Christ and stewards

---

[17] B. Ahern, "The Concept of the Church in Biblical Thought," *Proceedings of the Society of Catholic College Teachers of Sacred Doctrine* 7 (1961), 36-37.

[18] L. Cerfaux, *The Church in the Theology of St. Paul*, tr. G. Webb and A. Walker, (New York, 1959), 95-117; 207-227: the Church is described as the Church of Christ inasmuch as he is its very life.

[19] P. Benoit, "La primauté de S. Pierre selon le nouveau testament," *Exegèse et Théologie* 2 (Paris, 1961), 250-284.

of the mysteries of God. Now here it is required in stewards that a man be found trustworthy" (1 Cor 4. 1-2).[20] To all his converts he could say what he wrote to the Corinthians: "I delivered to you first of all what I myself *received*" (1 Cor 15. 3). He is a witness to the sacramental life of the Church: "The bread that we break, is it not the partaking of the body of the Lord?" (1 Cor 10. 16).[21]

The witness of the Christian community is distinct. The followers of Jesus are set apart from their fellow Jews by their preaching (*kērygma*) that the crucified Jesus had risen from the dead and had bestowed the messianic gift par excellence, the Holy Spirit (Acts 2. 29-36; 3. 12-16). This proved that he was truly Messiah and Lord, the only source of salvation for all men (Acts 4. 8-12; 5. 29-32). After accepting this truth there was further instruction drawn not from Judaism but from Jesus, known as the "teaching" (*didachē*) of the apostles" (Acts 2. 42).[22]

The Church's witness was distinct inasmuch as its teachers and directors were no longer the Jewish leaders or doctors of the Law but rather the qualified "witnesses of His resurrection" (Acts 1. 22; 5. 32).[23] The Twelve spoke for the community and intransigently witnessed all that it stood for.[24]

The community's rite of initiation and its central mystery, "the breaking of bread", also gave witness to its distinctiveness. Membership in the new community required the profession of faith in Jesus as the messianic Son of God and baptism (Acts 2. 38).[25] Continuance in the community meant frequent sacramental communion with the Lord through the "bread" which He had provided.[26] Although the followers of Christ prayed in the temple, they "broke bread" in their own homes (Acts 2. 42, 46).

[20] B. Ahern, *art. cit.*, 44.

[21] Cf. J. A. T. Robinson, *The Body: A Study in Pauline Theology* (Chicago, 1952).

[22] D. M. Stanley, "*Didache* as a Constituitive Element of the Gospel Form," *Catholic Biblical Quarterly* 17 (1955), 336-348; See Bo Reicke, "A synopsis of Early Christian Preaching," *The Root of the Vine: Essays in Biblical Theology*, ed. A. Fridrichsen (New York, 1953), 128-160.

[23] K. L. Schmidt. "The Church," *Bible Key Words* I, ed. J. R. Coates (New York, 1951), 13.

[24] B. Rigaux, *Les Epitres aux Thessaloniciens* (*Etudes Bibliques*: Paris, 1956), 154.

[25] O. Cullmann, *Baptism in the New Testament*, tr. J. Reid (London. 1960), 9-22).

[26] P. Benoit, "The Holy Eucharist," *Scripture* 8 (1956), 97-108.

While awaiting the Lord's imminent return (the *parousia*) they found strength and joy in their eucharistic communion with him (Acts 3.20).

Luke writes of the *koinōnia* of the early Christians (Acts 2.42) as evidence of the distinctively new mode of existence into which they had entered through faith and baptism in the name of Jesus and through the gift of the Spirit. This brotherhood or fellowship is not explicitly described as witness; it is explained as the effect of having received the apostolic witness to the exalted Christ. The apostolic witness is creative and communal; those who accept it are assimilated into the new witnessing community or *koinōnia.* Luke describes their unity: "The whole group of believers was united in heart and soul; no one claimed for his own use anything that he had, as everything they owned was held in common" (Acts 4.32).

The Lucan account of Jesus' teaching in Jerusalem presents the Church as the true Israel. Jesus not only cleanses the Temple but, with the witnesses who followed him from Galilee, takes possession of it and teaches in it.[27] Luke thereby implicitly asserts that the Church has replaced Judaism as the true Israel.[28] His account of the beginnings of the Church centers at the Temple.

IV.

Luke modified the Pauline concept of apostle by using the word in the restricted sense only of the Twelve, and by making association with Jesus during the earthly ministry a qualification for apostleship (Acts 1.21f.).[29] Nevertheless, for both Luke and Paul, the essential mission of the apostle consists in witnessing to the resurrection. The apostolic speeches of Acts do not emphasize witnessing to the earthly ministry.[30] In the Petrine speeches the only mention of that occurs in Acts 10.39. In Acts 10.39 Paul speaks of those who came up with Jesus from

---

[27] F.C. Burkitt, *Christian Beginnings II* (London), 194, 110.

[28] H. Conzelmann, *The Theology of Saint Luke,* tr. G. Buswell (London, 1960), 75.

[29] M.M. Bourke, "Reflections on Church Order in the NT", *Catholic Biblical Quarterly* 30 (1968), 498.

[30] See Acts 1.21 which G. Klein, *Die zwölf Apostel* (Göttingen: 1961), 204, calls the "Lucan Magna Charta of the apostolate of the Twelve".

Galilee to Jerusalem, in the post-resurrection period, as begin his "witnesses to the people." The Lucan portrayal of Paul as the one who carried out the final stage of the commission of Acts 1. 8 is problematic for those who hold that he did not consider Paul and apostle. It is through Paul that Luke traces the fulfilment of the Lord's commission to the apostles to be witnesses to him "... even to the ends of the earth" (Acts 1. 8). The three acounts of Paul's conversion in Acts, when taken together, show that he has fulfilled the basic requisites of apostleship: he has seen the risen Lord and he has directly received from him the apostolic commission (Acts 26. 16-18). In Acts 22 the Lord's commission comes during the Temple vision which directly follows the conversion account (vv. 17-21). With no mediation of the apostolic commission, Paul is clearly qualified as an apostle in the third conversion account. [31]

Witness to the ministry of Jesus is doubtless an important aspect of the apostolic mission in Luke's perspective, where such insistence is made on the reliability of the traditions handed down by those who were eyewitnesses from the beginning (Lk. 1. 2) of "all that Jesus began to do and teach" (Acts 1. 1). [32] However, the full apostolic mission involves witnessing to both the ministry and to the resurrection, and the latter is the more important object of witness. It is, in fact, the principal point in the apostolic speeches. Luke's not applying the word "apostle" to Paul may be based on the exceptional character of Paul's apostleship; nevertheless, Paul seems to regard his own apostleship as exceptional in I Cor 15. 8, where he writes of his "untimely birth". The apostleship of Paul is the mission to bear witness to Jesus' resurrection, a mission received from the risen Lord himself.

---

[31] This account is a Lucan composition. See E. Haenchen, "Tradition und Komposition in der Apostelgeschichte," in *Gott und Mensch* (Tübingen, 1965), 211-218.

[32] M. M. Bourke, "Reflections on Church Order in the NT", *Catholic Biblical Quarterly* 30 (1968), 497-8.

NOTES

P.-H. Menoud, "Jésus et ses témoins. Remarques sur l'unité de l'oeuvre de Luc," *Eglise et Théologie* 23 (1968), 7-20, affirms that the Church is found on the work of Christ and the testimony of the apostles. The Third Gospel bears witness to Christ's work; his Book of Acts, to the work of the apostles witnessing to Christ. Luke's purpose in Acts was to provide a compilation of testimony to Jesus' redemptive work. Christ first conferred the title and the mission of witnessing to His teaching and Resurrection only upon the small circle of chosen apostles. Later, he chose Matthias, Paul and Stephen in a special way. The structure of Acts is based on the witness of Peter, Stephen and Paul preaching successively to three categories of men: the Jews in Palestine, the semi-Jews in Samaria, the non-Jews in surrounding territories. All other witnesses and their activity are secondary to these great witnesses. For the benefit of future believers who would come to faith only through hearing the preached word, Luke set out to record how these first preachers witnessed to the redemptive work of Christ.

APPENDIX

ADDITIONAL ESSAYS ON SUBJECTS RELATED TO THE THEMES OF LUKE

21.

THE UNPRODUCTIVE WORD IN LK. 8.7

The Parable of the Sower (Mk 4.13-20; Mt 13.18-23; Lk. 8. 5-15) explains the different attitudes with which men receive the word of God.[1] This study investigates one of these attitudes: "... they are those who hear (i.e. the word of God), but as they go on their way they are choked by the anxieties and riches and pleasures of life, and their fruit does not mature" (Lk 8.14). The same attitude is also represented in the other synoptic accounts of the parable; however, the context of the Lucan Gospel deepens our understanding of why the word of God is rendered unproductive.

The basic presupposition is that the word of God, compared to a seed (8.11), produces something[2]. If it does not, the fault

---

[1] W.C. Robinson, *The Way of the Lord* (doctoral dissertation submitted to the Theological Faculty of the University of Basle), (Basle, 1962), p. 215: "The parable of the sower (Lk 8: 4ff) and its interpretation depicted the preaching of the church as the sowing of the word of God and the response of converts as receiving and observing the word (Lk 8:15; *cf.* 11:27f). In the case of Jerusalem Luke gave an example of divine visitation which required decision. The teaching of Jesus as Luke presented it laid emphasis not only on the radicality of man's decisions (Lk 9:57ff; 14:25ff) but also and especially on the grace of God (Lk 10: 29ff; 15: 11ff). In Jesus' ministry Luke presented the paradigm of God's gracious reign (Lk 4: 18-21; 7: 21f; Acts 2: 22; 10: 38). Christian life therefore should be characterized by joy (Lk 2: 10; Acts 2: 46; 8: 8; 13: 52; 15: 3) rather than by anxiety about the things of the world (Lk 8: 14; 10: 41f; 12: 1, 22f, 25f; 21: 34)."

[2] See L. Cerfaux, "Fructifiez en supportant (L'épreuve)," *Revue Biblique*, 64 (1957), 481-491: U. Holzmeister, "'Exiit qui seminat seminare semen suum' (Lc. 8, 4-15)," *Verbum Domini*, 22 (1942), 8-12.

A. Jones, *God's Living Word* (London, 1963), p. 7: "Scripture grows, ripens into Christ, for the Word of God is a seed. This agricultural image does not lie with the word of God, but rather with the personal character of the individuals who hear it.[3]

The word of God cannot produce its normal results in one category of persons who hear it because they are radically distracted from it by one of the following: (a) anxieties[4]; (b) riches[5]; (c) pleasures of life[6].

I

With regard to anxieties (= worries, cares, preoccupations), there are several illuminating parallels. The verb "to worry", or "to be anxious about" occurs in the Martha and Mary pericope (10. 32-42).[7] The Parable of the Sower was about the word of God; the story of Martha and Mary is about the word of Jesus. In each case, the word is associated with people who are distracted by worries, as well as with others who are ideally receptive. The abiding aspect of the word is also cited.

---

is common to both the Testaments; though the actual phrase belongs only to the New, its spirit is that of both. What in one is life-giving water is the very germ of life in the other."

[3] W. C. Robinson, Jr., "On Preaching the Word of God (Luke 8:4-21)," in *Studies in Luke-Acts,* ed. by Keck and U. J. Martyn, (New York, 1966), p. 136. Robinson maintains that to apply 8:41 strictly to the preaching of the church, Luke asserted the authority of that preaching by underscoring the gravity of rejecting it (8:12), and that he vindicated that authority by showing that the preaching was based upon those witnesses who were with Jesus when the nature of the kingdom of God was disclosed.

[4] The word for "worry" (*merimnan*) and its derivatives occurs five times in Luke's Gospel (10. 41; 21. 34); and three times in texts which parallel those in which the other synoptics employ the word (8. 14; 12. 11; 12. 22, 25). The word is translated by "concerns", "cares", "preoccupations", "anxieties", and their verb equivalents.

[5] The word for "wealthy" (*plousios*) and its cognates occurs fourteen times in Luke's Gospel (1. 53; 6. 24; 12, 16; 12. 21; 14. 12; 16. 1; 16. 19, 21, 22; 18. 23; 19. 2) and three times in texts which parallel those in which the other synoptics employ the word (8. 14; 3. 25; 21. 1).

[6] The word for "pleasure" (*edone*) occurs only once (8. 14) in the Gospel of Luke and is not found in the other synoptics.

[7] A. Plummer, *The Gospel According to Luke* (The International Critical Commentary) 4th ed. (Edinburgh, 1901), p. 291, comments: "The verb is a strong one, 'thou art anxious,' and implies division and distraction of mind (*meridso*), which which believers ought to avoid: Mt 6. 25, 28, 31, 34; Lk 12. 11, 22, 26; Phil 4. 26. Comp. *merimna,* 8. 14; 21. 34, especially 1 Pet 5. 7, where human anxiety (*mérimna*) is set against Divine Providence (*mélei*).

	Parable of the Sower	Martha and Mary
1.	*The word of God*	*The word of Jesus*
	"The seed is the word of God" 8. 12	"Mary sat at the Lord's feet and listened to his word" 10. 39
2.	*Anxieties, or cares*	
	"... as they go their way they are choked by the anxieties of life" 8. 14	"Martha was distracted by her many tasks" 10. 40; "Martha, you are anxious (*merimas*) and troubled about many things" 10. 41 [8]
3.	*Attentiveness to the word*	
	"But the seed in good soil represents those who bring a good and honest heart to hearing the word" 8. 15	"Mary ... listened to his word" 10. 39
4.	*Permanence of the word*	
	"they hold it fast, and by their perseverance yield a harvest" 8. 15	"The part that Mary has chosen is best; and it shall not be taken away from her" 10. 42

In contrast with Mary, who is listening to the Lord's words, Martha is described as busy over many things. Jesus prefers the attention of Mary to the distraction of Martha. His declaration that Mary has chosen the best part implies that it is the best part because "it shall not be taken away from her." Luke implies that Martha's preoccupations have a rather transitory, unlasting quality. Luke presents an antithesis on two levels. The attitude of tranquil attention is contrasted with that of an anxious preoccupation. On the second level, the consequences of these attitudes are contrasted. The former results in something lasting

[8] E. Ellis, ed., *The Gospel of Luke* (Century Bible), (London, 1966), p. 160: To Martha — and Luke implies, to all her daughters — the Lord offers a gentle rebuke: don't let ordinary dinners spoil your appetite for the real dinner."

A. Plummer, p. 291, notes that *Merimnas* refers to the mental distraction, and that the second verb (*thorubadse*) refers to external agitation. Martha complains of having no one to help her; but it was by her own choice that she had so much to do.

and inalienable; the latter, (it is implied) results in nothing of permanent value to the agent. Mary's attitude permits the word of Jesus to produce permanent, personal results. Thus, Jesus evaluates these attitudes in terms of their ultimate productivity.

In his eschatological discourse, Jesus underscores the permanence of his words and warns against the danger of becoming distracted by worldly pleasures and cares:

> "Heaven and earth will pass away; my words will never pass away.[9] Keep a watch on yourselves; do not let your hearts be dulled by dissipation, drunkenness and worldly cares (*merimais*), 21. 33-34. (The parallel text in Matthew [24. 50] omits *merimnais*.)

The word "worry" appears in other Lucan texts common to Matthew, which help complete the Lucan doctrine on this subject.

When condemned by civic and religious leaders, the Christian is not to worry (*me merimnēsete*) about what he should say in his self-defence. He should trust in the Holy Spirit who will teach him how to respond to his accusers (12. 11-12).

The spirit of a man can be discerned by worry. The worrier lacks faith and loving trust in God. "How little faith you have!" (12. 28), Jesus admonished those who have set their minds on food and drink (12. 29): "Do not set your mind on food and drink: you are not to worry."[10] If God cares for the lilies of the field, how much more He will care for us (12. 28). Thus, the care that God has for the Christian, rather than his care for himself, is the ultimate basis for freedom from anxiety. Worry reveals an absence of that absolute faith without which the word of God in Christ remains unproductive.

Those primarily preoccupied with food and drink are behaving like the heathen: "For these are things which the heathen run after" (12. 30). They are not the dominant concern of the authentic Christian. He is to trust in his Father's care: "... but

---

9 T. W. Manson, *The Sayings of Jesus* (London, 1949), p. 333 f.

10 A. Plummer, p. 325, divides this section as follows: God's Providential Care and the Duty of Trust in Him (12. 22-34) and of Watchfulness for the Kingdom (12, 35-48) which Christ came to found (12. 49-53). He comments: "It is more important to notice that covetousness and hoarding are the result of a want of trust in God (Heb. 13. 5) and that an exhortation to trust in God's fatherly care follows naturally on a warning against covetousness".

you have a Father who knows that you need them (i. e. food and drink)" (12. 30). Thus, basic concerns distinguish the Christian from the heathen, faith from unfaith.[11]

Christ expresses the Christian's basic concern: "Set your mind upon his (i. e. the Father's) kingdom, and all the rest will come to you as well" (12. 31). The Christian is commanded not to worry about "the rest": "Therefore I tell you, do not worry (*me merimnāte*) about you life, what you shall eat, nor about your body, what you shall wear" (12. 22 = Mt 6. 25).

Not to trust in God in these matters is absurd: "Is there a man among you whose worrying (*merimnōn*) can add a foot to his stature? if, then, you are unable to do such a little thing, why are you anxious (*merimnate*) about the *rest*?" (12. 26 = 6. 27).

For the disciples worldliness presents itself more often in an anxious attitude than in the overt materialism of the rich man. Life's essentials must not be life's mission or determine life's attitude (12. 29).

Jesus's reasoning is twofold: First, nature testifies to God's provision for the most inconsequential creation-life. To ape the "seeking" attitude of the pagans shows little faith in God's obviously much greater concern for his children's needs (12. 24-30).[12] Second, the follower of Jesus had been made aware of a higher goal, the kingdom of God, toward which his "seeking" should be directed (12. 31-34). Only in the light of the kingdom do other life-needs find a proper perspective and fulfillment.[13] For the threat to man's being, which motivates his ceaseless seeking for material security, is met only in this "treasure that does not fail". Jesus always requires from one just that earthly security

---

[11] A. Plummer, p. 328: "The heathen seek anxiously after all these things because they know nothing of God's providential care." Plummer notes that useless worry about food and clothing is contrasted to the concern that should be had in seeking the kingdom of God. The kingdom belongs to those who seek it, and with it God provides the necessaries of life. Those who neglect the Kingdom that they may secure the necessaries of life will lose both.

[12] A. Plummer, p. 326, comments: "By being anxious can add a *span* to his *age*." That *helikia* here means "age" (Heb. 9. 11; Jn. 9. 21. 23) and not "stature" (19. 3), is clear from the context. It was the prolongation of his *life* that the anxiety of the rich fool failed to secure. Not many people give anxious thought to the problem of adding to their stature."

[13] E. Ellis, p. 176.

upon which one would lean. Only in the context of abandonment to Christ's demand can one's basic life motivation really be "for the sake of the kingdom of God". Peter represents the true disciple who answers, "We have left our homes and followed you" (18. 28).[14]

II

Luke's attitude to wealth emphasizes its dangers. The rich fool is a fool because his life is rooted in his resources (Lk 12:16ff).[15] The rich man is worried and pleasure-bent: "... I will say to myself, 'Man, you have plenty of good things laid by, enough for many years: take life easy, *eat, drink,* and *enjoy* yourself'," (12. 19). Such preoccupation clashes with the words of Christ: "Do not set your mind on food and drink; you are not to worry" (Lk 12. 29).

The rich fool's land "yielded heavy crops" (12. 17), nevertheless he worries about obtaining more wealth: "I will pull down my storehouses and build them bigger" (12. 18). The fool's wealth creates his concern: "He debated with himself: 'What am I to do? I have not the space to store my produce'" (12. 17).[16]

Ironically, at the time of his death, the rich fool is condemned by his own standard: he is separated from all that gave his life meaning and value. He is meaningless and empty, a fool. Wealth and emptiness are associated by Luke: "The rich he has sent away empty" (1. 53).

The rich fool's wealth and worry do not profit him before God:

---

[14] *Ibid.*, p. 218.

[15] J. Jeremias, *Rediscovering the Parables,* Eng. trans. by S. H. Hooke (London, 1966), p. 130: "This rich farmer, who thinks that he need not fear bad harvests for many a year (v. 19), is a fool (v. 20) — that is, according to the biblical meaning of the word, a man who in practice denies God's existence (ps. 14. 1)". Jeremias does not think that Jesus intended to teach that death strikes unexpectedly. Rather does he wish to teach that we are just as foolish as the rich fool under the threat of death, if we heap up possessions when the deluge is threatening; cf. P. Joüon, "La parabole du riche insensé (Lc 12, 13-21)", *Recherches de science religieuse,* 29 (1939), 486-89.

[16] A. Plummer, p. 324, calls attention to the repetition of the word "my": "my crops, my barns, my goods, my soul." Through the repetition of this word Luke emphasizes the egoistic character of the fool.

"You fool, this very night you must surrender your life; you have made your money — who will get it now? This is how it is with the man who amasses wealth for himself and remains a pauper in the sight of God" (12. 20-21).[17]

Life, rather than wealth, is what really counts: "even when a man has more than enough, his wealth does not give him life" (12. 15).

Wealth is a transitory basis for happiness: "Alas for you who are rich; you have had your time of happiness" (6. 24).

Those who are dedicated to wealth and pleasure love unwisely, because they are improvident:

"Provide yourselves with purses that do not grow old, with a treasure in the heavens that does not fail ... For where your treasure is, there will your heart be also" (12. 33-34).

In contrast with the wealth of the rich fool which must be left to another, Mary possesses something of value "which shall not be taken from her" because she "listened to His words" (10. 39). The words of Jesus, rather than riches, yield man's only inalienable possession. They cannot influence men whose thinking and activity is dominated by wealth and pleasure.

The story of Zaccheus (19. 1-10) treats of a personal concern, wealth, the words of Jesus and their effectiveness.

Zaccheus has a special concern: "He sought to see who Jesus was" (19. 3). He is impeded: "... he could not (see Jesus), because of the crowd" (19. 3). He, nevertheless, overcomes the obstacles of the crowd and of his short stature: "... he ran on ahead and climbed up into a sycamore tree to see him, for he had to pass that way" (19. 4).

Zaccheus hears the words of Jesus, which take the form of a personal command characterized by urgency: "Zaccheus, *be quick* and come down; I *must* come and stay with you *today*" (19. 5).[18] Besides his use of the imperative, Luke accumulates

---

[17] A. Plummer, p. 325, comments: "Being rich toward God means being rich in those things which are pleasing to Him." (See Mt 6. 19 and 2 Cor 12. 14). Amassing wealth without reference to God who bestows it is foolishness. The life that Jesus teaches is worth living does not depend upon wealth; even mere existence cannot be secured by it.

[18] R. Schnackenburg, *The Moral Teaching of the New Testament*, Eng. tr. by J. Holland-Smith and W. O'Hara (New York, 1965), p. 31: "By his

three distinct elements (underlined) which clearly underscore the note of urgency in Jesus' words to Zaccheus.

Zaccheus responds to the words of Christ with promptness and joy: "He climbed down *as fast as he could* and welcomed him *gladly* (19.6).[19] (Luke often writes of joy at divine events [1.14, 44, 47; 6.23; 10.21].) Zaccheus does not have to be invited to distribute his goods to the poor, as the rich ruler (18.22), and to restore ill-gotten gains.[20] His responsiveness to Jesus appears in his new attitude towards his neighbor: "Here and now, Lord, I give half my possessions to the poor; and if I have defrauded anyone, I shall restore it four times over" (19.8).[21]

Zaccheus does not give away all his wealth: he gives *half* to the poor. From the remaining half, he will make restitution for his unjust acquisitions. How much this leaves Zaccheus is of no concern to Luke. What counts for Luke is his renewal of spirit: wealth is no longer the basis of Zaccheus' security. The new disposition of his wealth manifests his peace with God and with his neighbor, following upon his reception of Christ.

Salvation comes to Zaccheus, "for this man too is a son of Abraham" (19.9). The words of Jesus are effective in his life, because he receives them with a faith like that of Abraham.

---

call to repentence, Jesus compelled people to make an immediate decision. Those who heard it from his lips were there and then receiving the call of God's grace: a blessing for one who the voice of God and obeyed it, like the chief publican Zaccheus who, in the gratitude of a heart filled with love for God and his envoy, allowed himself to be inspired by the coming of Jesus to a noble action (Luke 19: 1-10)."

[19] W. C. van Unnik, "La notion de 'sauver' dans les synoptiques" in *La Formation Des Evangiles* (Recherches Bibliques), (Louvain, 1957), p. 192. Van Unnik observes that Zaccheus, who has been excluded from the kingdom by the Jews, is reintegrated into the kingdom of God *by the word* of Jesus. He has been delivered from evil through the word of Jesus.

[20] A. Descamps, *Sin in the Bible,* Eng. tr. by C. Schaldenbrand (New York, 1960), p. 81: "That fraternal charity is more precisely the antithesis of sin is suggested in Lk 6, 32-34, where we see that it is especially by a disinterested charity that the disciples are to be distinguished from sinners." Zaccheus' aid to the poor and his act of restitution to those that he had cheated are acts of fraternal charity which manifest his renewal of spirit. This may also be called his "conversion" or "salvation".

[21] G. E. Ladd, *Jesus and the Kingdom* (London, 1966), p. 205, remarks: "The salvation Jesus brought to Zaccheus was a present visitation, although its blessings reach into the future." Ladd also notes (p. 247) that Jesus has come as the shepherd (Mk 14.27; Jn 10.11) to 'seek and save the lost' (Lk 19.10) in fulfillment of Ezekiel 34.15, to rescue the lost sheep of Israel, to bring them into the fold of the messianic salvation.

The story of Zaccheus offers an interesting contrast to that of the rich ruler (Lk 18.15-26; Mt 19.16-29; Mk 10.17-30): [22]

	Rich Ruler	*Zaccheus*
1.	"All these (commandments) I have observed from my youth" 18.21.	"He has gone to be the guest of a man who is a sinner" 19.8.
2.	"You still lack one thing. Sell all that you have and distribute to the poor" 18. 22.	"Here and now, Lord, I give half my possessions to the poor; and if I have defrauded anyone, I shall restore it four times over" 19.8.
3.	"But when he heard this he became sad, for he was very rich" 18.23.	"... and received him (Jesus) joyfully" 19.6.
4.	"Jesus looking at him said, 'How hard it is for those who have riches to enter the kingdom of God! For it is easier for a camel to go through the eye of a needle than for a rich man to enter the kingdom of God!" 18.24-25.	"Today salvation has come to this house since he also is son of Abraham.[23] For the Son of Man came to seek and save the lost" 19.9-10.

The Zaccheus story outlines the salvation process. The arrival of Jesus and Zaccheus' determination in overcoming the obstacles to seeing him initiate the salvation process. When Jesus speaks, Zaccheus obeys and welcomed Him. He rejoices. His new relationship with Jesus produces a new relationship with his neighbors. In fact, his new responsiveness to the needs and grievances of his neighbors verifies the authenticity of new relationship with

---

[22] E. J. Tinsley, *The Gospel According to Luke* (The Cambridge Bible Commentary), (Cambridge, 1965), p. 172, contrasts Zaccheus to the rich ruler: "Here in Jesus is the coming of one who obeys the Old Testament summons to care for the oppressed and the outsiders. Zaccheus' response to this, giving away half his wealth, points to the self-giving of true discipleship (compare the rich ruler in 18:18-23). The whole incident is a pointer to the coming, in the *Son of Man*, of *salvation* to the *house*, (of Israel — Zaccheus is a *son of Abraham*).

[23] E. Ellis, p. 268.

Jesus. Thus, the word of Jesus, received with faith, produces salvation and peace with God and man.

For Luke, the permanence of what one possesses is a criterion of its value: what has value endures. Mary has chosen the best part because, as Luke implies, it will not be taken away from her. The rich fool, in contrast, loses everything at the hour of death: "You have made your money — who will get it now?" (12. 20). The rich ruler is encouraged to give all his possessions to the poor so that he may have riches *in heaven* (18. 22).[25] The superiority of riches is heaven is explained in terms of permanence: "Provide yourselves with purses that do not grow old, with a treasure in heaven *that does not fail*" (12. 33).

Like the rich fool (12. 16), Dives (16. 14-31) is a typical man of the world who finds his fulfillment in this age. Lazarus looks on in misery. In the next life Lazarus reclines with Abraham while Dives looks on in misery. Happiness is only as enduring as its basis. The rejection and misery of this age, as typified by Lazarus, may be only temporary because, as Luke implies, faith in the word of Jesus is the basis of inalienable happiness.[26]

The wealth and pleasure of Dives are of no ultimate value because they lack permanence.[27] The status of Dives and Lazarus after death is of incomparable significance because of its permanence.[28]

---

[24] *Ibid.*, p. 221-222.

[25] *Ibid.*, p. 114. The great reward of the righteous (6, 22) originates and presently exists "in heaven with God" (G. Dalman, *The Words of Jesus,* [Edinburgh, 1902], pp. 206ff.) as "in God".

[26] E. Ellis, pp. 202-207.

[27] J. Jeremias, p. 145: "In face of this challenge of the hour, evasion is impossible. That is the message of the parable of the Rich Man and Lazarus (Luke 16. 19-31). "For Jeremias, this is the parable of the Six Brothers (p. 147-48). The surviving brothers of the Rich Man, who have their counterpart in the men of the flood generation, living a careless life, heedless of the roar of the approaching flood, are men of this world, like their dead brother. Like him they live in selfish luxury, *deaf to God's word,* in the belief that death ends all (v. 28). No miracle, even a resurrection, would be of use to these skeptical worldlings. He who will not submit to the word of God will not be converted by a miracle. The demand for a sign is an evasion and an expression of impenitence. Thus, Jeremias' interpretation of this exclusively Lucan parable implicitly relates it to the problem of the unproductive word in Lk 8. 7. The lack of faith, which characterizes lives dedicated to selfish luxury, renders men unresponsive to the word of God.

[28] The second part of the story of Dives and Lazarus (16. 19-31) emphasizes the absolute seriousness and urgency of accepting the words of

III

The "pleasures of life", which impeded the word of God's efficacy in the Parable of the Sower, find their parallel in the "riotous living" (15. 13) which characterizes the alienation of the Prodigal Son from his father.[29] "After he had squandered all his property" (15. 13), the Prodigal's state suggests that of the rich fool whom Jesus regarded as "a pauper in the sight of God" (12. 21). Both are destitute; however, the Prodigal's misfortune is not permanent. There is still time to forsake his "riotous living" and return to his father.[30] Luke identifies the son's former condition with death: "Your brother was dead, and is alive" (15. 31). Thus, Luke again teaches the illusory character of pleasure as an enduring basis for happiness.

Worldly cares, wealth and pleasure are a hazard. They can all too easily prevent the word of God (8. 7) and the words of Jesus (10. 39) from producing that happiness which is our only inalienable possession. Faith is the essential condition for the

---

Moses and the prophets. Those who ask for a sign have all they need in the words of those whom God has sent to speak his word to them.

[29] A. Plummer, p. 373. The Prodigal leaves his father precisely because he wishes to enjoy the pleasures of life. He goes away from his father's care and restraint, aid from the observation of those who knew him. Plummer notes that it had cost the Prodigal nothing to obtain his share of the inheritance and he squanders it as easily as he had acquired it. The working of Providence is manifest. Just when the Prodigal had spent everything, a famine arose in precisely that land to which he had gone to enjoy himself, so that he and the entire country began to be in want.

[30] A. R. C. Leaney, *The Gospel According to St. Luke,* 2nd ed. (London, 196i), p. 218.

B. Gerhardsson comments on the Parable of the Sower in Luke's Gospel, noting that the phrase concerning those "choked with cares and riches and pleasures of life and bring nothing to fruition" (8. 14) reveals Luke's concern with the problem of property and the danger of riches. Luke can add, or preserve, the third phrase "pleasures of life" and this shows that he is exemplifying various aspects of worldliness. ("The Parable of the Sower and its Interpretation," *New Testament Studies* 14 [1968], 184.)

Luke is keen to preserve parables from the mouth of Jesus. His readers find them generously scattered throughout his Gospel. But when he comes to the special "parable chapter" in Mark, instead of sharpening and developing it as Matthew does he, on the contrary, shortens and minimizes it; it is cut down to fifteen verses with only one real parable and very sparse comment; no new traditions are introduced (cf. Gerhardsson, *art. cit.,* 182). However, the total context of the entire Lucan account gives the Parable of the Sower frame of reference and, therefore, new nuances of meaning.

efficacy of the word of God and the words of Jesus, however the Christian must safeguard it. Anxieties, riches and the pleasures of life threaten that freedom of spirit which faith requires for maturity (8. 14).

NOTES

P. Benoit, "'Et toi-même, un glaive te transperçera l'âme,' (Luc 2, 35)," *Catholic Biblical Quarterly* 25 (1963), 251-261. The sword which will divide Israel is the revealing word brought by Jesus and which results in salvation but also in judgment. These words derive from Ezek 14. 17 which describes the sword of God passing through the land as an avenging force. Mary, the Daughter of Sion, represents the land, and the destroying word consumes only the wicked and will leave Mary and the Remnant unharmed. Mary's suffering on Calvary portrays the value of Jesus' coming into the world which will rend the hearts of God's people.

R. E. Brown, "Parable and Allegory reconsidered," *Novum Testamentum* 5 (1962), 36-45. Brown answers the five arguments adduced as proof that the Church and not Jesus was responsible for the allegorical interpretation of the Sower and the Seed. Although the main point of the parable is the abundance of the harvest, that does not mean that the details of the parable cannot have meaning. Secondly, the complicated character of the allegory in contrast to Jesus' customary way of teaching is an illusion. When compared with the patristic elaborations, the Marcan allegory, is modest. Thirdly, the unevenness of style in contrast to Jesus' rhetorical ability shows that Mark was handling a revered tradition with which he did not wish to tamper. The address to the existing Christian community in the allegorical explanation of the parable reflects the continued validity of Jesus' teaching in the minds of his followers where his own allegorical explanation was readapted for a later time. Lastly, because the vocabulary contains nothing foreign to Jesus or to the Jewish mind, the parable could have appeared on Jesus' lips.

E. Ferguson, "Apologetics in the New Testament," *Restoration Quarterly* 6 (1962), 189-196. The New Testament apologetic showed that Christ fulfilled Messianic expectation by reading the Old Testament christologically (Acts 10. 43); by reading it eschatologically (Acts 3. 24); by interpreting it in terms of contemporary events (Acts 2. 16); and by choosing blocks of passages and understanding thems as wholes (Lk 24. 44). This constituted the Christian method of exegesis for constructing an apologetic for the Jews. The apologetic to the Gentiles appealed to the natural law and the Jewish concept of the Noachian Commandments (Rom 1-2: the Gentiles are without excuse; Acts 17 attacks idolatry on the basis of natural law).

H. Flender, "Lehren und Verkündigung in den synoptischen Evangelien," *Evangelische Theologie* 25 (1965), 701-714. In Luke alone do we find proclamation in the modern sense of personal encounter. Luke relates the present eschatological salvation to a lengthy world History. He gives the kerygmatic pronouncement an historical context. His distinction between pre-Temple and the Temple ministry of Jesus, especially in the Journey to Jerusalem, provides instruction for Christian life in the contemporary world.

G. Frost, "The Word of God in the Synoptic Gospel," *Scottish Journal of Theology* 16 (1963), 186-194. An examination of the expression *logos* in the Synoptics is made to discover its relationship in the thought of Jesus and the Evangelists with the being and person of Jesus. There is no basis for believing that Jesus employed *logos* to describe his own message. This use of the term is an assimilation to the usage of the early Church.

When the Synoptics employ *logos* for the message of Jesus, they do not restrict its meaning to the gospel preached by Jesus, but also include the fact that Jesus is the gospel. They hesitate to name Jesus the Word of God; however, Jesus is the Word: "what God does in Jesus, God does in the *logos*: Jesus is the one in whom *ho logos tou theou* decisively encounters mankind."

22.

PARALLELS BETWEEN MAN AND WOMAN

In Luke stories about a man are often paralleled by stories about a woman. These parallels generally occur in the exclusively Lucan material. Even if these stories were originally arranged this way in his source, a similar complementary parallelism in Acts indicates that Luke has purposely extended and developed this literary device.

According to Flender, Luke expresses by this arrangement that man and woman stand together and side by side before God. [1] They are equal in honor and grace; They are endowed with the same gifts and have the same responsibilites (cf. Gen. 1. 27; Gal. 3. 28).

Among these complementary parallelisms are the stories of Zachary and Mary (the angelic annunciation: Luke 1. 11-20 / 1. 26-38); glory to God: 1. 46-55 / 1. 67-79), Simeon and Anna (2. 25-38), the widow of Sarepta and Naaman (4. 25-28), the healing of the demoniac and Peter's mother-in-law (4. 31-39; cf. Mk 1. 29-31), the centurion of Capharnaum and the widow of Naim (Lk 7. 1-17), Simon the Pharisee and the woman with the leaven (13. 18-21), the good Samaritan and Mary and Martha (10. 29-42) the man with the 100 sheep and the woman with the ten pieces of silver (15. 4-10), the importunate woman and the publican (18. 1-14) or the friend at night (11. 5-8), the women at the tomb and the Emmaus disciples (23. 55-24. 35), the sleeping men and the women at the mill in the last judgment (17. 34f; cf. Mt. 24. 40f), Ananias and Sapphira (Acts 4. 1-11), Aeneas and Tabitha (Acts 9. 32-42), Lydia and the pearl seller and the Philippian jailer (Acts 16. 13-34), Dionysius and Damaris (Acts 17. 34) [2].

---

[1] H. Flender, *St. Luke Theologian of Redemptive History,* tr. by R. and I. Fuller (London, 1967), p. 10.

[2] *Ibid.,* p. 9.

The Feminine Advantage

In several of the Lucan parallelisms women show greater faith and love. Mary's faith excels that of Zachary; the sinful woman manifests a love which is not found is Simon the Pharisee. Simon of Cyrene is constrained to help Jesus carry his cross, whereas the Daughters of Jerusalem spontaneously mourn and lament over the suffering of Jesus in another complementary parallelism which reveals the participation of man and woman in the life of Christ.

Deeds have Word-character

The complementary parallelisms between man and woman are illuminated by Gerhard Ebeling's concept of the word-character of deeds: [3]

> Man's deeds have word-character. It can be learned from them whether he has understood something of the situation in which he finds himself, or whether he completely misunderstands it. It can become plain from a man's deeds — more clearly and more convincingly than by words — what is in the man. A very ordinary deed can be uncommonly eloquent and significant. It can awaken hope and plunge into despair, it can — not in its immediate effect as a deed, but in its effect on the understanding, and thus in its word-effect — open up a whole world, but also destroy a world.

The story of Simon the Pharisee and the sinful woman (7. 36-50) illustrates this common characteristic of the parallelisms. Although neither Simon the Pharisee nor the sinful woman had said anything, their deeds clearly revealed what was in them. Jesus himself interprets the word-character of their actions:

> I came to your house: you provided no water for my feet; but this woman has made my feet wet with her tears and wiped them with her hair. You gave me no kiss; but she has been kissing my feet ever since I came in. You did not annoint my head with oil; but she has anointed my

[3] G. Ebeling, "Die Evidenz des Ethischen," p. 344, quoted by R. W. Funk, *Language, Hermeneutic, and Word of God* (New York, 1966) p. 220.

feet with myrrh. And so, I tell you, her love proves that her many sins have been forgiven (7.44-46).

Wordless Giving, Wordless Receiving

The complementary parallelism between man and woman in the Good Samaritan and Martha and Mary pericopies reveals a second level of parallelism between the active and passive character of wordless deeds which are also language events. The active Samaritan goes about his compassion wordlessly; and Mary quietly sits at Christ's feet listening to him speak. Both of these events "bespeak" a world in which love is indigenous and made present to those hearing or reading these stories.[4] The wordless initiative of the Samaritan on behalf of his neighbor and the quiet receptivity of Mary to the word of God in Jesus communicate the meaning of that world in which God reigns.

Hope and Despair

The parallelism between the women at the tomb and the Emmaus disciples reveals how the same event, depending on the way in which it is interpreted, can awaken hope or plunge into despair. For the women, the events of passion and death of Jesus, interpreted in the light of their resurrection faith, opened a whole new world. For the Emmaus disciples the same events had destroyed a world of false hopes that Jesus was the man to liberate Israel; however, the word-character of the Lord's wordless deed in the breaking of the bread was so overwhelming that the same events of the passion and death were reinterpreted as a source of resurrectional joy.

Dual Witness

The complementary Lucan parallelisms between a man and a woman square somewhat analogously with his "dual witness" motif, a literary pattern common to the Old Testament and to Matthew and Mark.[5] Dual witness is encountered in the second

---

[4] Cf. R. W. Funk, *op. cit.*, p. 220.

[5] Cf. V. E. McEachern, "Dual Witness and Sabbath Motif in Luke," *Canadian Journal of Theology* 12 (1966), 267-280.

charge (10. 1 ff.), the double trial before Pilate and Herod (23. 1-16), the two Emmaus disciples (24. 13-35), and in Luke-Acts itself. Dual witness is strikingly apparent in the structural parallelism of two almost identical parables which both express the same invitation to the joy of God in the saving work of Christ (15. 4-10):

(Man)	(Woman)
Which of you,	Or again, what woman
if he has a hundred sheep	if she has ten silver pieces
and loses one of them,	and looses one of them
does not leave (...)	does not light the lamp (...)
until he has found it?	until she has found it?
(...)	(...)
he calls his friends and neighbors	she calls her friends and neighbors
and says to them:	and says to them:
"Rejoice with me,	"Rejoice with me,
for I have found my sheep	For I have found the silver piece
which was lost!	which I have lost!
In the same way, I tell you,	In the same way, I tell you,
there will be greater joy	there is joy
over one sinner who repents	over one sinner who repents.
than over ninety-nine righteous	(15. 8-10)
who do not need to repent.	
(15. 4-7)	

Luke's parallel stories about a man and a woman offer a type of dual witness to his interpretation of the kingdom of heaven. Man and woman stand side by side in witnessing to the truth of Christ. These complementary Lucan parallelisms of a man and a woman contain within themselves a certain word-character which implies that Christ is the Savior of all mankind and possesses a relevance which is both masculine and feminine. This instance of the "two-membered architectonic art of Luke" represents one aspect of Luke's distinctive universalism.[7]

The reason why Luke should choose to structure his work on the principle of two-foldness is given by Dr. Robert Mor-

---

[6] The parallelism of the literary structure in these parallels is taken from E. Rasco, "Les Paraboles de Luc XV," *Ephemerides Theologicae Lovanienses* (1968), p. 168.

[7] H. Flender, *op. cit.*, p. 8ff.

genthaler in the second volume of his two-volume work, *Die lukanische Geschichtsschreibung als Zeugnis* (Zurich, 1949), where he observes that Luke intends by means of his work to bear witness, and it is laid down in Scripture (Deut. 19. 15; Mt 18. 16; 2 Cor 13. 1; I Tim 5. 19; Heb 10. 28; I Jn 5. 6) that testimony is to be received *at the mouth of two or three witnesses.*[8] This principle underlies Lucan parallelisms, tautologies, doublets, and repetitions. Luke's art of two-foldness reveals that the only kind of testimony he means to offer is that which would satisfy a law-court, which demands twofold and threefold testimony.

Morgenthaler shows that Luke builds his work on the principle of pairs, or of doubling (Zweigliedrigkeit). He quotes Bussman's statement: "Luke has the greatest number of doublets of all the Synoptics, so far removed is he from any dread of doublets" (*op. cit.* i, p. 13)[9], and proceeds to substantiate this observation with reference to words, sentences, paragraphs, and overall composition. He holds that Luke's work may be analyzed as follows:

Scenes in Jerusalem I	Luke	1. 5 - 4. 13
Travel Narrative I		4. 14 - 19. 44
Scenes in Jerusalem II		19. 45 - 24. 53
Scenes in Jerusalem III	Acts	1. 4 - 7. 60
Travel Narrative II		8. 1 - 21. 17
Scenes in Jerusalem IV		21. 18 - 26. 32
Travel Narrative III		27. 1 - 28. 31

Morgenthaler shows close correspondences between the first two sets of Jerusalem scenes. In one Jesus is born in poverty; in the other he suffers and dies. In one he is in his humanity tempted by Satan; in the other it is the same. In the one, the Son of God through birth becomes man; in the other he is again exalted through resurrection. John is rejected in one; Jesus in the other.[10] The intervening travel narrative is also divided in two parts which contain numerous correspondences. Each begin with a rejection. At the beginning of the former stands the call

[8] On this theme see H. van Vliet, *No Single Testimony* (Utrecht, 1958), esp. n. 19.

[9] Cf. W. Bussmann, Synoptische Studien, I (Halle, 1925), p. 57. The author argues against Luke's alleged. *Duplettenfurcht* (pp. 6-66).

[10] R. Morgenthaler, *Die lukanische*, i, p. 168.

of the tax-collector Zaccheus. At the end of the former Jesus announces his approaching passion; he does so again at the end of the latter. Each contains two deeds performed on the Sabbath. Thus the Gospel can be more completely analyzed as follows:

Scene I:	Jerusalem narrative	1. 5 - 4. 13
Scene II:	On the road (Galilee)	4. 14 - 9. 50
Scene III:	On the road (Samaria)	9. 51 - 19. 44
Scene IV:	Jerusalem narratives	19. 45 - 24. 53

Morgenthaler next shows parallels between these Jerusalem and travel sections in the Gospel with those in Acts. The same pattern of two-foldness, and with it the same themes, of the fulfilment of Judaism, and the rejection by Judaism of its own fulfilment, together with the acceptance of the Gentiles, runs throughout the whole work. The Jewish question or the Gentile question constitute the meaning of the overall composition, depending on the direction in which one looks.[11]

---

[11] *Ibid.*, p. 190.

23.

PARALLELISM IN THE GLORY AND HUMILIATION OF CHRIST

Parallelism is a literary device which employs to present complementary truths.[1] Luke creates a didactic unity by balancing literary structures. This "diptych" unity is found in the parallelism of the infancy narratives of John the Baptist and of Jesus. The same angel announces God's extraordinary action to both Zachary and Mary. Both rejoice at the divine intervention with a hymn of praise, the *Benedictus* and the *Magnificat.* Luke relates the circumcision of each child as well as their hidden life, growth and development before God and man, and prophecies of their future greatness.

The Good Samaritan story (10:30-37) and the story of Martha and Mary (10:38-42) which immediately follows illustrate the "diptych development." The first story teaches that man's fundamental attitude toward his fellow man should be one of *giving;* the second episode suggests that man's relationship to God is one of *receiving.* Receptivity and responsiveness in faith should characterize the human relationship to God, whereas, in relation to other men, Luke gives the primacy to active generosity. Men can only give to others what they have received from God.

Luke treatment of the Transfiguration (1::28-36) and of the Agony in the Garden (22:41-46) illustrates the same didactic method. These two accounts are understood as a diptych illustrating the two complementary truths which make up the mystery of the Incarnation. The linking of two contrasting pictures into a single frame is characteristically Lucan.

---

[1] Cf. J. Navone, *Personal Witness* (New York, 1967), p. 80f.

Transfiguration and Agony

Parallels have been detected in all the Synoptic accounts of the Transfiguration and the Agony.[2] The Lucan treatment, however, is distinctive in its emphasis on prayer. Parallelism underscores the radical contrast between the glorification of Christ in the Transfiguration and his humiliation in the Agony. The Fathers used the first narrative against the Arians and the Nestorians; they employed the second against the Docetists and the Monophysites. The first episode represents the climax of the revelation of Christ's glory before the resurrection; the second, in a certain sense, expresses the climax of the revelation of his humiliation.

Both events take place on a mountain,[3] were witnessed only by Peter, James and John, were characterized by a spiritual experience of Jesus in which his appearance underwent a striking change (cf. 9:39 and 22:53).[4] After each event, Jesus resumes his usual appearance and demeanor: his glory fades and his disciples are told to have no fear; after his Agony, he delivers himself without fear into the hands of his enemies. In each case, Peter has a prominent role. At the Transfiguration Peter alone speaks to Jesus; in the garden he alone is addressed by Jesus.

In these two narratives Luke does not assert that Peter, James and John were the only witnesses of the agony. There are two coincidences between these pericopes which are peculiar to Luke. In each case, the narrative begins with Jesus and his disciples going to the mountain to pray (9:28; 22:39-40). Luke alone mentions that Jesus went to the mountain of the Transfiguration to pray. The Transfiguration is the fourth major event in the mission of Jesus which Luke marks by a reference to prayer.

The choosing of the twelve; Peter's act of faith at Caesarea; the Transfiguration; the teaching of the Lord's own prayer: these are perhaps the most important single events in the public min-

---

[2] A. Kenny, "The Transfiguration and the Agony in the Garden," *Catholic Biblical Quarterly* 19 (1957) pp. 444-452, is the primary source for this study. Kenny tends to press parallelisms between the Transfiguration and the Agony.

[3] H. Conzelmann, *The Theology of St. Luke*, tr. G. Buswell (2nd ed., London, 1966), pp. 44 f., notes that in contrast to the plain, which is the place where Jesus meets people, the mountain is the place where Jesus prays to his Father.

[4] Luke contrasts the brilliant whiteness of Jesus' garments at the Transfiguration with the power of darkness during the Passion (9, 38 and 22, 53).

[5] Cf. A. Hastings, *Prophet and Witness in Jerusalem* (London, 1958), p. 89 f.

istry as it appears in the Synoptics. Luke alone links each of them with the prayer of Jesus. Only he explicitly makes the prayer taught to the disciples a prolongation of Jesus' own, which it most truly was, for it began with the word "Father." Thus, this prayer is the sharing of the Lord's own prayer (Hastings, *Prophet and Witness in Jerusalem,* pp. 89f).

The second coincidence hinges upon the use of the *exodus.*[6] Moses and Elijah speak to Jesus during the Transfiguration of his decease, of his going away or *exodus,* which he would accomplish in Jerusalem.[7] This associates Jesus with Moses; both save God's people. Jesus will fulfill what Moses prefigured by leading the people out of Egypt.[8] His sacrificial, redemptive death is an *exodus,* a passing away, which enables men to pass from death to life. Moses, the symbol of the Law, and Elijah, the symbol of prophecy, are present. Thus, the Transfiguration narrative implies that both the Law and prophecy point to Calvary. The reason for both Moses and Elijah at the Transfiguration is disputed. A satisfactory hypothesis is that both — Elijah in Scripture itself (2 Kings 2:11; 1 Mac. 2:58) and Moses in Jewish tradition — had an "assumption," and in Luke the Transfiguration is an anticipation of the ascension.[9]

In the Transfiguration account Luke relates that "Peter and they that were with him were heavy with sleep." In the Agony account Luke remarks that the disciples' eyes were heavy with sleep.[10] This is the only other place where the idea occurs in

---

[6] G. Caird, *Saint Luke* (London, 1963), p. 132, observes that the word which Luke uses for death is unusual — *exodus;* and it is clear that he used it because of its Old Testament associations with divine deliverance.

[7] Cf. E. Tinsley, *The Gospel According to Luke* (Cambridge, 1965), p. 103. Tinsley cites the popular belief that Moses and Elias had never died, and that both would reappear as forerunners of the messianic age. Jesus is seen as the fulfillment of Old Testament law and prophecy, symbolized respectively by Moses and Elias.

[8] E. Ellis, *The Gospel of Luke* (Century Bible), (London, 1966), p. 142 comments on the "exodus": "It probably includes the whole of Messiah's redemptive work: death, resurrection, and ascension. The 'exodus' typology is clearly in view. Jesus is the new Moses who establishes a new Israel, gives a new covenant, and through his death and resurrection delivers God's people from the 'Egypt' of sin and death."

[9] Cf. *Studies in the Gospels,* ed. D. E. Nineham, G. W. H. Lampe, "The Holy Spirit in the Writings of St. Luke," (London, 1955), p. 176; cf. de la Potterie, *Exerpta Exegetica ex Evangelio Sancti Lucae* (mimeographed notes), (Rome, 1964), p. 19.

[10] Cf. D. Daube, *The Sleeping Companions,* in *The New Testament and Rabbinic Judaism* (London, 1956), pp. 332-335.

the New Testament. At the Transfiguration the disciples sleep while Moses and Elijah speak of the Passion; during the Agony they sleep while Jesus prays for deliverance.

The Prayer Theme

It would seem that Luke might have been aware of the complementary aspects of the mystery of the Incarnation and had chosen to underscore them by means of literary parallelism within the framework of his prayer theme, a favorite with the evangelist.[11] Luke alone affirms that Jesus prayed on the mount of the Transfiguration. More than the other evangelists Luke stresses Jesus' prayer during the Agony. Jesus, "being in agony, prayed the longer." The root word for "pray" in Greek, *proseuch* —, occurs five times in seven verses of the Agony narrative.[12]

The obviousness of the parallelism is found in the resemblance between Luke's version of the Lord's Prayer and the prayer of Jesus on the Mount of Olives:[13]

Father[14]	*Father*
Hallowed be thy name	If thou wilt
Thy Kingdom come	remove this chalice from me
(*Thy will be done*	but yet *not my will but thine be done*
as it is in *heaven*	and there appeared to him an angel
so also on *earth*)	from *heaven,* strengthening him.
Give us this day	And being in agony, he prayed the longer.
our daily bread.[15]	And his sweat became as drops
Forgive us our sins	of blood tricking down upon
for we also forgive	the *earth.* And ... he came
everyone that is	to the disciples and found
indebted to us.	them sleeping for sorrow.
And lead us not into temptation (11:14)	And he said to them, Why sleep you? Arise, pray, *lest*

[11] Prayer is a favorite Lucan motif: 3, 21; 5, 16; 6, 12; 9, 18, 28-29; 11, 1; 22, 41.

[12] Cf. D. Guthrie, *The Gospel and Acts*: *New Testament Introduction* (Chicago, 1965), p. 86 f.

you enter into temptation (22:41f.).[16]

This parallelism has been schematically arranged as follows:[17]

Father	Father
Hallowed be thy name	If you willest
Thy kingdom come	Remove the cup which brings the kingdom
Thy will be done	Lead us not into temptation
as it is in heaven	Not my will but thine be done
so also on earth	Heaven sends the angel to
Give us this day our	Jesus' service
eucharistic bread	The reconciling blood falls on the earth
Forgive us our sins	Christ sheds for us his eucharistic blood
	Christ wakes his disciples from sleep (sin)
	"Pray, lest you enter into temptation."

Other parallels which may be no less coincidental have also been noted:[18]

(1) *The association of the chalice and the kingdom.* These had been noted earlier in the same chapter: "And having taken the chalice, he gave thanks, and said: Take and divide it among you; for I say to you, that I will not drink of the fruit of the vine till the kingdom of God come" (22:17-18). The eucharistic

---

[13] Cf. A. Kenny, *art. cit.*, p. 450.

[14] Cf. J. Jeremias, *The Central Message of the New Testament* (London, 1965), I, "Abba". Jeremias notes that this expression reveals the foundation of Jesus' communion with God (p. 21). This expression of a boy addressing his father had never been employed by Jews addressing God. It expresses Jesus' perfect confidence and desire of fulfilling his Father's will.

[15] M. Dibelius, *"Die dritte Bitte des Vaterunsers," Die christliche Welt* 5 (1940) p. 53, maintains that the Lord's Prayer derives from the Mount of Olives pericope.

[16] A. R. C. Leaney, p. 272, maintains that the "temptation" (22.40) for which the disciples must prepare themselves with prayer refers to the fiery trial which should precede the kingdom, as, in Dan. 12.10; Zech. 13.9; 14. 1-3, and often in tse Old Testament and later Judaic works; Cf. A. George, *"Heure des ténèbres et règne du péché", Lumière et Vie* 1 (1952), pp. 41-64.

[17] Cf. A. Kenny, *art. cit.*, p. 452.

[18] *Ibid.*, p. 451.

word over the wine, in Luke's account, stresses the chalice: "This is the chalice, the new covenant of my blood." Luke stresses the word "chalice," using it twice with the article, whereas Matthew and Mark use it once and without the article.[19]

(2) *The division of the Lord's Prayer.* The first half prays for glory; the second half petitions human needs. A similar division occurs in the Agony account. The first half is Jesus' prayer; the second half relates Jesus' actions.

(3) The heaven-earth parallel. The angel from heaven shows how heaven does God's will; the blood falling on the earth inaugurates the new covenant between God and man.[20]

(4) *The bread and blood.* "Give us this day our daily bread" suggests the eucharistic body of the Lord given for our salvation. The sweat of blood is the beginning of the blood-shedding of the Lord, prophesied in the eucharistic word said over the cup.

(5) *Sin and sleep.* "Forgive us our sins" corresponds to the words of Jesus, "Why do you sleep? Arise." Sin and sleep are frequently linked in the New Testament. Sleep represents the lack of that attention which marks the true disciple.

(6) *Prayer and temptation.* The story of the Mount of Olives brackets Jesus' prayer with his admonition: "Pray that you may not enter into temptation" (40:45f).[21] Luke teaches that the trials which Christians are destined to endure can be overcome only through prayer. Eager to fight for God's cause with man's weapons (22:38, 49), the disciples can only fumble with the weapon that counts.

Only after the death and resurrection of Jesus would the disciples understand what the Transfiguration vision meant. Luke's

---

[19] Cf. L. Goppelt, *Theologisches Wörterbuch zum Neuen Testament,* ed. by Kittel and Friedrich, VI 148-158. The Chalice is a metaphor which represents either the divine wrath or the divine blessing.

[20] E. Rasco, *Synopticorum Quaestiones Exegeticae* (Roma, 1966), p. 228 f., notes that Jesus, as once the people of God, is comforted by an angel during a period of crisis (Deut 32. 43 LXX; Is 37. 36; 2 Kgs 19. 35; 2 Chr. 32. 21). In Dan. 10. 18f., appearing like "the Son of Man", tells Daniel not to fear and to take courage. H. Aschermann, *Zum Agoniegebet Jesu,* Lk. 22, 43-44, *Theologia Viatorum* 5 (1953-53), p. 146, notes that the angel on the Mount of Olives does not imply the subordination of Jesus, but rather the service which is due the representative of the new people of God.

[21] A. R. C. Leaney, *The Gospel according to St Luke* (London, 1966), p. 272, notes that Luke does not mention Gethsemane but makes the arrest take place on the Mount of Olives. Thus, the parallelism with the Mount of the Transfiguration is maintained.

account places more emphasis on Jesus, who, facing death, found in prayer with his Father the confirmation of his salvific mission. The prayer motif of the Lucan Gospel grounds the diptych development of the two complementary aspects of the Incarnation mystery.

Never in his public ministry did Jesus appear nearer to the Father than at the Transfiguration. From the glory of the mountain to the agony of the Mount of Olives the greatest of all his words was about to be accomplished, and hence he prayed. In these moments of intense prayer his glory is revealed and we enter into the realms of mystery, whether the mood be gladness or sorrow. Whether in glory or in agony, Jesus is fully divine; he can send the Spirit, can be transfigured, can talk as an equal with his Father.

24.

THE TRADITIONS COMMON TO THE GOSPELS OF LUKE AND JOHN

John A. Baily, in his book *"The Traditions Common to the Gospels of Luke and John,* shows how the Fourth Gospel, although containing more genuinely Palestinian material, drew upon Luke's Gospel and hence should be dated after A. D. 80. In the thirteen chapters of this study Baily, under the tutelage of his mentor, O. Cullmann, affirms that evidence of this dependence is particularly noticeable in the parallel Passion accounts beginning with the Anointing of Jesus and is clear to in the Resurrection narratives. Literary and historical similarities are the major preoccupations of the dissertation (Supplements to *Novum Testamentum* [Leiden: Brill, 1963], VII and 121 pp.). Resemblances in theological viewpoint are for the most part excluded.

Baily affirms that John knew Luke's gospel, and that he drew on Luke for elements in his account of the anointing of Jesus (Lk 7. 36-50/Jn 12. 1-8), of the Last Supper and Last Discourse (Lk 22. 14-38/38Jn 13-17), of the high priestly prayer, of the arrest (Lk 22. 39-53a/Jn 18. 1-12), of the trial before Pilate (Lk 23. 1-25/ Jn 18. 29-19. 16), of the crucifixion, death and burial (Lk 23. 25-26/ Jn 19. 17-42), and of the appearances of Jesus in Jerusalem (Lk ch. 24/Jn chs. 20f.). Not all the similarities, Baily asserts, are to be so explained. At a large number of points — as regards the people's wondering who the Baptist was, the fishing miracle, the approach to Jerusalem, Jesus' serving at the Last Supper and the chronology of the events there, the hearing before Annas, the charge against Jesus that he claimed to be king, the two disciples' going to the grave and the words the risen Christ speaks to Peter — Luke and John bring traditions with, though related, came independently to the two of them. The means by which this happened vary. In the case of the approach to Jerusalem (Lk 19.37-40/Jn 12.12-19) the two evangelists drew on similar, but not identical, written accounts of the event, whereas they both knew the same oral account of the Last Supper and the same written account of Jesus' examination before Annas. What characterizes the instances of related material, according to Baily, is the variety of the means by which the relationship came about; there is no evidence for either Luke's or John's having drawn such material from a continuous source which one of them or both knew. Rather the evidence of Bailey's analysis points to the existence in the Church at the time both evangelists wrote of many isolated written and oral traditions — the former having been written for catechetical or liturgical purposes — on which (in addition to Mark) the two writers drew. The period in which isolated stories circulated as such was a long one, perhaps fifty years after the resurrection. Bailey's evidence indicates that virtually all the traditions coming independently to Luke and John originated in Jerusalem; it also is a check to those critics who, at the expense of Luke and John, regard Mark as *the* historical gospel.

The subject of Lucan-Johannine parallels has once before been extensively examined by Julius Schniewind in his monograph *Die Parallelperikopen bei Lukas* und Johannes (Leipzig, 1914). Schniewind maintained that John did not know Luke's gospel, and that another explanation for all the agreements must be found. Bailey demonstrates that Schniewind was mistaken on this point, though indeed John's knowledge of Luke by no means explains all the points of similarity. The scope of Bailey's work is larger than Schniewind's, in that it is not limited to an analysis of the passages where some verbal similarity appears, but also treats the two gospels at points where they contain related elements which, while not verbally similar, yet raise historical questions concerning the events of Jesus' life, e.g. Jesus' activity in Samaria. However, Bailey does not treat purely theological similarities, such as those which exist between the doctrines of the Spirit of the two gospels because that would have entailed a work much longer than necessary for the scope of his dissertation. The similarities and the dissimilarities between the theologies of the two evangelists constitute an interesting subject which would require a book in itself.

For the sake of brevity this author has avoided making comparisons between the Lucan and Johannine treatment of common themes. Bailey's competent work should provide at least partial satisfaction for those who wish to pursue this comparative aspect of the thematic study of Lucan theology.

BIBLIOGRAPHY

Abbreviations

BC	*Black's New Testament Commentary*
BJ	*Bible de Jérusalem*
CB	*Century Bible*
CLB	*Clarendon Bible*
CBC	*Cambridge Bible Commentary*
CGT	*Cambridge Greek Testament*
DSB	*Daily Study Bible*
EB	*Études bibliques*
EGT	*Expositor's Greek Testament*
ET	*English Translation*
IB	*Interpreter's Bible*
ICC	*International Critical Commentary*
JB	*Jerome Biblical Commentary*
KEK	*Kritisch-exegetischer Kommentar*
LHB	*Lietzmann's Handbuch zum Neuen Testament*
MC	*Moffatt's New Testament Commentary*
NLC	*New London Commentary*
NTD	*Neue Testament Deutsch*
PBC	*Peake's Bible Commentary*
PGC	*Pelican Gospel Commentaries*
SB	*Sainte Bible*
TBC	*Torch Bible Commentary*
WC	*Westminster Commentary*

Commentaries

Adeney, W. F., *St. Luke* (CB), 1922.
Arndt, W. F., *The Gospel according to St. Luke,* 1956.
Balmforth, H., *The Gospel according to St. Luke,* (CLB), 1930.
Barclay, W., *Luke* (DSB), 1953.
Browning, W. R. F., *The Gospel according to St. Luke* (TBC), 1960.
Bruce, A. B., *The Synoptic Gospels* (EGT), 1897.
Burton, H., *The Gospel according to St. Luke* (EB), 1909.
Caird, G. B., *St. Luke* (PGC), 1963.
Creed, J. M., *The Gospel according to St. Luke* (MC), 1930.
Easton, B. S., *The Gospel according to St. Luke,* 1926.
Ellis, E., *Luke,* 1965.
Farrar, F. W., *St. Luke,* 1895.

Fishinger, D., *Das Lukasevangelium,* 1962.
Geldenhuys, J. N., *Commentary on the Gospel of St. Luke* (NLC), 1951.
Gilmour, S. M., *The Gospel according to St. Luke* (IB), 1952.
Grundmann, W., *Das Evangelium nach Lukas,* 1961.
Harrington, W. J., *The Gospel according to St. Luke,* 1967.
Hauck, F., *Das Evangelium des Lukas,* 1934.
Klostermann, W., *Das Lukasevangelium* (LHB), 1929.
Lagrange, M. J., *Évangile selon saint Luc* (EB), 1921.
Lampe, G. W. H., *Luke* (PCB), 1962.
Leaney, A. R. C., *The Gospel according to St. Luke* (BC), 1958.
Loisy, A., *Évangile selon Luc,* 1924.
Luce, H. K., *St. Luke* (CGT), 1949.
Lüthi, W., *Das Lukasevangelium ausgelegt für die Gemeinde,* 1958.
Manson, T. W., *The Gospel of Luke* (MC), 1930.
Marchal, L., *Evangile selon saint Luc* (SB), 1946.
Osty, E., *Evangile selon saint Luc* (BJ), 1961.
Plummer, A., *Gospel According to St. Luke* (ICC), 1896.
Ragg, L., *St. Luke* (WC), 1922.
Rengstorf, K. H., *Das Evangelium nach Lucas* (NTD), 1967.
Schlatter, A., *Das Evangelium des Lukas,* 1931.
Schmid, J., *Das Evangelium nach Lukas,* 1955.
Stöger, A., *Das Evangelium nach Lukas,* 1964.
Struhlmueller, C., *The Gospel of St. Luke* (JB), 1968.
Tinsley, E. J., *The Gospel according to Luke* (CBC), 1965.
Valensin, A., and Huby, J., *Évangile selon saint Luc,* 1948.
Weiss, B., *Lukasevangelium* (KEK), 1901.
Wellhausen, J., *Das Evangelium Lucae,* 1904.
Wright, A., *St. Luke in Greek,* 1900.
Zahn, T., *Das Evangelium des Lucas,* 1920.

Books

Albertz, M., *Die Botschaft des neuen Testament,* I, 1947, II, 1952.
Bailey, J. A., *The Traditions Common to the Gospels of Luke and John,* 1963.
Barrett, C. K., *The Holy Spirit and the Gospel Tradition,* 1947.
—, *Luke the Historian in Recent Study,* 1961.
Bartsch, H. W., *Wachtet aber zu jeder Zeit,* 1963.
Bouwman, G., *Das dritte Evangelium,* 1968.
Brown, S., *Apostasy and Perseverance in the Theology of Luke,* 1969.
Bundy, W., *Jesus and the First Three Gospels,* 1955.
Burrows, E., *The Gospel of the Infancy,* 1940.
Burton, H., *The Gospel according to St. Luke* (EB), 1909.
Cadbury, H. J., *The Style and Literary Method of Luke,* 1919.
—, *The Book of Acts in History,* 1955.
—, *The Making of Luke-Acts,* 1927.
Carpenter, S. C., *Christianity according to St. Luke,* 1919.
Chapman, J., *Matthew, Mark and Luke,* 1937.

Carter, C. W., and Earle, R., *The Acts of the Apostles,* 1959.
Cerfaux, L., *La communauté apostolique,* 1953.
—, *Recueil Lucien Cerfaux,* 1954.
—, and Dupont, J., *Les Actes des Apôtres,* 1958.
Conzelmann, H., *The Theology of St. Luke* (ET), 1960.
Cullmann, O., *Early Christian Worship* (ET), 1953.
—, *Christology of the New Testament,* (ET), 1963.
Dalman, G., *The Words of Jesus,* 1902.
Daube, D., *The New Testament and Rabbinic Judaism,* 1955.
D'Aygalliers, A. W., *Les Sources du Récit de la Passion chez Luc,* 1920.
Degenhardt, H.-J., *Lukas, Evangelist der Armen,* 1965.
Delling, D. G., *Worship in the New Testament,* 1962.
Dodd, C. H., *According to the Scriptures,* 1952.
—, *New Testament Studies,* 1953.
Duncan, G. S., *Jesus, Son of Man,* 1948.
Dupont, J., *Les Béatitudes,* 1954.
Flender, H., *St. Luke Theologian of Redemptive History* (ET), 1967.
Ford, D. W. C., *A Reading of St. Luke's Gospel,* 1967.
George, A., *L'Annonce du salut de Dieu,* 1963.
Grant, F. C., *The Gospels, Their Origin and Growth,* 1957.
Green-Armytage, A. H. N., *Portrait of St. Luke,* 1955.
Gollwitzer, H., *La Joie de Dieu* (Fr. trans.), 1958.
Haenchen, E., *Der Weg Jesu,* 1966.
Hannam, W., *Luke the Evangelist,* 1935.
Harnack, A., *Luke the Physician,* 1907.
Hastings, A., *Prophet and Witness in Jerusalem,* 1958.
Howard, W. F., *The Gospel according to St. Luke: Interpreter's Bible,* VII, 1951.
Javet, J. S., *L'Évangile de la Grâce,* 1957.
Jeremias, J., *The Eucharistic Words of Jesus* (ET), 1955.
Keck, L. E., and J. L. Martyn (eds.), *Studies in Luke-Acts,* 1966.
Knox, W. L., *St. Luke and St. Matthew,* 1957.
Koh, R., *The Writings of St. Luke,* 1953.
Ladd, G. E., *Jesus and the Kingdom,* 1966.
Laurentin, R., *Jésus au Temple,* 1966.
—, *Structure et théologie de Luc, I-II,* 1957.
Lenski, R. C. H., *The Interpretation of Luke's Gospel,* 1946.
Lohse, E., *Die Auferstehung Jesu Christi im Zeugnis des Lukasevangelium,* 1961.
Lundstrom, G., *The Kingdom of God in the Teaching of Jesus,* 1963.
McLachlan, H., *St. Luke: the Man and his Work,* 1920.
McNiele, A. H., *An Introduction to the Study of the New Testament,* 1927.
Manson, T. W., *Jesus the Messiah,* 1943.
—, *The Servant-Messiah,* 1953.
Miller, D. G., *The Gospel of Luke,* 1959.
Morgenthaler, R., *Die lukanische Geschichtsschreibung als Zeugnis,* I, II, 1949.

Morton, A. Q., and MacGregor, C. H., *The Structure of Luke and Acts,* 1964.
Noack, B., *Das Gottesreich bei Lukas,* 1948.
Ott, W., *Gebet und Heil,* 1965,
Perry, A. M., *The Sources of Luke's Passion Narrative,* 1920.
Powell, C. H., *The Biblical Concept of Power,* 1963.
Price, J. L., *Interpreting the New Testament,* 1961.
Ramsay, W. M., *Luke the Physician and Other Studies in the History of Religion,* 1908.
Ramsey, A. M., *The Glory of God and the Transfiguration of Christ,* 1949.
Reicke, B., *The Gospel of Luke* (ET), 1965.
Robertson, A. T., *Luke the Historian in the Light of Research,* 1920.
Robinson, W. C., *Der Weg des Herrn,* 1964.
Salm, C. L., (ed.) *Readings in Biblical Morality,* 1967.
Schürmann, H., *Der Passahmahlebericht,* Lk. 22: 15-18, 1953.
—, *Der Einsetzungsbericht,* Lk. 22: 19-20, 1955.
—, *Jesu Abschiedsrede,* Lk. 22: 21-38, 1957.
—, *Das Gebet des Herrn,* 1958.
Selwyn, E. C., *St. Luke the Prophet,* 1901.
Shedd, R. P., *Man in Community,* 1958.
Stonehouse, N. B. *The Witness of Luke to Christ,* 1951.
Talbert, C. H., *Luke and the Gnostics,* 1966.
Taylor, V., *Behind the Third Gospel,* 1926.
Tittle, E., *The Gospel according to Luke,* 1965.
Walls, A. F., *The Gospel according to St. Luke,* 1965.
Wickenhauser, A., *New Testament Introduction* (ET), 1958.

Select Doctoral Dissertations

Cottle, R. E., *The Occasion and Purpose for the Final Drafting of Acts* (University of Southern California), 1967.
Crockett, L. C., *The Old Testament in the Gospel of Luke: With Emphasis on the Interpretation of Isaiah 61. 1-2.* (*Volumes I and II*), (Brown University), 1966.
Davis, E. C., *The Significance of the Shared Meal in Luke-Acts* (Southern Baptist Theological Seminary), 1967.
Harris, O. G., *Prayer in Luke-Acts: A Study in the Theology of Luke* (Vanderbilt University), 1966.
Kaylor, R. D., *The Ascension Motif in Luke-Acts, The Epistle to the Hebrews, and The Fourth Gospel* (Duke University), 1964.
Prevallet, E. M., *Luke 24:26: A Passover Christology* (Marquette University), 1967.

AUTHORS

AUTHORS IN NOTES

Imprimi potest: Romae, die 7 febr. 1970. Hervé Carrier, S. I., *Rector Universitatis*
Imprimatur: E Vicariatu Urbis, die 16 febr. 1970. ✠ Hector Cunial, *Vices gerens*